"Spiced with wit and mellowed with charm, Coren's anecdote-laden survey of canine–human interspecies history is a solid read. . . . The tales are well told and thoughtfully constructed, nicely balanced with solid historical research. Each chapter works nicely as a self-contained essay, and these vignettes build to tell an informative and entertaining story of canine camaraderie."

—*Publishers Weekly*

"This delightful chronicle offers a rich and surprising cavalcade of canines who touched the lives of such famous people as Richard Wagner, Alexander Pope, Alexander Graham Bell, Frederick the Great, and Sigmund Freud."

—*Booklist*

"A true-tales look at the fascinating role of dogs in history."

—*Seattle Post-Intelligencer*

"Well documented and humorous. . . . Coren gives every dog its day."

—*Maclean's*

"Little known and private moments give this book its power. . . . We hear our own humble love of dogs echoing through the ages."

—*BARK* magazine

"Mr. Coren's records give flesh and feeling to historical personages that might otherwise be names on a page."

—*The Vancouver Sun*

The
PAWPRINTS
of
HISTORY

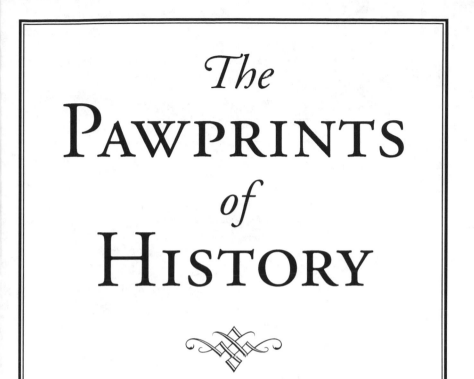

*DOGS AND THE COURSE
OF HUMAN EVENTS*

STANLEY COREN

ILLUSTRATIONS BY ANDY BARTLETT

ƒP

FREE PRESS

NEW YORK • LONDON • TORONTO • SYDNEY • SINGAPORE

This book is dedicated to my loving mother,
Chesna Coren, who is no longer here to read it,
and to my cherished father, Ben Coren, who is.

ƒP

FREE PRESS
A Division of Simon & Schuster, Inc.
1230 Avenue of the Americas
New York, NY 10020

First Free Press trade paperback edition 2003

FREE PRESS and colophon are trademarks of Simon & Schuster, Inc.

For information regarding special discounts for bulk purchases,
please contact Simon & Schuster Special Sales:
1-800-456-6798 or business@simonandschuster.com

DESIGNED BY KEVIN HANEK

Manufactured in the United States of America

10 9 8 7 6 5 4 3 2 1

The Library of Congress has cataloged the Free Press edition as follows:
Coren, Stanley.
The pawprints of history : dogs and the course of human events / Stanley Coren ;
illustrations by Andy Bartlett.
1. Dogs—History. 2. Animal intelligence. 3. Behavior, animal. 4. Dogs. I. Title.
SF422.5 .C67 2002
636.7/009—dc21   2002283337
ISBN 0-7432-2228-8
0-7432-2231-8 (Pbk)

CONTENTS

PREFACE

⚜

T HIS IS A BOOK about the history of humans and dogs—or, more pre-
cisely, about how dogs have influenced and changed human history. The
concept comes out of a melding of my passions for history, biography, psychology, and (of course) dogs. Although humans and dogs have lived together for
more than fourteen thousand years, accounts about how dogs have changed our
world are not usually highlighted in academic histories and biographies. Occasionally, however, there are hints that some digging might unearth an interesting
story.

Much of the material presented here comes from the personal papers of the
people involved. In letters and diaries, people are more likely to reveal secrets
that they would not utter in public—like their feelings about a favorite dog, and
how they might have changed some aspect of their life in response to living with
a dog.

This book is filled with stories of kings and queens, presidents, prime ministers, war heroes, scientists, social activists, authors, and musicians, all of whom
have had their lives changed by one or more dogs. By influencing their lives,
their four-footed companions also changed history.

There are some technical things that must be noted for my academic colleagues and for scholarly historians. First, although the research for this book has
been thorough, and I have tried to ensure that all of the material is as accurate as
possible, I have not extensively annotated or referenced this work in the text.
Some of the more important references have been provided in a set of annotated

endnotes, which are keyed by chapter. Second, I have occasionally translated centuries-old quotations into contemporary language, grammar, and spelling. Thus if I were to quote Edward, the second Duke of York, writing about hunting dogs in 1406, the original would read, "Rennyng hondis hunten i dveris maners, . . ." and I would present it as "Running hounds hunt in different ways, . . ." The reason for both of these choices is that I have focused on being more of a storyteller than a historian. It is the flow of the story, the interactions between dog and master, and the effects that the interplay between humans and dogs ultimately have upon history that I care about here. Numerous footnotes can be distracting to the reader's enjoyment of the tale, while archaic language can slow or even limit a reader's understanding. My academic associates may think that this is a less than scholarly way to proceed, but I believe that my dog-loving readers will appreciate this less formal account of some little-known but fascinating aspects of history where dogs played a significant role.

Finally, I must provide a few warm acknowledgments and notes of thanks. The first goes to my wonderful wife, Joan, who (as she has done in the past) has gone over my chapters and pointed out the convoluted passages that need modification or elimination. Second I must thank my brother, Arthur, for his support during this project, including his help in keeping out the pressures of the world so that I could write in peace. In addition I must thank him for finding Andy Bartlett, an animation artist and director who has taken the time from his busy life to draw the illustrations for this book. Finally I must acknowledge the contributions of my own dogs, Dancer and Odin, who help to keep me sane and happy—and also Wizard, who after changing my life for the better has now himself passed into history.

PROLOGUE

A GRIZZLED, UNSHAVEN MAN sits in a crude hut and huddles next to a tiny fire. He is clothed only in the skin of an animal. Nearby his wife sleeps, and on the other side of the shelter sleeps his nearly grown son with his younger son and tiny daughter.

Sharing the fire with him is a dog with pointed ears, but of no recognizable breed. It has just awakened and is now standing and looking in the direction of a faint sound, one too weak for the man to hear. The dog sits back down, its head still cocked to follow the sound. Then, as humans have always done, the man speaks to the dog quietly: "What do you hear, my dog? You will tell me if I should worry?"

Bones and artifacts suggest that this scene could have taken place in Iraq fourteen thousand years ago, in France or Denmark twelve thousand years ago, in Utah eleven thousand years ago or in China ten thousand years ago. It has been that long that the group of animals that we know as dogs have been sharing our living space and shaping the individual and collective histories of humans.

As the scene (which could have happened thousands of times in our past) unfolds, the man looks at the guardian and hunter beside the flickering fire. Talking to the dog again for company, he asks: "What would life be like without you?

"I remember the stories of the grandfathers. They said that there was a time when there were no dogs. Then men had no warning when animals came to hunt them, or when other tribes came to raid us. But then your grandfather came with his family. They ate the garbage, the bones and skin from our hunts that we tossed outside the village. My grandfathers thought that this was good. It kept the smells down and kept the insects away. They said that because you ate the leavings, we could stay in a village for a much longer time before we had to move.

"Then my grandfathers heard you bark. Every time an animal or a man approached, you barked. What a wonderful thing, they thought. If you stayed close and barked, then nothing could surprise us in the dark. So, to keep your family close we threw extra food to you. Soon the grandfathers took some of your ancestor's puppies and brought them into their homes. They thought, 'If a dog will protect the village with its bark, then another dog will protect my own home.' Soon the puppies who lived with us were no longer wild.

"The grandfathers say that it happened one day that we were chasing a wounded deer, and your grandfathers had trailed behind us. The deer was clever, like many are, and turned off the path. My grandfathers did not see this and ran past, but your grandfathers knew in their noses where the deer had gone and ran after it. My grandfathers followed your ancestors, and ever since we have learned to hunt together.

"The grandfathers say that there used to be other, ugly men [Neanderthals] here. But they are gone now because they never had dogs to protect them or help them hunt. So they were killed by great beasts or men who hid in ambush, and when the animals that we hunt became few, they starved.

"Today I watched you and your brothers hunt the little sheep. I saw how you circled their flock to keep them together, then drove them toward the trees where you could slow them and scatter them to make them easier to kill. And I thought, my dog, if I could get you to do this gathering of sheep without killing them, then perhaps we could keep some alive, to give birth to other sheep. Then we would not need to hunt so often. We must try this soon."

The dog settled to the ground, placing its head down on its paws, and the man knew that there was no danger near. He yawned and stirred the fire, then lay down to sleep as well, secure in the knowledge that his guardian would warn him if anything dangerous lurked by. In the morning they would hunt together and, if they were successful, in the afternoon his dog and his daughter would have time to play together. His rough hand reached out and stroked the dog's fur, and that touch made them both feel content.

The history of men and dogs had begun. Their fates would be entwined as long as each species chose to share the other's company. At some time in the far future, the history of even kings or nations might show the pattern of a dog's pawprints on it.

CHAPTER ONE

SENTINELS AND SYMBOLS

OW MANY TIMES has the fate of a man, or even a nation, hung from the collar of a dog? Had it not been for dogs, the last imperial house of China might not have fallen; Columbus's first attempts at colonizing the Americas not have been so successful; some of Wagner's operas might never have been written; the American Revolution might not have been fought; the freeing of the American slaves might have been delayed for decades; the way that we educate deaf children might be different; and great and well-loved books like *Ivanhoe* might never have been written.

Most people know and accept in a general way the fact that dogs have changed human history by fulfilling needed functions in human activities such as hunting, herding, exploration, or the waging of war. When it comes to political, social, or cultural history, however, few people would expect any evidence of canine influences. Yet there are many instances where the actions of a single dog changed the life of a single human, who in turn went on to shape human history. These seldom-told stories are the most fascinating.

Consider, for example, the case of Alexander Pope, the brilliant satirist who is considered by many to be the greatest English poet of the eighteenth century. One of the most quotable poets of all time, Pope is the source of such familiar epigrams as "A little learning is a dangerous thing," "To err is human, to forgive, divine," and "Fools rush in where angels fear to tread." Many of his poems, such as *The Rape of the Lock* and *The Dunciad,* as well as his *Essay on Man* and *Essay on Criticism,* are still popular classics and required reading for anyone seeking a degree in literature in most universities.

Pope was born in London in 1688. His interest in literature and writing was probably in part the result of his poor physique. While still quite young, Pope developed a form of tuberculosis that affects the spine. This condition stunted his growth; his full-grown height was only four feet six inches. In addition, Pope was condemned to suffer from headaches throughout his life, and he was abnormally sensitive to pain. His spinal condition made bending and physical exertions a source of agony. He often needed assistance to rise from his bed or chair and was obliged to have a servant help him dress and undress.

Nevertheless, Pope could be a charming social companion and host. Despite his lack of height, he had a handsome face and an attractive appearance so that people did not feel uncomfortable in his presence. At his large estate at Twickenham on the Thames (only a short distance from London), Pope entertained many celebrated guests, from poets and philosophers to high government officials, society belles, and even royalty. On any visit to him one might have met the likes of Jonathan Swift, the satirical author of *Gulliver's Travels;* Henry St. John the Viscount Bolingbroke, a statesman and orator who later became an author; Robert Harley, the first earl of Oxford, who would one day be the Lord Treasurer; and even Frederick, the Prince of Wales. Pope's many visitors would often convene in the great garden that he had carefully designed, and then the whole party would spend hours in sprightly conversation.

When he was not in a social setting, however, Pope's painful physical condition made him touchy and easily angered. Close associates would hear him rage at even the slightest perceived insult. His temper would often flare at a critic, then be redirected to whatever innocent target happened to be near—frequently a servant. The resulting high level of turnover among his personal staff as employees quit or were fired made maintenance of a household routine difficult.

Pope had other personal quirks as well. Despite his personal wealth and his lavish entertainment of guests, for example, he was quite miserly in some of his personal habits. Thus he often would not buy writing paper, but rather write his poetry on old envelopes from his voluminous correspondence. He distrusted financial institutions, such as banks, and only did a minimal amount of business with them. Instead, he kept much of his wealth in a strongbox built into a wall of the mansion, wearing the key on a chain around his neck at all times.

Although he loved dogs all of his life, Pope's favorite was an unlikely choice, given his size and physical condition. It was a large Great Dane that he named Bounce. When Bounce and Pope stood facing each other, their eyes were nearly at the same level. Bounce, however, proved to be a fine companion. He was quiet and unobtrusive when his master worked, but was always present to greet company and to socialize when anyone showed him any attention. Prince Frederick was so impressed by Bounce's good manners and stately appearance that he expressed a desire to own a dog just like him. Pope was flattered, and some time later the prince returned from a visit to Twickenham carrying one of Bounce's puppies—a gift from the poet. The puppy was installed at the royal kennel at Kew, which was the summer residence of the royal family. Shortly thereafter, Pope sent another gift, a collar for Frederick's dog with the following couplet engraved on it:

I am his Highness' dog, at Kew.
Pray tell me, sir, whose dog are you?

Although Bounce was generally friendly, he could be quite protective of his master. Since Jonathan Swift was now around sixty and had grown quite deaf, Pope had to raise his voice to communicate with him on his visits. This shouting made Bounce very suspicious of Swift, and so he would protectively lie between his master and the writer. If Swift gestured too broadly as he spoke, Bounce would rise to his feet as if ready to intervene on Pope's behalf and might even give a warning growl.

Although Pope did not need protection from Swift, Bounce's role of guardian would ultimately prove to be a blessing. One day, the temperamental poet had dismissed his latest valet, amid some name-calling and abusive language. When a new manservant was quickly hired from a short list of available applicants, Bounce sniffed at the man, then withdrew beside his master in an untypical show of dislike. Nonetheless, the valet seemed to know his job and appeared to be quite conscientious. As night fell, the valet lifted Pope from his chair and assisted him to the bedroom, where he helped the poet undress for the night and placed him on his bed. After pulling the heavy curtains around the canopied bed to shut out the night drafts, the valet quietly slipped out of the room.

Bounce, who normally stayed downstairs by the fireplace at night to soak up the last heat of the dying embers, abandoned his usual place of rest this evening. As the valet left, the dog slipped into Pope's bedroom and crawled under the bed to sleep. Much later that night, Pope thought that he heard a noise. When he slightly parted the bed curtains to peek out, what he saw paralyzed him with fear. The dark figure of a man stealthily approaching the bed was dimly visible. In his hand, Pope could make out the shape of a large knife, glittering in the moonlight. Because of his physical frailties, the poet was helpless to rise and protect himself. He could only scream for his valet, who slept in the next room, to come and help him.

At the sound of his master's cry, Bounce sprang from under the bed and leaped at the man, who toppled over and lost his grip on the knife. Then Bounce held him there on the floor, alternately growling at the man and barking loudly for help. When the commotion brought other members of the household staff to the rescue, the man with the knife turned out to be the new valet of whom Bounce had been suspicious. Hearing that Pope kept a great deal of money in the house, the man had decided to kill him, steal the strongbox key that he wore, and then flee before anyone else awakened.

Because of Bounce, Pope would live to write more great poetry. In addition, another epigram would be penned by the dog's master, who wrote, "Histories are more full of examples of the fidelity of dogs than of friends."

The concept of a dog as a protector is found in virtually every culture. For many people, the most important function a dog serves is to warn its family of any danger. An example of this view can be found in a story that was being told by the Mik'Maq Indians of North America long before the Europeans reached the American continent.

The legend begins with Gisoolg, the great spirit god and creator, who created Ootsitgamoo (the earth), then filled it with all sorts of animals. The work was difficult, so he rested and slept awhile. While Gisoolg was sleeping, though, the great snake that he had created became ambitious and greedy. It used magic to add deadly venom to its bite, so that it could kill the largest animals and in this way become the chief among all living things.

When Gisoolg awoke, he decided to make some beings that would rule over the animals. So first he gathered some clay from a sacred hidden place, and then he spent a full day forming the shape of a man from the clay. He gave the man life, but the man was too weak to move yet, so he lay on the ground gathering his strength. Gisoolg then went to sleep again.

The snake did not like the idea that Gisoolg was creating a creature that would be more intelligent and more powerful than any of the animals, so in the dead of the night it crept up and killed the man. When Gisoolg awoke he was distressed at the loss of the man, but spent another long day shaping another and then again went to sleep. Again the man became the victim of the cunning snake. On the third day Gisoolg rose early, and before he began to recreate the man, he first created a guardian in the form of a dog. By the time he had re-formed the man, the dog had gathered enough strength to stand watch. So again Gisoolg went to sleep.

Now the snake again approached through the long grass, with murder in its heart and venom dripping from its fangs. But this time it was confronted by the dog, who barked loudly to sound the alarm and then slashed at the snake with its teeth. Now the serpent was slowed by its wounds and had lost the element of sur-prise. Even worse, the dog's barking awakened Gisoolg, who came forward at once.

"Evil serpent, you have no right to interfere with that which I am creating. As a penalty for your wickedness I will strike off your legs, so that you, and all of your family after you, will be forced to slither on your bellies for eternity. Fur-thermore, be warned that I have given the man, whom I shall name Glooscap, this guardian, E'lmutc. The dog will be with him always and keep him safe. If you are foolish enough to try to hurt Glooscap or his family, E'lmutc will know that you have come. He will sound the alarm, and I will grant Glooscap the wisdom and the weapons to protect himself. Be warned, serpent, next time, if E'lmutc's teeth do not slay you, then Glooscap's hand will."

In this story, there would have been no humans at all if not for the protec-tion provided by a dog. While this is obviously just a myth, the idea that a dog's God-given duty is to serve as a guardian of man somehow comes to mind when one reads the lives of many historical individuals.

The biography of Saint Giovanni Melchior Bosco (commonly called Don Bosco or John Bosco) has a dog that appears from nowhere, like a guardian an-gel, to protect him. The story begins in the 1840s, when the slums of Turin, Italy, were rife with the kind of poverty and cruelty that one finds associated with sweatshop factories—their hazardous machinery, their abusive practices of child labor, and their starvation wages. When he was a young boy, Bosco was inspired by a series of dreams to help young children who had been trapped in this terri-ble poverty. After he had taken his vows as a priest, Bosco wandered the streets, visiting factories and prisons where young boys in trouble were to be found. He soon arranged to meet weekly with a growing band of ragged youngsters. In the beginning these meetings floated from place to place. There was no one perma-nent home for the group because in those troublesome times people were afraid of a large gathering of poor working boys. Bosco would convene the group in a different place every Sunday—sometimes a city church, or a cemetery chapel, or even an empty lot. There, the priest would hear their confessions and say a simple Mass for them. This would be followed by an hour of religious instruction, which was presented in plain language and often punctuated with a bit of juggling or a magic trick to keep the boys' interest. Then Bosco would take his ragtag band out to the countryside near the city for an outing with food and games.

By 1846, Don Bosco managed to raise enough money to buy a lot in an underdeveloped section of the city. Empty except for a ramshackle shed, it was next door to a saloon and across the street from a hotel with a shady reputation. It was a beginning, however, and furthermore, he had been assured in a dream that this was holy ground because it was the burial ground of the martyrs of Turin. Bosco then proceeded to convert the shed into a chapel, digging out space for a congregation to gather, and a tiny anteroom. Now every Sunday around five hundred poverty-stricken boys would squeeze into it for Mass.

It was around 1848 when the dog who played a role in his life appeared. He was a huge hulking gray mongrel whom Don Bosco would give the name "Grigio." Where Grigio came from originally, no one seems to know. His pedigree, parentage, and origin were as obscure as those of the many homeless children that the saint tended to gather around him.

Grigio's involvement began one evening as Bosco wended his way through the narrow streets toward his chapel. Unfortunately, some of the more criminal elements in the neighborhood had concluded that between his building and his provision of food for the children, Don Bosco must have accumulated a lot of money. As he passed by a dark alley, a man leaped from hiding. He grabbed the future saint and demanded money. Don Bosco virtually never had any money of his own, since all that he obtained went immediately to the children he was trying to help. When he denied having anything to give his attacker, the thief waved a knife in the priest's face: "If you have no money then you are of no use to me and I will kill you. Give me money, or show me where you have hidden it in that little chapel of yours, and you can buy your life." Bosco would later remember only that he closed his eyes and murmured a prayer, knowing that his life was about to end.

Suddenly, a savage gray blur hurled itself at the thief, knocking him down and causing the knife to fall from the man's hand as he crashed to the ground. The blur turned out to be a huge, snarling mongrel, which interposed himself between the priest and his attacker. The thug made one lunge toward the knife, but a growl and the snap of the dog's teeth made him reconsider any attempt at continuing his original course of action. He quickly clambered to his feet and then disappeared down the street, running as fast as he could.

Don Bosco did not know whether to be thankful or even more terrified. As the dog turned to face him all that he could focus upon was the dog's great muzzle and long teeth and the priest considered joining the thief in flight. However, the dog closed its mouth, lowered its head slightly, and gave a reassuring wag of its tail. Bosco then, hesitantly, reached out and stroked its coarse gray coat, and the dog responded with a contented whimper. It then silently followed the saint home to share a humble meal.

From that moment on Grigio was always at hand when Bosco was in danger—which apparently was quite often, since others in the vicinity would sometimes try to accost him and to steal his nonexistent wealth. He was also often with Bosco on those rare occasions when he actually had to carry valuables for those in his care, and few would approach with harmful intent given the size of the dog. Often the dog would seem to wander off, but suddenly appear (as he had on that first day) to defend Bosco from attack.

At times, some of the more unscrupulous local factory owners believed Don Bosco's ministry was becoming intrusive. His attempt at raising the standard of living of the children in the area was threatening their supply of cheap labor. On one evening Bosco was returning from a visit to a sweatshop, where he had lectured the owner about the dangers that the children were facing because of unsafe equipment and the long hours that they were required to work. As he was about to turn down a street that he always used on his return home, Grigio sprang forward and blocked his way. The priest tried to push past him but the big dog would not allow him to continue. Since both Don Bosco and Grigio were familiar sights on the street, this disagreement between them drew the attention of passers-by, and the small crowd attracted a policeman. Someone from one of the houses then turned up a light—and there, lurking in the shadows, were two armed men. It would later be learned that they had been hired to set an ambush by one of the factory owners who wanted the meddling priest killed.

Ultimately, Don Bosco convinced the government that he could be trusted to run his schools. His educational and other projects were now functioning well and safe from interference. In addition, the general public and even the criminal element recognized Bosco's altruistic motives, and so they no longer treated him as either a threat or a target of opportunity. If one had a bent toward a mystical connection associated with Grigio's appearance, then one might conclude that now, with things beginning to go well, the dog's heroic services were no longer needed. Be that as it may, as the saint sat in the refectory one evening at dinner-time, Grigio came to him once more. The dog rubbed his grizzled gray head against the saint's habit, licked his hand quietly, and placed a tentative paw on his knee. Then, without a sound, the huge brave dog turned and wandered out into the night, never to be seen again.

By the time of Don Bosco's death in 1888, there were 250 houses to help underprivileged and undereducated children under the auspices of what had come to be known as the Salesian Society. These hospices and schools were scattered through several different countries. The total number of children in their care was around 130,000, from which 18,000 finished apprentices left annually with the knowledge that they needed to earn their own living. In the main house in Turin, Don Bosco had placed the brightest of his pupils and had taught them Italian, Latin, French, and mathematics. This group eventually formed a teaching corps for the newer homes. By the time that he died more than six thousand priests had completed the seminary program at Don Bosco's institutions, twelve hundred of whom had remained in the society. Yet none of this might have come to pass had it not been for a mysterious dog named Grigio.

It is not only big dogs, like Pope's Great Dane or Don Bosco's great gray mongrel, that can intervene to save their master's life and thus let him continue on some history-shaping mission. Even small lapdogs can change the future, as in the case of William I, Prince of Orange (who is also called William the Silent) in the Netherlands. William is known as one of the principal founders of Dutch independence and is also remembered for the first formal attempts to institutionalize religious tolerance.

William was born in 1533 and, although his parents were Protestant, he was reared as a Roman Catholic and sent to the court of Holy Roman Emperor Charles V at Brussels. William soon became the emperor's favorite, performing well the social, military, and diplomatic duties that were expected of him. He continued to do so under Philip II, the emperor's son and successor as king of Spain and lord of the Burgundian dominions. In part because of this service, in 1555 William was made *stadtholder* (the equivalent of governor and commander in chief) of Holland, Zeeland, and Utrecht.

By the 1560s, William and the other principal lords of the region began to offer some opposition to Philip's rule. Philip was hard and inflexible and did not like to share power. Civil rights were being suspended, there was no true local representation in government, and personal freedom (as it was then known) was being threatened. Furthermore, because Philip would not tolerate any deviation from strict Catholicism, the Spanish Inquisition had been brought to the Netherlands, and many Protestants and even "moderate" Catholics were being tried and executed for heresy. Having been influenced by the thoughts of the humanist philosopher Desiderius Erasmus, William leaned toward more religious tolerance. When popular resistance arose to the harsh controls he had imposed, Philip appointed the Duke de Alba to quell the dissent. The duke set up a special court, the Council of Troubles, to try all cases of rebellion and heresy, and this court was responsible for more than a thousand executions.

With both political liberty and religious freedom at issue, William took the field against Philip. It would be a long fight, with many military reverses and political intrigues. Ultimately, the Spanish would be pushed out and a peace treaty, the Pacification of Ghent, would be the result. It would provide for the union of the seventeen states that were called the Netherlands under one national government. William would survive all of the dangers of that period and become the hereditary ruler of the Netherlands—however, for this to happen required the intervention of a dog.

As many rulers of his time, William had a variety of dogs. Many were used in hunting, but William also had small dogs (which he referred to as "indoor" dogs) simply for companionship. His favorites were the pugs, which had recently been introduced from China. These little dogs were then called Camuses, which means "flat-nosed." William often took one or more of these dogs with him as company, even on military maneuvers. The incident that we are interested in occurred in 1572, when William had set up camp at Hermingny. In 1618 Sir Roger Williams, who had served with William and knew him well in later years, described what happened in his history *Actions of the Low Countries:*

> The Prince of Orange being retired into the camp, Julian Romero [one
> of de Alba's most daring generals], with earnest persuasions, procured
> licence of the Duke de Alba to hazard a *camisado* or night attack upon
> the Prince. At midnight Julian sallied out of the trenches with a thou-
> sand armed men, mostly pikes, who forced all the guards that they
> found in their way into the place of arms before the Prince's tent, and
> killed two of his secretaries. The Prince himself escaped very narrowly,
> for I have often heard him say that he thought but for a dog he should
> have been taken or slain. The attack was made with such resolution that
> the guards took no alarm until their fellows were running to the place

of arms with their enemies at their heels, when this dog [who always slept on the bed with the Prince], hearing a great noise, fell to scratching and crying, and awakened him before any of his men; and though the Prince slept armed, with a lackey always holding one of his horses ready bridled and saddled, yet at the going out of his tent with ado he recovered his horse before the enemy arrived. Nevertheless, one of his equerries was slain, taking horse presently after him, as were diverse of his servants. The Prince, to show his gratitude, until his dying day, kept one of that dog's race, and so did many of his friends and followers.

An effigy of William with his pug at his feet is carved over his tomb in Delft Cathedral. When his son and successor, William II, landed at Torbay to be crowned as king of England he brought with him a full retinue, which included a number of pugs. Because of this royal patronage, pugs would be a fashionable breed in England for several generations.

This same story, where a small and apparently insignificant dog saves the life of an individual who changes the world, has been repeated many times in many different cultures around the world. For example, in the seventeenth century the fifth Dalai Lama, Ngag-dbang-rgya-mtsho, had engaged in a series of political actions that would lead to a political alliance with the Mongols. While these steps resulted in political dominance of his religious order in Tibet, they also earned him a number of bitter enemies. The Dalai Lama kept as companion dogs the little Lhasa Apsos, who actually get their name from the city of Lhasa, where the Lama built his summer palace. It was there, that one night, while the Dalai Lama was sleeping, assassins stole into the wing of the palace that held his living quarters. They silently killed the group of soldiers on the outer perimeter, then stealthily approached guards outside the Lama's bedroom. Suddenly a loud barking broke out from one of the little Lhasa Apsos who slept in the Lama's chambers. This alerted the Lama's personal guards to a problem and caused others to come from nearby, foiling the attack. It was in this way, as the personal watchdog of the ruler of a nation and the leader of a religion, that a dog which is only ten inches at the shoulder and weighs less than fifteen pounds, could shape the destiny of a region of the world. This brave act is commemorated in Tibet in the name which they give to this tiny breed of dog, *abso seng kye,* which translates as the "barking lion sentinel dog."

While we have seen that a single dog can save the life of an individual and thus alter history, it is also the case that a single dog, acting in its traditional task of sentinel, can save whole cities. From the earliest times of our association with dogs they have served as perimeter guards for villages and settlements, ready to sound the alarm if any invaders should try to approach. Dogs are convenient in this regard since they require only a minimal amount of human control to perform such sentinel duty.

One example of this involved the city of Corinth, which is now a hub of communications between northern and southern Greece and is the primary point of export for local fruit, raisins, and tobacco. In the year 456 B.C., during the Greco-Persian wars, Corinth was strategically important because it controlled not only the land traffic between Attica and the Peloponnese, but also the traffic between the Aegean and Ionian seas. Because of Corinth's location on an isthmus, ships and cargoes could be speedily moved by being hauled overland on the stone roadway between the harbors on either side of the city. This process spared seafarers the arduous voyage around the southern tip of the Peloponnese.

Approximately fifty dogs were posted around the city to warn if any invaders appeared. One night, the Persians sent a small company of invaders to steal in under cover of darkness, then hold the city long enough so that a larger army might launch a quick surprise attack on Greece. The Persian intelligence had indicated the existence of the canine sentinels, and so the first task of the invaders was to eliminate them and prevent the rallying of any organized defense. Although the dogs were well trained, the invaders managed to kill all but one of them—a dog named Soter, who managed to escape and to wake up the soldiers. Thus alerted, the Corinthian garrison successfully repelled the invading forces; they also had time to send messengers to bring reinforcements from nearby allies before the city gates were sealed. Soter was honored with a pension and a silver collar inscribed, "To Soter, defender and savior of Corinth, placed under the protection of his friends." More than two thousand years later, Napoleon would remember this incident and post dogs around the perimeter of Alexandria to alert his garrison of any attempted surprise attacks.

Yet sometimes the influence of a dog on a person (and on history) is much more indirect. It can occur when the dog is acting not as a guard, but as a companion and a comfort in times of stress. It can happen when the dog is simply doing its job as a shepherd or hunter. It can happen when the dog misinterprets an event and acts rashly. It can also happen when an event involving a dog takes on a symbolic meaning. It is in the subtle role as a symbol that a dog affected a young girl who would go on to save many lives.

Most people remember Florence Nightingale, the English nurse who is considered to be the founder of modern nursing. Her life was dedicated to the care of the sick and war-wounded. She is best known for her activities during the Crimean war, when in 1854 she organized a unit of thirty-eight female nurses. By war's end she had become a legend. She was remembered by so many soldiers for her habit of carrying a lamp at night as she visited the wounded that she ultimately was given the nickname "The Lady of the Lamp." After the war she established a nursing school at St. Thomas's Hospital in London, where her contributions were so great that in 1907 she became the first woman to be given the British Order of Merit. Yet none of this might have happened except for her encounter with a dog.

Florence Nightingale was born as the second daughter of William Edward Nightingale and his wife, Frances, during a brief stay in Italy. Named after the Italian city in which she was born, Florence grew up in the countryside of Derbyshire, Hampshire, and in the city of London; her well-to-do family maintained comfortable homes in both locations. She was educated largely by her father, who taught her several languages (including Greek, Latin, French, German, and Italian) as well as history, philosophy, and mathematics. Throughout her life she read widely; however, her social life was generally unsatisfying, and she felt unfulfilled.

One afternoon in early February of 1837, when Florence was seventeen years of age, she had an encounter that foreshadowed her future. It involved a sheepdog named Cap. The dog was owned by a shepherd named Roger who lived near Matlock in Derbyshire, not far from the place where Florence's parents had a home. Roger lived alone except for his dog in a cottage near the edge of the woods. One day some village boys noticed Cap sleeping on the doorstep; in an act of cruel mischief, they began to throw stones at him. The dog stood up to dodge the onslaught, but one of the stones hit Cap's leg, damaging it so badly that he couldn't put it down on the ground. Despite his love for the dog, Roger couldn't survive without a working sheepdog, and he was too poor to keep a dog that couldn't work. With great regret, he went off to pasture the sheep by himself, and to get a bit of rope to hang Cap.

While Roger was out with his sheep, Florence rode past the field in the company of a local clergyman. Since they knew the shepherd, they stopped to chat for a few minutes. Florence liked dogs and had often stopped to play a bit with Cap, so she asked where the dog was. As Roger told them his story, Florence grew extremely distressed. As she and the clergyman continued their travels, she convinced her companion that they ought to at least take a look at Cap and see if anything could be done. The two of them rode over to Roger's cottage after borrowing a key from a neighbor to get in.

As the pair entered the room, Cap recognized them and crawled out from beneath the table to give them a pained greeting. While Florence held Cap's head, the clergyman examined the dog's leg. He explained to the young woman that the injury was not a break in the bone, as Roger had assumed, but merely a bad bruise. He predicted that hot compresses would cure the dog in a few days. Then, under his direction, Florence tore up some old flannel for bandages, lit the fire with the shepherd's tinderbox, and boiled some water. She then applied the bandages, wrung out in hot water, to the injured leg.

As they left the cottage to return home, they met Roger, who was walking with his shoulders slumped and ominously carrying a piece of rope. They persuaded Roger not to hang his dog and promised to return the next day to renew the compresses with fresh flannel. Two days later, on February 6, they met Roger and his flock on the hillside. An excited Cap, still limping slightly but clearly almost healed, bounded up to Florence and expressed his gratitude by leaving pawprints on her dress. She looked down at the first patient that she had ever nursed back to health and grinned happily.

The very next night, on February 7, 1837, Florence Nightingale had a dream—or perhaps it was a vision—that caused her to believe she had heard the voice of God informing her that she had a mission. Perhaps it occurred simply because she was still bathed in the warm feeling from having saved Cap's life. Into her mind sprang the belief that this whole incident was a sign from God to tell her that she should devote her life to healing others. Her father, however, refused to allow her to study nursing at a hospital, pressuring her to pursue a study of parliamentary reports instead. She reluctantly agreed, and after only three years of such study, influential friends regarded her as an expert on public health and hospitals.

It would not be until nine years later that her sense of mission would return. In 1846, a friend sent Florence the yearbook of the Institution of Protestant Deaconesses at Kaiserswerth in Germany. This was a group that trained country girls of good character to nurse the sick. That night she remembered the vision that had been triggered when she had nursed the sheepdog, and this time she could not be talked out of her decision. A short time later she entered the institution, went through the full course of training, and began her career as a nurse. Once again, as in the case of Saint Giovanni Bosco, the combination of a dog and a dream would change history.

THE SAINT AND THE
IRISH DOGS

TRADITIONALLY DOGS ARE supposed to be able to see evil approach, which is why the howling of a dog is often believed to be an omen that something bad (such as a death in the family) is about to happen. The flip side of this coin is that dogs are similarly supposed to be able to recognize sanctity and truth. It is in this way that dogs have worked their way into the lives of many saints and holy people.

Some stories of dogs and saints are well known, such as the tale of Saint Roche. He was born at Montpellier around 1295, and had a bright red mark on his chest in the shape of a cross. Many people believed this mark indicated that he would be a holy man who was destined to do great deeds. When he was about twenty years old, his parents died. He wondered whether their early deaths may have been a judgment visited on him because he had failed to follow the life in the church that had been suggested by his birthmark. (He had instead taken an easier path to a career in government, which was available to him because of his father's position as governor of the city.) Reconsidering his life, he decided to distribute his fortune among the poor, and to hand over all government responsibilities to his uncle. Keeping only the family dog as a reminder of his past life, he dressed himself simply and set out on a pilgrimage to Rome.

On the way he stopped at Aquapendente, where the population was suffering from the Plague of the Black Death. He tried to offer assistance to plague victims in the usual ways of that time. He noted, however, that his dog had no hesitation about approaching the sick and licking at the abscessed spots on their skin. People did not withdraw from this, because there had been a long tradition (going back to the temples of Asklepios in Athens) where the lick of a dog was used to cure wounds and heal sores. We now know that this has some true medicinal effect—not just by acting to clean out the wound, but also because scientists have actually found a chemical in dogs' saliva that seems to inhibit infections. To Roche, however, this ministration of the dog seemed to represent a sign that what was needed was his touch. So he carefully traced the sign of the cross on each sick individual's body while praying for deliverance. The effect was miraculous, for the sores began to heal and people began to recover from their illness. He next visited Cesena and some of its neighboring cities, finally making his way to Rome. In every city the story was the same. Roche and his dog visited the places where the sick had gathered. Then, his touch, his prayers, and the sign of the cross seemed to drive the sickness away. He now felt that he knew what his mission was in life, and he and his dog continued to go from city to city on his healing mission.

Unfortunately, near Piacenza, Roche himself was stricken with the plague. He considered going into the city, but he felt weak and did not want to impose his own suffering on others. Instead he found a small hut, the kind of rude shelter that is used by foresters as a temporary shelter when the weather is very bad, or to store cut wood until it is dry and ready for sale. He crawled inside, covered himself and went to sleep. Soon he awoke. There was a rain barrel nearby, so that Roche had water, but he was now too weak to get up to scrounge for food. His dog licked at his open sores and seemed to want to comfort him.

As the sun began to go lower in the sky, Roche's dog got up and left his feverish master. He wandered down the road, not more than a mile, to a castle owned by a minor aristocrat named Gothard. The dog entered the main gate and then walked into the building. People were gathering in the dining hall for dinner, and as they watched in amazement, the dog placed his paws on the edge of the table and helped himself to a loaf of bread. Then, without stopping to eat it, he trotted back out of the open door. Gothard was amused, but his amusement turned to astonishment when this theft was repeated several days in a row. The aristocrat went to the window to watch the dog leave and was amazed to see that the dog never stopped to take a bite out of the bread, but rather proceeded down the road and disappeared along a path into the woods. On the fourth or fifth night that this had occurred, the nobleman followed the dog. The faithful animal went directly back to the shelter where his master lay. Gothard watched the dog drop the bread and then proceed to tenderly lick Roche's plague sores.

Gothard was so moved by the care shown by the dog that he set about to have Roche's needs supplied. To the amazement of everyone, Roche recovered and did not even show any of the scars that the abscesses caused by the plague usually left. Gothard would be so inspired that he eventually entered the service of the church himself.

Eighty-seven years after Roche's death, the plague returned and hit the city of Constance. The city council ordered public prayers and processions in honor of Saint Roche, and immediately afterward the plague ceased. The dog, whose name has not been preserved, was not mentioned during the prayers. However, it does live on in most of the artistic representations of Saint Roche, which show him being gently licked by his faithful companion.

Often the influence of a dog involves a life of companionship but only one or two notable incidents, as in the legend of Saint Margaret of Cortona. She was a beautiful peasant girl who was born in Tuscany in 1247. Her father was a farmer, and her mother died when she was seven years old. Her father remarried, but his new wife gave little attention or affection to the high-spirited girl. Margaret was one of those people who crave affection and so sought it outside of the home. When she was about seventeen years of age she made the acquaintance of a young cavalier. They had a passionate relationship that continued for several years, resulting in the birth of a son. Although she frequently tried to convince her lover to marry her, he always avoided the issue. Despite this, she was really quite devoted to the cavalier, and her kindly nature also endeared her to the residents of the castle and the surrounds. She often went out walking with one of the young lord's favorite dogs and would pleasantly socialize with peasants and nobles alike.

After nine years of living with her lover, he disappeared. He had actually been murdered under mysterious circumstances, and the body was not immediately discovered. The cavalier's dog, the one who had been the favorite of both his master and Margaret, still continued to search for the nobleman. Eventually he found the body, and then sought out Margaret. The dog tugged at the hem of her skirt until she followed it to the place where her lover lay dead.

Margaret was devastated. She began to loathe her own beauty, which she felt had drawn her lover away from a more acceptable way of living. Ultimately she returned all the jewels and property he had given her to his relatives, then left his home. She took with her only some clothes, her little son, and the dog who had discovered the crime. Her stepmother rejected her, though, when she tried to return to her father's home.

Without any means of sustaining herself, Margaret became quite desperate. She thought about trading on her beauty, and went into town with the idea of getting employment in a local bordello simply to stay alive. On the way, however, the dog once again grabbed the hem of her skirt and began to pull her. Remembering the previous time this had happened, she allowed the dog to lead her to the door of a church. Puzzled, she wandered inside and knelt down to pray.

As Margaret prayed for guidance, she believed that she heard a voice telling her to seek absolution. She rose, lovingly stroked the dog, and set off to put herself under the spiritual direction of the Franciscan friars at Cortona. She later took the veil and led a life of extreme piety, which eventually led to her sanctification. She would ultimately become the patron saint of the homeless and single mothers. The dog remained with her throughout its life, serving as a comfort and companion. Most of the traditional drawings and sculptures of Saint Margaret usually include the dog pulling at her hem, or on a leash by her side.

For some holy people, the contributions of dogs are woven tightly through the fabric of their lives. Perhaps one of the most striking examples of this was a young man, named Sucat at birth, who would later become Saint Patrick, the patron saint of Ireland. There is much that we do not know about Patrick's life, but from his sparse writings, the written records of others, and the ballads and oral histories that have been retrieved, it appears that his life and his legends are strangely entwined with dogs.

Patrick was born around the year 387 A.D., at a place not far from Dumbarton in Scotland. His father, Calpornius, was originally from an aristocratic Roman family and held the office of deacon in Britain. His mother, Concessa, was from a devout family and a near relative of the man who would become Saint Martin of Tours, the patron saint of France. Perhaps because of this, the young boy received some Christian education. Patrick's normal upbringing and education were all cut short at the age of sixteen, however, when he was abducted by Irish marauders.

Upon their return to Ireland, the raiders sold Patrick as a slave to a local chieftain named Milchu, and he was set to work as a shepherd. For the next six years he tended Milchu's flocks near what is now the town of Ballymena. This was lonely work, and for weeks at a time his sole companion was a black and white, longhaired sheepdog. During his long vigils he had time to meditate, and this strengthened his faith. At other times he would practice speaking the Celtic language of Ireland by having "conversations" with his dog, during which he instructed his companion about his insights regarding God and Christianity. How much enlightenment the dog achieved through these passionate preachings, we will never know. Patrick did achieve a perfect fluency in the Celtic tongue through these sermons, however, and this would serve him well in the future.

Around 407 or 408 A.D., Patrick had a dream (or was visited by an angel), receiving the clear message that he must travel to the coast. A ship that would be waiting there would be the first step in his return home and his entrance into his service of God. Although he had been torn from his family and pressed into slavery, Patrick still felt an obligation to his master, Milchu, who had treated him relatively fairly by the standards of the time and had not abused him. Obviously, if he took the time to return the flock to Milchu's holding, suspicions would be aroused, and it would be more difficult for him to escape his situation. Thus all he could do was to entrust the flock to his faithful sheepdog. He whispered in its ear, "Guard them well and take them home," and then murmured a prayer to God to guide the dog to do what had to be done. With several glances over his shoulder to make sure that the dog was not following him, he set off on his escape. Two hundred miles later in Westport, Patrick found the ship his dream had told him about.

To understand what happened next, you must understand some changes that had taken place during the Roman domination of Europe. Hunting was the most important sport of the aristocracy, while the principal amusement of the general population was the gladiatorial games. Over the years the novelty of seeing men in combat in the arena had worn off, so often exotic animals were brought in to fight. Dogs were popular combatants and often put on performances that excited the spectators. As the demand for new and more powerful canine gladiators began to grow, the prices that were being offered for large dogs (such as the heavy mastiff types and tall wolfhounds) began to rise sharply.

Changes in the nature of the hunt also increased the demand for dog breeds that were not common in the Roman Empire. As first practiced by the Romans, hunting was a very slow operation that involved the setting up of snares in advance. Beaters (men with drums or other noisemakers) and dogs (principally greyhounds) would then be used to drive the game in the direction of the nets. The function of the hunt was to obtain meat and to control animals that might damage crops or livestock, rather than the sporting enjoyment of a lively chase. This all changed when Rome expanded into Gaul (which is now mostly France) and Britain. There the Romans found several varieties of hounds, from which we would later develop deerhounds, wolfhounds, and harriers—dogs that are designed to chase game. By the end of the first century A.D. the hunt had become a wild scramble that required fast horses and accomplished riders to keep up with the fast-running hounds being imported from these provinces. This new manner of hunting made for great entertainment among those who could afford to keep the horses and hounds that would be needed. Thus Hadrian, the Roman emperor whose reign extended from 117 to 138 A.D., wrote about the thrill of riding his favorite horse, Borysthenes, who would "fly across the plains" in close pursuit of the dogs who had flushed out deer or wild boar.

The Romans' desire for swift and powerful dogs was insatiable. Julius Caesar mentioned dogs as among the better prizes to be won by expanding westward and into the British Isles. There are some reports that the Roman emperors actually maintained a special officer at Winchester whose title was *Procurator Cynegii,* or "Procurer of Dogs." His sole function was to select and export large mastiffs to fight in the arena, and fleet-running hounds for the nobility to use on their hunts.

The demand for fast hounds from the British Isles outlived the Roman Empire and the Roman gladiatorial games. Dogs that were not only fast but also strong enough to take on stags and wild boar were bringing fabulous prices on European markets. Because these quarry were themselves very powerful and dangerous even the best of dogs were at risk of being injured or killed in the hunt. This meant that the useful life of a hunting dog was only three to five years, and since packs often included several dozen dogs, the demand far exceeded the available supply. There was also a certain glamour associated with having the largest, fastest, and strongest dogs in a region, and the wealthy were willing to pay large sums of money for that honor.

The dogs that fetched the highest prices were the ones that we know today as Irish wolfhounds. The ship that Patrick found as he fled his slavery was a *curagh,* just like the one used by the Irish raiders that had carried him off. The boat was moored and waiting because the captain was trying to get a full cargo of wolfhounds to take back with him to Gaul. Taking advantage of this delay, Patrick approached the captain to ask if he could journey with the ship when it sailed. It is not surprising that being only a penniless runaway slave, he was received rather unsympathetically. He had no experience as a sailor, so the idea of exchanging his labor for the cost of the trip was out of the question. Patrick was saddened, and his faith was weaker, as he walked down the gangway to leave the ship. He had barely taken a step on the shore, though, when he was unexpectedly called back. The reason was the dogs.

Not only was the boat similar to those used by Irish raiders, but the morals of the captain, it seems, were similar to those of the marauders that took youths such as Patrick as slaves. To maximize his profit, the captain had opted for stealing, rather than purchasing, many of the hundred-plus Irish wolfhounds that now packed the holds and filled the deck of the ship. Wolfhounds are not toy dogs or spaniels that are easily ignored. Among today's dog breeds the Irish wolfhound is known as the tallest dog, with a shoulder height that can exceed three feet and a weight of about 135 pounds. However, this modern version is a reconstruction, since by the middle of the nineteenth century the breed had become almost extinct. The near extinction of the breed was due to the fact that the wolves, boar, and elk that it had been used to hunt for were now gone from the scene. A few samples of the breed were found and saved by a Scottish dog fancier, Captain George A. Graham, who altered the shape of the dog to its present, more manageable size. From descriptions of the dog that were written during the fourth century, however, we are led to believe that the earlier dogs were actually taller by about five inches and heavier by about thirty-five pounds. Obviously, a dog of that size could be difficult to handle if it were upset or angry.

Taken from their masters and familiar surroundings, the giant dogs on the boat were frantic and furious, and the situation was becoming intolerable. Some of the sailors had noticed that during Patrick's brief visit, however, he had spoken with some of the dogs and seemed to have a calming effect upon them. For the first time since they had been on board, some of the dogs actually wagged their tails as they allowed the young man to approach. Perhaps it was, as legend tells us, that the dogs recognized the saintly nature of this ragged person, or perhaps spending the last six years mostly in the company of animals provided him with some empathy for them. Whatever the reason, it seemed as if he could safely interact with the dogs and keep them under control. Therefore, in exchange for Patrick's services (which would involve feeding, cleaning up after, and otherwise caring for the dogs), he was given passage to the continent.

The anchor was lifted that same day, and the journey began. The ship was badly underprovisioned because it had taken longer than expected to get a full cargo of dogs, and furthermore, the huge dogs themselves consumed much more than the captain had expected. After only a few days of sailing, food began to run short, and fresh water was also becoming a problem. At the first opportunity that presented itself, the ship landed on a deserted piece of the coastline of Gaul. Such stretches of shore with few inhabitants were not unusual because the ceaseless activities of barbarian sea-raiders often made living near the sea quite dangerous unless you were in a fortified city. Patrick's ship arrived with its stores completely exhausted, and there had been nothing left to feed dogs or men for a day or so before landfall. Furthermore, the hungry voyagers could see no sources of replenishment on this barren shore.

Because the dogs were worth more than the ship, the crew took as many of the animals as they could handle, abandoned the vessel, and set off inland on foot. Unfortunately, after a long day they could still find neither inhabitants nor food in the area. Now the dogs and men were all in jeopardy of starvation.

The shipmaster, who had learned that Patrick was a Christian, then taunted him by saying, "If your God is so great, then pray to him to send us food." Patrick was not dismayed at this request, and he began to pray out loud. Tradition has it that as a result of his prayer a miracle occurred, although a skeptic might suggest that it was just a chance occurrence. Out of the trackless wilderness, a herd of wild pigs appeared, seemingly from nowhere. Instead of bolting and running, as one might have expected, the swine stayed within reach long enough for the starving men (with the assistance of the dogs) to kill a number of them. This provided meat, comfort, and salvation for all of the members of the party, canine and human alike.

As you might guess, the crew's opinion of Patrick rose considerably. They had considered selling him as a slave in the first town that they reached in order to make up for some of their costs, but now he was treated as one of the regular crew. After the dogs were marketed, the sailors even gave some food and a bit of money to help him on his way.

Patrick's association with dogs did not end in Gaul, however. Many years later, after a number of adventures and extensive training in church doctrine under the guidance of Saint Germain, he returned to Ireland. He had been having dreams in which he heard the people of Ireland calling him, saying, "O holy youth, come back to Erin, and walk once more amongst us." Now he had been charged by the church to "gather the Irish race into the one fold of Christ." This had already been tried before, but those who had gone to preach Christianity in Ireland had been met with fierce opposition. The local chieftains who still believed in the old religion of the Druids felt no moral restraint about taking any action, including murder, to ensure the supremacy of their religion. It had now fallen to Patrick to take on the daunting task of bringing Christianity to this hostile realm.

It was probably in the summer of 433 that he landed again in Ireland with a small band of other priests. The local Druids immediately began to mount a resistance. Strangely, Patrick's first victory would come because of his rapport with dogs. It seems that there was a certain Irish chieftain named Dichu who was told that a strange ship had just landed. From this ship there had emerged white-robed men with shaved heads, and these men chanted in a strange tongue. The Druids assured him that they had come to attack the old religion and would bring ruin to the country. This rallied Dichu, who then went to the coast to see if some action was needed.

Dichu reached the edge of the rocky shore just as Patrick's party was approaching. As always, his favorite dog, Luath, a large Irish wolfhound known for his ferocious nature, accompanied Dichu. Luath wore a heavy metal collar with sharpened spikes, and also hardened leather body armor to protect him from blows and knife wounds when he went into battle. He had often been used against Dichu's opponents, and the sight of such a great beast never failed to terrorize the people that he was sent against.

As he observed Patrick's missionary group, Dichu decided that the simplest course was to kill these odd clerics and be done with it. With a wave and a shout, he signaled Luath, who leaped forward in full fury with a growl that sounded like the roaring of a tiger. Dichu drew his sword and waited for the priests to scatter in response to the dog's attack, at which point he would order his men to charge and easily dispatch them. Tradition has it that it was then that Patrick's first miracle in Ireland occurred. According to the story, Patrick knelt down and uttered a short prayer. As if mesmerized, the dog halted, then quietly approached and nuzzled Patrick's hand. Dichu, whose sword was already raised, was frozen in place by the scene in front of him and could not move for many seconds. A skeptic might note that Patrick already had a history of dealing with large, angry dogs, most of which were the same breed as Luath. By kneeling and remaining still, he showed the dog that he was no threat. Whether Patrick was actually uttering a prayer or was simply making calming sounds would make no difference to the dog, since the soft singsong tones of a gentle human voice can often soothe and pacify dogs. But whether the event was due to divine intervention or the knowledge of an experienced dog handler, the effect was the same. Dichu was emotionally touched by this scene and suspended the attack. In fact, he was so impressed by the event that he asked for instruction in this new religion.

A short time later, Dichu gave Patrick a barn to serve as his church and meeting place. This sanctuary established Patrick's credibility and gave Christianity its first real foothold in Ireland. In later years, this hall would become one of the saint's favorite places to return to for meditation. A monastery and church were erected there. The Celtic word for barn is *sabhall* (pronounced saul), and, even today, this site is still known under the name Sabhall.

Much of Saint Patrick's life is known only through legend and oral tradition, so it is difficult to separate the myths from the reality. However, if we believe some of the legends, he had two more significant encounters with dogs. The first occurred at Ard Mhacha, which we now call Armagh. It was here that Daire, the chieftain of the district, had given Patrick some land to construct a church. The land was in a valley at the foot of a hill, but for some reason Patrick was not happy with this site. He was walking the area with Benan, a young convert, who would later become one of the saint's successors in the church hierarchy. Patrick was musing about the site of the new church as the afternoon grew late and the sun sank toward the horizon.

"This place is not right," he said. "We need a special place to sing praises to our Lord." At that very moment they heard a loud and ecstatic howling, and the two men looked up the hill. There, at the very top, was a great gray dog with a white blaze on its chest. The white patch was oddly shaped, being wider in the middle than at the top or bottom, so that to the two men it looked like a cross. Patrick took this as a sign that the church should be placed on the hilltop, where this dog was now singing praises to God. He would later convince Daire that this was a true message from heaven, and the most significant church in Ireland would be constructed on that hilltop in Armagh.

The story of Patrick's death and burial, at least according to tradition, includes this same dog. The saint's health was failing when he had a vision of the angel Victor, who told him that he was destined to die not in Armagh but at Sabhall, his first church in Ireland. Patrick then instructed the faithful Benan that when he was dead, his body was to be laid on a wagon hitched to two oxen. These beasts were not to be guided by Benan or any other man, but instead allowed to pull the wagon wherever they chose. Where they finally stopped was to be the place where Patrick should be buried.

On March 17, 493, Patrick died. Benan did as he was told, and all that night a shimmer of angels kept the darkness from falling on his body as it rested outside on the oxcart. Just as the morning sun rose, a great gray dog appeared. Benan was astonished, because it appeared to be the same gray dog with the blurry white cross on its chest that he and Patrick had seen before—but that had been nearly fifty years earlier! The dog walked up to the wagon, stopped, and then, as if it had been planned, he took a position in front of it. The oxen fell in behind him, and this funeral procession began to move. They walked slowly and deliberately for about two miles until they reached a place known as Dún Leathghlaise, or the "Chieftain's Fort." At that point the dog stopped, gave a howl (which sounded to Benan much like the one he remembered from the top of the hill at Armagh so many years before) and then dashed away. The oxen moved no farther, so there St. Patrick was laid to rest.

The place, which this dog had designated, was clearly a most holy place, since it is said that in this very location the body of two other saints would later be buried—namely Saint Bridget and Saint Columbia. However, no legends suggest that the bodies of these other holy people were guided to their final resting place by a great gray Irish dog or a dog of any other sort.

CHAPTER THREE

THE ANGRY PRINCE

AND THE WELSH DOG

T HE STORIES OF THE SAINTS in the last chapter were drawn from a the smattering of writing and correspondence that they left us, from witnesses or those who spoke to witnesses about the events, and from the oral record that has come down to us as a mixture of history, legend, and mythology. Although the rest of this book will be about dogs' contributions in matters where historical documents can be produced in great abundance, so that even the cynical reader can verify the accuracy of the narrative, I do want to tell one more story in which the point where the facts leave off and the legend begins is a matter of debate.

There is a story of medieval Wales that always stirs controversy among historians, literary scholars, and professors of classical studies. Much of this controversy comes from the actions of an innkeeper who was trying to attract visitors, and a poet who recorded and embellished the tale. The poet was William Robert Spencer, and his ballad *Beth-Gêlert* was the tragic saga of a heroic dog (named Gelert) and his angry, misguided master. Much like Hollywood screenwriters of today, Spencer made up details and modified names and places to create a wonderful story, but one that has obscured some of the true history. Let me tell the tale the way that I learned it from some sources that were found for me by a professor of history and a professor of classics, both on the faculty at the University of Cardiff in Wales some twenty years ago, and both of whom had researched the story.

Prince Llywelyn the Great was a long-reigning and highly successful ruler of the ancient Welsh kingdom known as Gwynedd. Protected on the north and west by the sea and on the south and east by formidable mountain ranges, Gwynedd was a natural fortress that could (and did) resist invaders for centuries. One of these protective mountain ranges, known as Snowdonia, includes Mount Snowdon, which is the highest peak in either England or Wales. The valleys are full of good pasture for animals, and grain can be grown easily on the nearby island of Anglesey.

It appears that Llywelyn was born at Dolwyddelan castle. In the time when he was growing up, there was not much peace in this region, and power struggles among the nobility were common. In fact, Llywelyn took advantage of a dispute among his uncles to seize control of the region in the year 1202. The battle with his family was fierce, and Llywelyn was ruthless, exiling or executing any who opposed him. He soon developed a reputation for having a quick temper, and for acting without careful consideration of alternatives. Nonetheless, his courage and energy gave him a number of military victories, and after the death of Lord Rhys he emerged as the most powerful of all the Welsh rulers.

At that time, the king of England was John, brother of Richard the Lionheart. Watching Llywelyn expand his empire, John noted that he might soon be a threat. Llywelyn was clever enough to recognize this growing tension between himself and the English king, and tried to ease matters with a politically inspired marriage to John's daughter. Llywelyn then went on to assist John in a military campaign against King William of Scotland.

For Llywelyn's help as an ally, as well as to honor his new family tie, King John gave him a young Irish wolfhound, which Llywelyn named Cylart. Cylart was sometimes referred to as being a greyhound, but only because any large dog who was not too square or bulky was often called a greyhound at that time (in much the same way that many people today refer to all breeds of northern dogs with bushy hair, a pointed face, pricked ears, and a plumed tail that is carried curved over its back as a "Husky"). The label seems to have stuck for Cylart, however, since later engravings and ballads all make him out to be a greyhound. Cylart soon became a trusted companion and guard who was with Llywelyn almost continuously.

Cylart was said to be unusually intelligent, and would pick up voice intonations or other cues to form opinions about individuals. When people with hostile attitudes toward Llywelyn were in his presence, he would always stand between his master and the antagonist, growling if voices rose too quickly. Such outbursts of anger were common. This was understandable because Llywelyn rose to his position by force, which earned him respect but little love from the nobles. These nobles owed their own positions to their hereditary right to own land, which in turn gave them power over their tenant farmers and slaves. Their only duty to the king was to repair bridges and roads on their lands, and to provide service and troops in time of war. The king could choose to ignore or rescind these obligations as a favor, or a noble might feel powerful enough to resist his monarch's attempts to enforce them. Those who chose to test their power against Llywelyn found that he was quick to express his displeasure, which would often turn to wrath and bring him off his throne to face the offender. At such moments of anger Llywelyn would instinctively reach for his sword, and when confronted by this physically powerful man with a sword in hand, and a large gray dog snarling protectively by his side, most opponents quickly backed off and became more respectful.

Cylart also appointed himself the bodyguard of Llywelyn's wife, Joan, and his new young son, Dafydd, whenever they were near. Dafydd was still really a baby, not capable of walking more than a few steps. Several times Cylart had saved Dafydd from harm, once by dragging him back from the edge of a high staircase when he had crawled too close and was in danger of falling. Another time, a spark from the fireplace had ignited a rug on which the child's bed rested. It was then Cylart who sounded the alarm that brought the household in time to put out the blaze before much damage was done.

In addition, Cylart had killed more than one rat in the nursery. Rats were common at that time. They particularly liked being around the places children frequented since it was there that bits of food were most likely to land on the floor. However, the rats of that time were brazen. People, particularly children, were known to have been bitten by rats in their sleep, and such bites could often cause infections that might cost the loss of a finger or limb or even result in death. Thus Cylart's guardianship of Dafydd and Joan was a comfort to Llywelyn if only because he could be a shield against common household calamities.

Over several years, the situation with King John changed. Llywelyn had been expanding his territory, capturing land from some of the minor lords who had been installed on Welsh land by John. Furthermore, Llywelyn was consolidating his political hold on the country by sharing his conquests with the lesser nobles, thereby gaining their loyalty and support. Llywelyn had been offered the title of King of Wales by his allies; however, he modestly declined and accepted the title of Prince of Wales—although King John would not acknowledge such claims of royal status. Both cruel and ambitious, John decided to take back the lands he had lost, and if possible destroy Llywelyn in the process. By 1210 he had begun a series of raids and encroachments into Wales, which would turn into a full-scale invasion the following year.

Safety was steadily becoming more of an issue, and Llywelyn was leading small groups of armed men to stop the various raids upon his territory. Since Joan was pregnant again and had been having a difficult time, she had been sent to the nearby abbey, Beth Kelert, for both care and safety. The English raiders had come very close to Llywelyn's home, and the prince had sent his household servants to a nearby stronghold. However, he had decided to keep Dafydd, who was the heir to the throne, with him. At the foot of some hills, the prince's party noticed signs that their enemy might have passed close by. Llywelyn decided that a quick reconnaissance would be needed to see if any English troops were still in the vicinity. Not wishing to expose Dafydd to the fatigue of a rough expedition over the hills and steep places where a man needs hands as well as feet to scramble along, he decided to leave the child behind. A shelter in the form of a roughly put-up tent was quickly assembled, and Llywelyn decided to leave the baby in the care of a guardian as faithful and trustworthy as any of his followers— namely, his stalwart dog, Cylart. He had done this before, and Cylart appeared to be a competent baby-sitter. Besides, the child was effectively penned inside his bed, and the tent was hidden behind an outcropping of rock and would be out of sight to any casual passersby. The baby was given his fill of goat's milk, and left under the guard of Cylart.

The expedition was only supposed to last for a couple of hours. Llywelyn's men came upon some English soldiers, however, and by the time they finally made their way back to the camp after a skirmish and a brief chase, evening was falling and the light was beginning to wane.

As they rounded the rocks that shielded the camp from view, they immediately knew that something was wrong. The tent had been knocked over, and the fabric was ripped in several places. Even more frightening were the reddish stains visible on the surface of the cloth, and the large and obvious pool of blood oozing from beneath the toppled shelter. A glance at Cylart immediately associated him with the carnage. His fur, lips, and fangs were covered with the sticky red of blood that has just begun to congeal. Instead of leaping forward to greet his master with a wagging tail, he remained sitting by the torn and bloodstained tent, with ears pulled back, giving only a few glances down and a single hesitant thump of his tail.

Llywelyn was naturally hotheaded, and this day had not gone well at all. His routine reconnaissance had turned into a fight, and one of his men was wounded. This alone would have made him irritable and susceptible to fatigue and worry. Now the scene in front of him, combined with his dog's strange behavior, excited his suspicions and led to a horrifying conclusion. He stared at the dog and then cried out, "My God, Cylart! You monster! You have killed my child!" Overwhelmed by rage, he snatched the spear from the man beside him and rushed at the dog. The fact that the dog did not bound out of the way should have provided one last clue, but Llywelyn was blind to all thoughts except for grief and revenge. With a yelp, Cylart fell beneath his master's thrust.

Llywelyn's next act—and no one more than he wished it had been his first— was to look within the folds of the tent. The baby he had thought killed (and perhaps devoured) uttered a loud cry as his cover was pulled up. Lying near the child was a mangled wolf, whose size and vicious teeth made him appear to be terrible even in death. It was now clear to Llywelyn's horror-struck eyes that the blood which covered everything was from this attacker who had tried to take his child, and from the dog who had defended him.

Llywelyn had been quick to strike with his spear, but now he seemed even quicker in racing to the dying Cylart. As his hands moved over the dog, he now felt other wounds, the legacy of the struggle to save his son. The wounds that he had received from the attacking wolf accounted for the dog's odd behavior; he was simply in too much pain to come forward to greet his master. The warrior prince, who could be quite merciless, sat with the crumpled body of his dog and cried. As the tears fell, Cylart lifted his head for one last time. He gently licked the hand that he had loved so well, and which in an act of mindless rage had ended his life.

It is recorded that Llywelyn mourned over Cylart as he had over the death of his brother. The dog was buried by a favorite tree near Llywelyn's home.

Traditionally, the story of the events that took place in 1210 ends here. Close to six hundred years later, though, the landlord of the Goat's Inn became involved in the tale. By this time, because of a chain of mispronunciations, Cylart's

name had been changed in the retellings to Gelert. The name of this region in
Wales had now become known as Beddgelert, with the translation accepted as
being "Gelert's grave," while in fact the region was originally called Beth Kelert
after the abbey that had been there for so many generations. So in 1794, the
innkeeper told the inhabitants of the town that he "felt compelled by the crav-
ings of tourists to invent a grave." That empty grave, and a stone marker retelling
the version of the story that Spencer would use as the basis for his poem, can still
be seen in Beddgelert today. Spencer was interested in the dramatic aspect of the
story, so perhaps he can be forgiven for designating the wrong location for the
events, the wrong breed of dog, the wrong dog's name, and other details of
the incident that are also not quite correct. He did accomplish his goal, after all,
in that he did pen a moving and memorable poem.

However, Cylart's contribution to Welsh history gave us more than a pretty
piece of poetry and a tourist trap. To begin with, by saving Dafydd's life he ensured the orderly succession of the throne. A much more immediate outcome
was the influence that Cylart would have on Llywelyn's behavior in later years.

At the end of the year King John invaded, and Prince Llywelyn was forced
back toward the western mountains. Because John had troubles with the Pope,
King Philip of France, and even with some of his own barons, however, he could
not press the advantage any farther. This gave Llywelyn the chance he needed to
capture back the land that he had lost.

Norman lords (known as the Marcher Lords) appointed by the king had
been installed on strategic properties and thus controlled most of the English
land bordering Wales. With his recent successes, and with an alliance of Welsh
princes, Llywelyn felt that this was the time to strike against these minor nobles.
He held a meeting to discuss the plans for his campaign. As he outlined his plans
to attack immediately and decisively to let the English king know that his actions would not go unpunished, Madog ap Gruffudd, the lord of one of the
northern provinces, spoke up. Madog had been Llywelyn's faithful ally almost
from the beginning of the prince's rise to power. He had also met Llywelyn on
his return from that fateful expedition when he carried home the body of Cylart.

He solemnly stood and began to speak. "My lord, I hear you say the words
'strike quickly' and also say the words 'we shall have our revenge.' Once before
you struck quickly, to revenge an act of violence and that cost you the life of Cylart, who had been so true and faithful and to whom you owe the life of your

oldest son. For the sake of that memory, let us pause and consider if there are any alternatives before we act."

Prince Llywelyn did respond to this plea. He did not attack the Anglo-Norman lords, but instead sought to establish alliances. Eventually he consolidated his position by marrying his daughters into the families of the Marcher Lords, bringing relative peace in a period when conflict was the norm. Ultimately his hallmark became the careful consideration of alternatives before taking any rash or violent actions—the very kind of judicious behavior that could have saved Cylart's life. It served him in good stead. By judiciously joining the barons' party in England, Llywelyn secured three clauses for Welsh rights in the Magna Carta of King John. Upon the death of John, Prince Llywelyn (now acknowledged as a true prince) paid homage to young King Henry III and lived in peace until his death at Aberconway abbey in 1240.

It is said that all of his life Llywelyn regretted the rash behavior that killed his heroic dog. Perhaps it is for that reason that Cylart lives on today in a Welsh expression: *Yr wŷn edivaru cymmaint âr Gwr a laddodd ei Vilgi,* which translates roughly as "I am as sorry and remorseful as the man who slew his greyhound."

CHAPTER FOUR

THE DEVIL DOG OF THE

ENGLISH CIVIL WAR

D OGS DO HAVE A WAY of weaving their influence through human events and subtly altering the course of history. When you look for evidence of this in standard historical and biographical books, however, you will seldom find dogs mentioned. For most historians the only important matters are political, military, or social movements (or the technical aspects of music, art, or science if the topic is in those realms). The only players in history are people, the thinking goes. The fact that these people had dogs with them is taken as being of no more consequence than the fact that they always had shoes on their feet. Of course there are a few events, such as when a dog becomes a symbol for something, that might force a mention of a dog in a biography—but if so, it will be brief, and then the historian will turn back to matters of greater scope. However, by overlooking the contributions of dogs one often misses much of the flavor of the times and sometimes neglects influences on events that may turn out to be of great significance later on. In addition, by ignoring a loved dog, one often loses a chance to understand the personality of the historically significant individual. Let's begin with a situation where dogs played a role in starting a revolution, and a role in losing a war.

When historians speak of the English Revolution or English Civil War, they are most apt to focus on the clash between Parliament and the king over funds (taxes and levies), military operations, and religious practice. Some historians will emphasize the personality of the ill-fated Charles I and his father, James I. Both were completely inflexible in their belief in a divine right of kings to govern as they see fit, without any interference or controls from other government bodies. Obviously, such an attitude would incense the parliamentary ministers.

Historians will also point to another source of stress that contributed to the uprising against the monarchy. Specifically, Charles also believed in the ultimate authority of the Church of England, and as its head, he maintained that it was in his power to unilaterally determine the nature of religious practice and observance in his nation. His attempt to impose a new liturgy based upon the English Book of Common Prayer, for example, was interpreted by the Scots as an attack on their Presbyterian religion.

All of these elements did have a major impact on the events to come. It is certainly true that by the middle of the seventeenth century, dissatisfaction with the Stuart dynasty had risen to the point that outright rebellion seemed to be an acceptable alternative. However, historians and political scientists seldom mention that dogs had a major role to play in the general discontent that led to the English Civil War.

The canine influence on events began with James I, the father of Charles I. Prior to James, most hunting by nobles was done in a manner that was efficient, but not very exciting. In their search for entertainment and sport, the aristocrats of James's era modified this mundane activity and turned it into a combination of spectacle and shooting gallery.

The new "hunting pageant" would be staged entirely on wooded land owned by a noble, or in a protected royal park. Special shooting platforms (called pavilions) were constructed to place the courtiers well out of danger from the animals. Men with noisemakers and dogs would force the game to travel along narrowly defined paths in front of the platforms. As the deer passed, the lords and ladies would open fire with steel crossbows that were handed to them—already cocked and loaded with heavy darts capped by sharpened metal heads. The nobility simply waited until the pursuing dogs brought the quarry to within range and then tried to bring it down with a clean shot through the heart or throat. Unfortunately, not all of the gentry were good shots, and often it would be one of the hounds following the deer that would end up wounded or killed by the bolt.

Regardless of what one might think about the morality of such sport, it was at least a pastime that did not intrude upon the general population. The noble who had convened the hunt would bear the expense, and all of the activities would be conducted on private land, out of sight of the common subjects living in the countryside.

With the crowning of James I, the formal pageant would disappear, and the limited scope of the hunt would widen to involve the private fields and meadows of all English subjects. James had been hunting since he was a child, and in fact his first portrait, which was done when he was eight or nine years of age, shows him as a falconer. He would continue to hunt up to the year of his death in 1624. The hunting style that captured his interest (just as it had captured the attention of many post-conquest Roman citizens centuries earlier) was that of the French, where riders would spur their horses to breakneck speed to keep up with their speedy hounds. Virtually the first thing that James did when he succeeded Elizabeth I was to set up a vast hunting establishment. Since he wanted to hunt in the French style, he felt that it would be sensible to import some French hounds to begin with, as well as some French huntsmen to instruct his own hunters in the techniques of the chase. For his own special enjoyment he also went so far as to import close to fifty red deer from the French king Henri IV's protected forest at Fontainebleau. In addition, he brought in a separate huntsman and a special pack of hounds for his queen, Anne of Denmark. This infusion of new huntsmen, new dogs, and new ideas would completely change the English style of hunting.

The array of dogs that James kept for his hunting pleasure was astonishing. His kennels contained many dog breeds that we can recognize today, including greyhounds, Irish wolfhounds, deerhounds, harriers, otterhounds, field spaniels (to accompany the hawks), water spaniels, setters, beagles, and a variety of terriers. In addition, he kept some breeds that have disappeared from the scene, such as liamhounds, sleuthhounds (an ancestor of our bloodhounds) and boarhounds.

Some of the enemies of James maintained that he virtually lived in the saddle in part because he did not look very impressive when he was on foot. A defect that he developed either in early childhood or at birth gave him a shambling gait when he walked, and his hands moved in an odd fashion as he tried to keep his balance. He often had to lean his weight on the person beside him in order to walk in a straight line. But whether he felt that riding made him look more respectable or because he simply loved to hunt, what is important is that James spent as much time hunting as he could. In this way, James was not much different from many of the country squires of his era. Hunting was all that these landed gentlemen seemed to care about. If one wrote to another without mentioning his most recent hunts, his friend's reply might well contain a query such as, "Does all go well with you? In all your letters I find not one word of horse, hawk, and hound."

James's passion for hunting with his dogs would ultimately have some consequences that would change history. The French kings, including William the Conqueror, Louis XI, and Charles VIII, had asserted that the right to hunt was a "royal prerogative," meaning that it was a privilege reserved for—and controlled by—the nobility. The aim of hunting was no longer to provide food; it was now a sport. As a formal royal activity it was expected that the subjects of the realm, including other nobles, clergy, and of course all of the commoners (including bailiffs, farmers, and foresters) would be expected to assist and provide service. This was essential because of the great distances that were often traveled during a fast hunt. It was not unusual for the hunters to be so carried away by the fever of the chase that by the end of the day they might find themselves twenty to fifty miles from their starting place. With the huntsmen, dogs, and horses all dead tired and so far from home, it was necessary to be able to claim hospitality from those who lived nearby. Soon the expectations associated with this forced lodging gradually escalated. No longer satisfied with a simple meal and a place to rest, now these self-invited guests felt that they should be provided with all that was needed for a feast, a long bout of drinking, and a night of revelry.

When James embraced the French style of hunting he also adopted the attitudes of the French nobility, along with the expectation of support from his subjects. A stream of orders and demands on the population preceded each royal hunt. If James was going to hunt deer, or to use hawks and spaniels on partridges or other birds, the farmers in the local region would be ordered not to plough their land in narrow ridges, and to put rings on their pigs to keep them from digging holes as they rooted in the ground—since furrows and holes could prove to be hazardous to the king when he was mounted on a horse and moving quickly. Local residents also were required to take down walls, fences, or hedges that might hinder His Majesty's ready passage. He even went so far as requiring landowners to put up locked gates between fenced fields and to make sure that only the royal huntsmen had keys to these gates. The orders would change depending upon the game being hunted. Thus, during the otter-hunting season James would order the millers to shut down their watercourses to prevent the otters from using them as hiding places or escape routes.

Even worse than the restrictions was the expense involved in the hunt. The "old fashioned" hunts were restricted affairs, but this new kind of hunt was different. It was conducted outside of parks and noble estates. In hunting deer, the royal huntsman would first assemble a pack of twenty to thirty hounds, then he would select a deer from the royal herd. Once the deer was set loose, the dogs were put on its track and the horsemen followed behind. This was a fast pursuit, and the hunt traveled at a speed that made it impossible to avoid considerable damage to property that it passed over. Crops were trampled down, fences were damaged, gardens were destroyed, and flocks of sheep and herds of dairy cows were scattered—all causing great expense and distress among farmers, herdsmen, and the owners of small estates in the countryside.

Not only did the common people have to suffer this damage to their property without any compensation, they also had to provide beaters and other workers to assist in the hunt. This would take people away from their work, often at critical times of the year. Even worse, the population was supposed to also provide food and forage for the hunters, horses, and dogs. This was not a trivial matter, since James had numerous huntsmen and falconers. A simple day spent falconing typically involved the services of twenty-four falconers (with an appropriate number of dogs and horses) and a dozen attendants, plus guests and so forth. The cost of providing for such a party for a single day could be a massive burden for a farmer and his neighbors; however, the expense would often be a repeated one since it was the king's habit to hunt several times each week.

When the country folk tried to appeal to the king, if not for payment—at least for some temporary relief from these expenses—their messages were either ignored or simply intercepted by intermediaries and kept from the king. Once, in desperation, some of the citizens who were being hurt by these activities tried to use one of the king's own dogs as a messenger. During one hunt, the huntsman noticed at the end of the day that one of the king's favorite hounds, a dog named Jowler, had gone missing. The next morning, just as the hounds were being readied for the field, Jowler turned up again. The king noticed that a piece of paper had been tied to the dog's collar. When it was brought to him, he found a message that read as follows:

Good Mr. Jowler, we pray you speak to the King, for he hears you every day, and he does not hear us. Ask that His Majesty be pleased to go back to London, or else this countryside will be undone. All our provisions are used up already, and we are not able to entertain him any longer.

Unfortunately, James simply took this as joke, laughed heartily, and then went on with the hunt. For the people he was imposing upon, however, this was no longer a laughing matter.

Perhaps the worst insult to be borne by his English subjects had to do with the way James acquired the dogs that he used in his sporting activities. Although he did keep his own kennels, he often had to augment the royal packs with additional dogs that were simply seized from the ordinary citizens who owned them. In 1616 he gave Henry Mynours the commission of Master of the Otterhounds, with the very broad entitlement "to take for us and in our name in all places within this realm of England . . . such and so many hounds, beagles, spaniels and mongrels, as well as dogs and bitches fit for hunting the otter as the said Henry Mynours shall think fit." Even if a citizen had a dog that would not be desirable for the hunt (such as a guard dog or a sheepdog), it could be seized and perhaps summarily killed, since the commission further read, "And we do also hereby authorize the said Henry Mynours to seize and take away all such hounds, beagles, and other dogs as are or may be offensive to our game and sport." This caused dogs to be confiscated from people all over England.

Some people may have had some solace that at least their loved companion dog might have a good life and be well cared for as a member of the king's hunting pack. In other cases, however, they watched their dogs taken away and sent to a sure death, because James had still another dog sport that he forced the population to support as well.

Early in his life, James had developed a fondness for bull- and bearbaiting. Animal baiting was probably the last vestige of the Roman games, where combat—often to the death—was viewed as a sport. In Rome, the nature of this combat could involve any combination of human warriors and animals. The British, being more civilized, simply took the humans out of the arena and let the animals serve as gladiators. For example, in bullbaiting, dogs were placed in a pit to fight a tethered bull. If a dog could grab the bull by the nose or throat and force it to its knees, then the dog was said to have won. If the bull killed or badly wounded the dog, then obviously the bull had won. Sometimes, instead of a bull, a bear would be put in the pit for a fight, or the combat might simply be a dog pitted against another dog. These battles were not merely spectator sports but were the basis for high-stakes gambling on winners, fight length, who drew first blood, and so forth.

James had become addicted to this "sport" and was always seeking ways to make the fights more exciting. At one point he came across a statement by the sixteenth-century travel writer Abraham Ortelius, in which it was claimed that the English mastiff was just as courageous as any lion. Finding that some lions were kept in the Tower of London, he ordered a combat between three mastiffs and a lion. The dogs were let loose against the lion one by one. The first two did not survive the combat, but the third did manage to bite the great cat so severely that it sought refuge in a den that had been provided. The dog was then declared the winner and given a comfortable retirement (because the king felt that any dog that had successfully fought a lion should never be matched against any inferior creature). This dog was extremely lucky, since the usual reward for a victorious dog was another, stronger opponent in the next match. It was not expected that dogs would survive more than a few fights.

In much the same way that James appointed Henry Mynours to confiscate hunting dogs for the king's pleasure, he appointed Edward Alleyn as the "Chief master, ruler and overseer of all and singular games, of bears and bulls and mastiff dogs and mastiff bitches." With this commission, Alleyn had unlimited authority to snatch any dogs that he felt were suitable for the baiting ring.

Seizure of dogs for the king's hunt or for the baiting ring was extremely unpopular. Many of the people who were forced to contribute dogs for the king's sport did so with little grace. With increasing frequency, officials who appeared to enforce these dog levies would be openly opposed, perhaps even attacked and beaten. The opposition was spreading so widely that local justices often refused to bring the offenders to trial. Some towns reached a grudging accord with the officials, agreeing to send a few good dogs for the king's service as long as none of the hated officers set foot within the boundaries of the township.

Another source of opposition was also becoming more visible. The Puritans, who at that time held the majority in Parliament, felt that hunting was a sin. They reminded James that God condemned the Old Testament figure King Nimrod. Nimrod was described as a mighty hunter, and it was his hunting that the Puritans interpreted as being his sin. The argument offered was that God intended the living beasts of this world for man's delight and improvement, but not for slaughter or cruelty. The only concession that James offered in response to the resulting public pressure was to ban animal baiting on Sundays. All the rest remained the same.

When James died in 1625, his ill-fated son, Charles I, ascended to the throne. It was a time of great social, financial, and religious turmoil, and, unfortunately, Charles was not temperamentally suited to deal with the situation. Just as his father before him, Charles was completely inflexible in his belief of the divine right of kings to govern as they see fit. He simply dissolved Parliament when it tried to curtail his activities, a tactic that brought him into an escalating conflict with successive Parliaments. His continuation and extension of the unpopular policies toward dogs and forced public support of the royal hunt increased the nation's negative feelings toward his reign. All of this contributed to the passions that ultimately made the idea of civil war acceptable to a large segment of the population.

Charles also made no attempt to stop animal baiting since, like his father, he was a devotee of that cruel pastime. He continued seizing dogs to fill out his own hunting packs, in much the way that James had. Only three years into his reign, the issue of the seizure of dogs brought Charles into direct conflict with a member of the family of the man who would ultimately topple his monarchy and order his execution. This man was Oliver Cromwell—not the general and revolutionary, but the Puritan country squire who was the uncle and godfather of the namesake who would lead the forces against the king during the English Civil War. During the reign of James, Cromwell had been called upon to present the king with "swift and deep-mouthed hounds" more than once. These were to be offered as "gifts" for the king. When Charles took the throne he found that more such "gifts" were no longer being volunteered, so he ordered the dogs to be requisitioned. He appointed Lord Compton as the Master of His Majesty's Leash, and gave him a commission to seize "greyhounds and other dogs for his Majesty's sport and recreation." One of the targets of this was the elder Oliver Cromwell, who, rather than provoke open conflict, offered the dogs as required—but only after a contingent of Lord Compton's armed officers arrived at his door.

You can readily imagine the feelings of Cromwell and the other country squires who found themselves the unwilling patrons of Charles's royal hunt. The bitterness was increased by the fact that they were losing their favorite animals. The animals that were being taken were not only an integral part of the people's own ability to participate in smaller-scale hunting but often were valued family companions.

These same gentlemen would have to suffer yet another insult (the brunt of which would also be borne by their dogs) when Charles decided to extend the range of the royal forests. Although he already owned sixty-eight forests, he wanted to expand them to the wider borders that had been relinquished centuries earlier. In part this was done to improve revenue, since Charles's conflicts with Parliament had incited the ministers to withhold his rights to collect many forms of taxes and tariffs. The people who lived in the annexed area became "tenants of the crown," owing rent and fees directly to the king.

This action affected dog owners outside the forests themselves because the laws protecting these royal preserves included the restriction that no human or animal could hunt the game there except the king or those granted a royal permit. Specifically, the law read that any large dogs within or near a royal forest would have to be maimed or mutilated to destroy their ability to hunt anything within the royal preserve. Foresters had the right to lop three foreclaws off the dog, to cut the hamstring muscle of a leg, or cut out the balls of the dog's feet. Each of these injuries would reduce the dog to a slow limp and would thus prevent it from successfully hunting deer or anything else that moved swiftly.

With the extension of the forest area, landowners who had lived on their family lands for hundreds of years now found themselves faced with the withdrawal of their hunting rights, and the prospect of being forced to allow the king's foresters to mutilate their dogs. This policy was so unpopular that it often required force of arms to carry it out, and many of the aggrieved dog owners would later express their anger by joining with the revolutionary forces against the king.

The English Revolution began in October of 1642. The supporters of Parliament were called Roundheads, because many of the Puritans trimmed their hair by using a bowl as a guide, so that a curved edge would lie against the neck. The supporters of the king were known as Cavaliers, a term that originally was used for mounted soldiers and knights. Although it originally had connotations of being gallant, in the context of the revolution the term *cavalier* would come to be used by the opponents of the king as a derogatory term for anyone who acted in an aristocratic or haughty manner. There was some small military comfort for the royalist side, in that the transformation of English hunting style to a wild ride behind dogs had produced a highly proficient cavalry force.

Now we move from the unrest caused by the king's treatment of many dogs and their people, to one dog and his influence on the war of revolution that had just begun. Dogs have often served as mascots in wartime, either boosting morale among the troops or providing comfort and companionship for a military leader. However, in these capacities dogs seldom get more than a casual glance or an acknowledgement from the enemy, and certainly have no effect on the opposition's morale and spirit. The exception to this rule involved the companion of Prince Rupert of the Palatinate—a dog who came to be known as the "devil dog of the Cavaliers."

Prince Rupert of the Palatinate made his mark as the most talented of the royalist commanders during the English Civil War. His tactical genius and his daring as a cavalry officer brought him many victories early in the war. Rupert was born in Prague in 1619. His father, who was then elector of the Palatinate, ultimately would become Frederick I, king of Bohemia. Rupert's connection to the English royal line was through his mother, who was Charles's much-loved sister Elizabeth. Rupert visited Charles in 1636 and the handsome and high-spirited young man became a favorite of his uncle.

Rupert had been trained for military service since he was a young child. His intelligence, ability to command, and his bravery (combined, of course, with his royal connections) earned him an officer's rank at the age of eighteen. Hunting behind swift-running packs of dogs turned him into a superb horseman, which confirmed his suitability to command cavalry troops. Within a year of his commission, he was called upon to fight in the Thirty Years' War in support of the elector and against the imperial forces. During this campaign, he distinguished himself with his daring (some might say reckless) actions. He also showed a clever tactical sense, and an ability to rally his troops behind him. He speedily rose to command a regiment of dragoons, the most heavily armed of the cavalry troops. When the imperial troops broke the siege at Lemgo in Münster, Rupert and the remaining forces were ordered to withdraw. Due to inadequate intelligence information and some dubious tactical decisions by his commander, General James King, the troops were sent in the direction of the main enemy force. In the resulting battle at Vlotho near the Weser River, Rupert found himself outnumbered and surrounded. He was captured there, then held captive for the next three years at Linz in Austria.

At that time, captured royalty were not usually imprisoned in musty dungeons or camps. Although confined, they were treated civilly and had certain amenities granted to them. It was expected that such prisoners would ultimately be returned to their home after a ransom was paid or some concession was gained. Rupert was allowed to practice his military skills, and, under supervision, he could still occasionally ride and hunt. Much of the time he was confined to his rooms, however, and he had only limited access to social interactions of any sort. It was here that a dog enters the scene.

At that time Lord Arundell was the English ambassador to Vienna. Charles had asked Arundell to look after Rupert as best he could until matters could be resolved. To provide some companionship for Rupert the ambassador brought him a dog named Boye, described in written histories as a large white poodle. Though Boye certainly looks like a poodle in the caricatures of the time and in the portrait later painted by Princess Louise, he was quite large for his breed— indeed, big enough and strong enough to run with his master's horse. According to the Countess of Sussex, who accompanied Rupert some years later on a hunt in Buckinghamshire, Boye supposedly helped to pull down five red deer bucks (no mean feat for any poodle!).

During Rupert's imprisonment Boye was a great comfort, and the prince spent many hours training him. This established a bond that would last throughout Boye's life and also made the dog extremely responsive to Rupert's moods and desires.

When Rupert was released, he almost immediately went to England to assist his uncle Charles in the civil war that was beginning. Although he was still only twenty-three years of age, on the basis of his performance in the elector's army, he received command of the cavalry. Meanwhile, his curly-coated white dog remained with him almost continuously. When Rupert ate his meals, Boye was there. When Rupert attended councils with the king or with his military commanders, Boye was there. When Rupert attended church, the dog was with him, as he was when he visited his soldiers or formally reviewed his troops on the parade ground. He even slept beside his master in the same bed.

Boye was apparently quite an amiable dog. Much like a politician, however, he knew who the important people were. After Rupert himself, Boye singled out King Charles as the person that would receive most of his affection. Charles, whose love of dogs was deep, responded very favorably to the dog's affection. It was observed of the king that "he himself never sups or dines, but continually he feeds him. And with what think you? Even with sides of capons, and such Christian-like morsels." At other times Charles would slide over in his great, thronelike chair and invite Boye to sit upon it with him as he conversed with those around him. One Roundhead sympathizer wrote, "It is thought the King will make him Sergeant-Major-General Boye. But truly the King's affection to him is so extraordinary that some at court envy him."

Boye's size and white color made him visible at great distances across the field. Because his visibility meant that Prince Rupert was also near, the sight of the dog became a comfort and a rallying point to the Cavalier troops, who loved and respected the prince. With Rupert and Boye leading the royalist offensive, the swift-moving Cavalier forces won a series of brilliant victories at Bristol, Birmingham, Newark, and Lancashire. Soon Boye had become the unofficial mascot of the army. After each victory, the roistering Cavaliers would toast the dog and were sometimes seen "upon their knees, drinking Healths to Prince Rupert's dog."

The same visibility and presence near Rupert that caused Boye to be loved by the Cavaliers caused the opposing forces to hate and fear him. They attributed to this "devil dog" all sorts of supernatural powers. Rupert always seemed to anticipate the movements and plans of the parliamentary armies, and the Roundheads soon were whispering rumors that Boye had special abilities: "He can go invisibly himself, and make others do so too." The fear was that the dog and his master were stealing into their camps under the cloak of invisibility conveyed by Boye's evil magic, and in that invisible form they were able to gather vital intelligence for Prince Rupert to use.

The fact that Rupert had never been wounded, although he was always out front with his troops, led the parliamentarian forces to suspect that Boye had other powers. The revolutionaries thought that by his very presence, Boye protected his master. A person who called himself T.B. and purported to be a Roundhead spy described Boye this way: "He is Weapon-proof himself and probably hath made his master so too. My self, and the rest whom you have employed to be of the conspiracy against him have always failed in our attempts, as if something more than Witchcraft watched over him."

Sir Edward Southcote would note in his memoirs that Boye was almost more feared than Prince Rupert: "The Roundheads fancied he was the Devil, and took it very ill that he should set himself against them!" John Cleveland would celebrate these feelings in his poem *Rupertismus,* noting, "they fear even his dog, that four-legged Cavalier." Cleveland added that the parliamentarians believed that Boye "is a devil without doubt."

The sight of Boye became so disheartening that the revolutionary armies effectively put a price upon his head. Soldiers were instructed that if they saw the dog they should ignore all other targets and try to kill him—even if it meant sacrificing the opportunity to attack Rupert or another high-ranking officer. None other than Sir Thomas Fairfax, the commander in chief of the Roundhead forces, was reported to have told his officers, "It has occurred to certain of us that only with the death of that hound from Hell can our victory be secured."

Unfortunately, on July 2, 1644, Rupert's string of victories, Boye's life, and the royalist hope of victory would all end on Marston Moor. Despite the early military successes, the Roundheads were showing no signs of giving up the struggle, and King Charles was feeling desperate. This caused him to write a letter that Rupert interpreted as a direct command to march at once to York and not only relieve the besieged city, but also directly attack and defeat the main body of parliamentary forces. Rupert's creed had always been loyalty and obedience, and although his own judgment of the situation did not give him much hope of success, he felt compelled to obey.

Rupert's brilliance and bravery did allow him to outmaneuver the city's besiegers, and to relieve the threat to York. His own assessment of the situation was that he should stop and consolidate his forces with that victory; however, his orders required him to pursue the parliamentary forces. After a chase of seven miles, on Marston Moor, the full force of the parliamentary armies under Sir Thomas Fairfax, combined with a Scottish army under Alexander Leslie, managed to surprise Rupert with an early-evening attack. Oliver Cromwell commanded the left wing of the parliamentary forces, which managed to turn and scatter Rupert's cavalry, and then Cromwell continued closing to the right until his forces enveloped the royalist center. This was not merely the first major military loss of the Cavalier forces—it was a disaster. The Royalists suffered heavy casualties with close to four thousand killed, a similar number taken prisoner, and most of their cannons captured. Charles ultimately lost control of not only York but the entire northern part of the country.

The impact of the Cavalier defeat at Marston Moor for two of the participants in the battle was great. Oliver Cromwell emerged as the leading parliamentary general due to his success. Prince Rupert, however, took this defeat as a major personal disaster, since it not only badly damaged his army but cost him his beloved companion, Boye.

There are several stories as to how Boye's death came about. Some suggest that someone simply forgot to tie the dog up prior to the battle or that he simply slipped his leash, and thus ended up among the combatants. Others say that as Rupert's mascot, the dog was allowed to follow him into battle, and this time he just came too close to the fighting. One Roundhead officer claimed that a contingent of armed men was deliberately sent to where the dog was most likely to be kept, with the idea of capturing him and bringing him back alive to demoralize the Cavaliers. (Perhaps they also feared they would need assistance from their priests to kill the demon that they felt inhabited the dog.) This force had actually reached the dog when they were detected, and rather than chance his return to Rupert, the Roundheads turned their muskets on him. Whatever the truth, Boye's body was recovered with multiple bullet wounds and several stab wounds, suggesting that his attackers wanted him dead very badly.

When Rupert heard the news, he could not control the tears that came to his eyes. In an attempt to keep his emotional state from being detected, he tried to treat the occurrence as merely another bad event on that tragic day. He did this with the greatest tribute that a cavalry officer could give to a mere animal, saying, "Rather I would have lost the best horse in my stable." Unfortunately, as he uttered this statement his voice broke, and the tears started to flow again. Instead of continuing and giving any further appearance that might suggest weakness to his assembled officers, he turned and walked away.

When the news of the events at Marston Moor reached the Parliament, the rejoicing among the Roundheads knew no bounds. While pamphlets sang the praises of their generals, the extreme Puritan elements were particularly happy about the death of Boye and about Rupert's obvious grief. A poem soon began to circulate with the title "A Dog's Elegy, or Rupert's Tears." A few lines of it will indicate how elated the Roundheads were:

Lament poor Cavaliers, ay, howl and yelp
For the great loss of your Malignant Welp,
He's dead! He's dead! No more alas can he
Protect your Dammes, or get Victory.
How sad that Son of Blood did look to hear
One tell the death of this shaggy Cavalier,
He raved, he tore his wig, and swore,
Against the Roundheads that he'd ne'er fight more

The fact was that Rupert's spirit seemed broken. He had few personal confidants, and Boye had served to provide him with a comfort and companionship that was not available from human sources in his daily life. It also appeared that Boye's loss challenged the young commander's feeling of invulnerability; in future military situations he would take fewer risks. He would also, throughout the rest of his service with Charles, appear to be much more subject to bouts of depression. Sometimes, when he was dining, he would be seen taking a morsel of food in his hand and looking mournfully down by his side, where Boye would usually post himself to beg for such treats. Rupert's troops were disheartened as well. The light morale-boosting banter about "our curly flag of victory" and the toasts to the health of "our hero and our hero's hound" were gone forever.

The parliamentary forces believed that the death of Rupert's "witch dog" took away any supernatural support that the Cavaliers might have had. Their fear dispersed, they could fight on in high spirits. At the battle of Nasby, perhaps the final decisive defeat of the royalist forces under Rupert, the Roundheads rallied their troops with the cry, "Rupert's white witch is dead. They can be defeated!"

Prince Rupert would never again win a victory against the parliamentary armies. The royalist forces would lose the war, and Charles would ultimately be executed. It was a war that was, at least in part, started by the love of two kings for dogs and hunting. It was a war that may have been lost, at least in part, by the death of a curly-haired white dog on the field at Marston Moor.

CHAPTER FIVE

THE COMPANIONS OF
THE PRUSSIAN EMPEROR

K ING FREDERICK II of Prussia is remembered as a brilliant military
leader who proved himself in a number of campaigns that greatly expanded Germany's empire and influence. He was also a social reformer
who practiced an unusual degree of religious tolerance for a European of that
time. He composed music and poetry, in addition to writing histories and many
books on government, politics, and military strategy. He also introduced important legal, agricultural, and mercantile reforms, and much more—all of which
would eventually earn him the title of Frederick the Great. In 1772, the French
writer and philosopher Voltaire described Frederick as a man who "gives battle
as readily as he writes an opera. . . . He has written more books than any of his
contemporary Princes has sired bastards; and he has won more victories than he
has written books." On the day of his coronation Frederick remarked, "A crown
is merely a hat that lets the rain in," while on another day he noted, "I never met
a dog that I never liked." The same early experiences that led this man to a casual
acceptance of his royal office also gave him a distrust of relations with other
people. He compensated for his lack of intimate human relationships by developing an abiding love for (and perhaps even a psychological dependence upon)
his dogs. In this history the dogs are not so much an agent of events but rather
an integral part of the life of this very successful but wounded man.

The children of royalty are not immune to abuse during their formative years. In some ways, especially in earlier eras, the degree of abuse that a prince might suffer may even be greater than that of a commoner. Even in those days, the police and the legal system would respond to complaints that a child was being severely mistreated (even if only to caution or offer public censure), but who would dare call the local constabulary when the abuser was the king himself? Young Frederick would be the target of much psychological and physical torment, and it changed him forever. The "why" of this abusive upbringing is the story of his father, William I, and grandfather, Frederick I.

Frederick was born in 1712 in Potsdam, near Berlin. He had two older brothers who did not survive early childhood. His older sister, Wilhelmina, was very close to him, but he himself felt much more loyalty and fondness for his younger brothers and sisters than they appeared to feel for him in later years. The most dominant force in Frederick's first twenty-eight years of life would be his father, King William.

His grandfather, Frederick I, had been greatly concerned with pomp and fashion and the trappings of royalty. He had a love of art and culture and used the style of France's Louis XIV as the model for the operation of his own court. There were many ministers who took care of the daily business of the state, and who were rewarded with titles, estates and rich pensions. Ultimately this left the finances of the country in a disastrous situation. William felt that Frederick I was irresponsible and, after his own accession to the throne, he immediately began to act in what he felt was a more responsible manner.

William was a harsh, militaristic man who was committed to the success and integrity of his country. He reduced the powers of ministers, or took over their departments himself. He was not a good communicator (which made things difficult for everyone, since he seldom wrote out his dictates), but he did have a talent for finance and administration and also understood the foreign affairs of the time. He explained that a king must not lead an easy "woman's life," but instead must be in full control. He claimed, "I am the King of Prussia's finance Minister and his Field Marshal." These policies served him well, and he instituted building programs to create homes, factories, arsenals, and hospitals to attract people back to the towns that had been depopulated during the Thirty Years' War. Soon he had a sound economy and full treasury. He began to expand and reorganize the military, doubling its size. He created two regiments of dragoons, thus giving the army the maneuverability and assault power of mounted men carrying muskets as well as swords, which was a novel concept at that time. He also introduced the most advanced fighting principles from leading military theorists, so that his troops learned to march in step and also how to perform bayonet charges.

Everything that his father had liked, King William hated, especially anything having to do with French culture, traditions, and even food. The French style of education also was distrusted, including education in the classics (Latin, the arts, music and so forth). Court privileges were abolished, and William came down heavily on all signs of luxury to the point where he sold off the silver from all of the royal residences, insisting that his family and guests eat off of wood and pewter. He avoided ornate clothing for himself and his sons since he considered such items effeminate.

It was in this austere climate that the crown prince Frederick would be raised. William had an inflexible idea about how the prince must develop if he was to be a good ruler and general, and he enforced his ideas with a heavy hand. It seems likely that William was suffering from porphyria, which is an upset in metabolism resulting in inadequate utilization of chemicals known as porphyrins. In certain people this condition leads to severe abdominal pain, intermittent paralysis, urinary problems, and mental disturbance. This was the illness that George III of England had, and seems to be traceable through the British royal family back to Mary, Queen of Scots. During the early stages of the disease it often leads to fits of temper, which in the case of William resulted in violent abuse of his children.

When the disease drove the king into a rage, blows and kicks punctuated everything associated with Frederick's upbringing. It soon became apparent that the crown prince was going to grow up as a small and delicate boy, who hated rough ways. Although he liked being around dogs and horses, and he enjoyed riding, he disliked hunting, which was considered to be one of the few acceptable entertainments for a virile man. Frederick much preferred reading and loved music. Frederick's mother, Sophia Dorothea, wanted him to grow up with a literate and cultured education. Thus, behind her husband's back, she arranged for him to learn French and Latin, as well as how to play the flute, lute, and piano. Frederick's confidant was his older sister, Wilhelmina, and with the aid of their mother she would provide the prince with access to books, mostly in French.

Whenever his father would discover the prince doing something that smacked of culture, or that showed any lack of what the king considered "manly

reserve," Frederick would get into trouble. He was beaten for reading French poetry, for eating with a silver fork, for wearing gloves in cold weather, and even for
throwing himself off a bolting horse. Most of this humiliation was quite public,
occurring in front of other family members, courtiers, soldiers, or even visitors.
No interaction with his father was safe for the prince. Thus one day William was
feeling particularly paternal and was instructing him about his future, telling
him, "Believe me, don't think of vanity, but keep to what is right. Always maintain a good army and have enough money, therein lies the peace of mind and
security of a Prince," and then he could not keep himself from punctuating the
point with a slap to the child's face.

The king tried to keep very tight control over Frederick. The prince's tutor
was beaten and dismissed from service for allowing Frederick to read a history
that was written in Latin. The new tutor was Jacques Duhan de Jandun, a
Huguenot soldier who had come to William's notice after he had distinguished
himself at the siege of Stralsund. De Jandun's father had been secretary for the
great French general Turenne, so it was believed that he would set the right tone
for someone who was being groomed to be a great general also. At the age of six,
Frederick was given his own company of cadets (131 boys) to drill. This was not
done as a playful act, but to remind the prince that the army, with its discipline
and command structure, was to be the main focus of his future life.

Frederick did not have much of a social life as a child. The only person he
could speak openly to was his sister, Wilhelmina. His mother provided some
support, but she was mostly involved in her own social life and with her political schemes to get her children married off into the best families possible. Since
the prince was so carefully watched by his father, there was little opportunity for
Sophia Dorothea to make her presence felt anyway, so she spent what time she
could with her other children. Thus, except for those acquaintances that he made
as part of his military training, Frederick grew up in relative isolation.

Under such conditions, it is not surprising that the lonely young boy might
seek out the company of a dog to provide some solace. When Frederick was
quite young, he was allowed to keep an Italian greyhound, which appears in a
portrait of him and Wilhelmina when he was around four years old. The Italian
greyhound is the smallest member of the greyhound family and today tends to
stand about twelve to fifteen inches at the shoulder. Although the name of the
breed seems to indicate that its origin was Italy, it appears likely that the breed
originated in Egypt, since mummified remains of a similar dog have been found

in the tomb of a pharaoh. The Italian connection comes from Roman soldiers apparently bringing these miniature greyhounds home with them. They soon became quite popular as gifts exchanged between wealthy families, and ultimately this little hound became associated with royalty because James I of England, Catherine the Great and Peter the Great of Russia, and Anne of Denmark, among others, owned such dogs. It appears that Frederick's uncle, George II of England, gave him his first dog as a gift. This early exposure to the breed left Frederick with a love of Italian greyhounds for the rest of his life.

Unfortunately, Frederick would not long be permitted to have his companion. In the eyes of the king, this was a small, useless dog that was not fit for hunting—merely a parlor companion for women and very young children. Thus, when Frederick was only six or seven, he was told that the dog would remain with one of his aunts in Potsdam. The boy was quite distressed and asked one of the royal servants who was making a trip to retrieve the dog for him. He did, and the king was infuriated, as he often was by his son's actions. The servant was beaten and fined a month's pay. Frederick was also beaten, and the dog only had its life spared because of its connection with the British royal family. Nonetheless the dog was again sent into exile, and the only companion dogs that Frederick had access to during his boyhood were those owned by his sisters and his mother.

The continuous criticism, social restriction, and physical violence that he suffered from his father eventually caused Frederick to resort to tactics of evasion and deceit—sometimes with the aide of his sister, Wilhelmina. At the age of eighteen, however, his family situation seemed hopeless. He began to plot an escape that would involve fleeing to France or Holland, then eventually making his way to England, where his uncle George II was the king. He reasoned that he could find temporary refuge there until his father died and then, with the help of such a powerful ally, return to assume the throne.

With the help of two of his military friends, lieutenants Hans Hermann von Katte and Peter Charles Christopher Keith, the plot was set in motion. Unfortunately things rapidly unraveled, and Keith panicked and revealed the plan to William. He even provided the king with a letter written by Frederick to von Katte outlining the prince's plan to leave and later return. Frederick was apprehended and taken to the king's yacht, where a formal reception was in progress. When William saw his son he flew into a violent rage, accusing him of treason and drawing his sword. General Henrick Magnus von Buddenbock threw himself in front of Frederick, shouting, "Over my dead body." William dropped the sword and grabbed a cane—and by the time the general and others could extricate Frederick to the safety of another yacht, his face was red with blood. In the end, Frederick was imprisoned in the fortress of Küstrin. Von Katte was brought there as well, and Frederick was forced to watch while his friend was beheaded.

For a short time there was the very real possibility that the prince would share his friend's fate. He was a clever young man, however, and eventually he tried to reconcile with his father. As a punishment for what William viewed as a betrayal of himself as king as well as his duty as the heir to the throne, Frederick was deprived of his royal privileges and his military rank, and forced to accept a commoner's job as a junior official in the local political administration. The loss of status and control was devastating. Furthermore, since those who worked with him knew his parentage and feared that any social approaches might be misconstrued either by the prince himself or others around him, they avoided all interactions with him. Thus, even though he was surrounded by people, he was again isolated. This condition continued for close to a year until his father was partially pacified by Frederick's agreement to return to full military duties and royal responsibilities. In addition the prince also had to agree to an arranged marriage.

It is difficult to measure with any accuracy the effects that the violent bullying of his father had upon Frederick. It is also difficult to know what the effects of the social controls and isolation from intimacy had on the young man. However, it is clear that he viewed the marriage merely as a means of eluding his father's control, by allowing him to move out of the royal residence.

Frederick had no desire to marry Elizabeth Christine of Brunswick-Bevern, who was a member of a minor princely family. He considered his new wife dull and unappealing, and from the first she was systematically neglected. He immediately left her in Berlin for a year of active service under the great Austrian commander Eugene of Savoy, who was campaigning against the French army in the Rhineland. On his return Frederick took up residence in the castle of Rheinsberg near Berlin. The next few years were the only time that he lived continuously with his wife. Elizabeth Christine had six ladies in waiting and a chaplain, but there was no affection and little intimacy from Frederick.

For Frederick, however, the Rheinsberg years were among the best in his life. For the first time he could live according to his own tastes. He read voraciously about military tactics, government, international relations, and economics for six to eight hours of each day. The ideas that he absorbed during this time would guide him throughout his own reign as king. It was also during this period that he wrote his first book, *Antimachiavell.* Published in 1740 with the encouragement of Voltaire, it idealistically opposed the political doctrines of the Italian statesman and philosopher Niccolò Machiavelli, favoring peaceful and enlightened rule. Ultimately Frederick would publish many books, tracts, and articles; his collected works amount to thirty volumes. He also played the flute and composed music, not only for chamber ensembles but full operatic works.

His social interactions were kept to a minimum. He corresponded with some of the leading thinkers of the time but did not have many visitors. Formally, his companions were officers in the army, and several of them formed a loyal bond with the prince that would continue to the end of their lives. Although he could be an entertaining and amusing conversationalist, he had difficulty showing much sincere warmth, probably because of his lack of social experience and his abusive childhood.

Frederick did not suffer from the complete absence of affection that had characterized his earlier life. Relief from emotional isolation came when he accepted the gift of a female Italian greyhound from his sister Wilhelmina, and then shortly afterward when he purchased another to be its companion. These two would be the first of some thirty-five dogs of this breed that would live with him over his adult life. They became his constant companions. Each morning when he arose, they would come to him, and later they would run barking beside him when he went off on his daily ride. When he was reading the dogs would curl up on the sofa next to him, or lie at his feet when he was sitting on a chair. Visitors and associates noted that Frederick spoke more frequently to the dogs than he did to his wife, and more fondly to them than virtually anyone else residing or working at Rheinsberg. This was the beginning of a pattern of behavior that would become quite familiar over the next forty-eight years of his life.

William died in 1740. When Frederick assumed the throne, he immediately made it clear to his ministers that he alone would decide government and military policies. One of Frederick's first official acts was the abolition of torture, except for crimes such as murder and treason. He permitted some freedom of speech and press and decreed broad religious tolerance, even welcoming Jesuits into his predominantly Protestant country. He also established impartial and efficient court procedures and reorganized the existing laws into a single code. He was not, however, simply an ardent social reformer. He defended traditional distinctions of rank and privilege, in part because he relied on the nobility to staff his bureaucracy and officer corps.

He reorganized his personal life as well. The same day that he learned that William was dead, Frederick sent his wife a note telling her that although "your presence is still necessary," she should go to the palace at Berlin and establish her residence there. He thus began his effective separation from her. She would live in the palace at Berlin during the winter and at Schönhausen in the summer, still receiving all of the honors due a queen. Foreign diplomats reported to their governments that any politeness shown to her was noted and well received by Frederick. Although the new king would occasionally reside in the same home with the queen, they would never share a bedchamber.

Frederick's bedchamber would not, however, be devoid of companions. Two ornate silk-padded chairs were placed near the bed. These were the sleeping accommodations for his dogs. A footstool was placed in front of each to make it easier for the dogs to reach the chairs. Later, a similar footstool would be placed next to the king's bed to allow a favorite dog to sleep with him.

Having taken care of his domestic affairs, both personal and national, it was only a matter of months before Frederick went to war. The Holy Roman emperor Charles VI, of the Austrian house of Habsburg, died, leaving as his heir the archduchess Maria Theresa. Frederick demanded that Maria Theresa give Prussia the province of Silesia (now part of Poland) in exchange for ratification of a treaty that gave her control over most of the Austrian dominions. When she refused, Frederick initiated the War of the Austrian Succession, using the well-disciplined army and full treasury his father had left him. Frederick turned out to be a fine military leader and strategist, and Prussia now became a respected force in Europe. Although he was a brilliant campaigner, Frederick acted with utter disregard of his allies. For example, he snubbed his French allies twice by concluding separate peace treaties with Maria Theresa (in 1742 and 1745) to accomplish his goal of gaining all of Silesia for Prussia.

During this war the number of Italian greyhounds that he owned increased from two to four. They were his source of personal comfort, so it was not surprising to find that he even took them with him on his military campaigns. The dogs had been given a separate carriage, drawn by six horses, and his coachman was ordered to address them with the utmost courtesy. For example, if the dogs were barking too loudly, the proper response on the part of the coachman was, "Mademoiselle, would you please try to stay calm and not bark so loudly?"

The care of all of the dogs was mostly left with Frederick's private chamberlain, who also had two liverymen to assist him. However, Frederick preferred to feed the dogs himself whenever possible. At one time, when he was in residence in Rheinsberg, the Marquis d'Argens had been invited to the king's private apartment. He found Frederick sitting on the floor with a big platter of fried meat in his lap. In his hand he had a little rod, which he used to keep the milling group of dogs in some kind of order. He would also use the rod to spear morsels of meat to give to the dogs. The Marquis could easily pick out Frederick's favorites, since they were given the best bits.

It was during this period of time that Frederick built his magnificent palace, Sans Souci (French for "without care"). It included a huge terraced garden with greenhouse windows to allow the growing of tropical plants. It had a music room where many of Frederick's compositions would be played. It also had a separate gallery specifically set aside for the dogs. With some of his dogs having litters of puppies and going through teething episodes, the furniture and the curtains suffered quite a bit. Frederick simply laughed at the situation, replacing items when they became too tattered.

One of Frederick's dogs, Biche, would actually contribute to Prussia's wartime difficulty. Probably his all-time favorite, Biche was with Frederick all of the time, wherever he went. She often sat on his lap while he discussed state affairs. Although some of his ministers thought that this was a bit odd, Frederick justified his behavior in a letter to his sister, saying, "Biche has good sense and understanding, and I see every day people who behave less rationally than her. If this dog has guessed my feelings towards her, at least she returns them graciously and I love her for that all the more."

Frederick's political situation was getting to be more difficult, however. Maria Theresa wanted to recover Silesia, and formed an alliance with Russia. France was wavering over which side to take. At this point an event occurred in which Biche was central to the loss of France as Prussia's ally. There was a great dining hall in Sans Souci where guests—politicians, ambassadors, philosophers, and military men—would be invited to dinner and would engage in conversations with the king. He was always fond of matching wits with others during discussions about the state of the world, the state of the arts or literature, philosophical theories, or simply gossip and speculation about local and international political issues and people. Virtually no females were ever invited to such dinners except for Frederick's Italian greyhounds, all of whom were female.

At one such meeting, talk had turned to the state of the French court under King Louis XV. Louis's relationship with Madame de Pompadour had become an item of gossip. Born Jeanne Antoinette Poisson, Madame de Pompadour was a brilliant woman, politically astute, well cultured, and ambitious. Louis XV had her installed in an upstairs room out of the main flow of traffic at the palace of Versailles, and she used the opportunity to get to know everyone of political importance during that time. After approximately five romantic years as Louis's mistress, he had her moved downstairs to a regal apartment. Soon afterward Louis conferred upon her the title of Marquise de Pompadour, after the name of the manor (Pompadour) that the king had purchased for her. Louis XV began to take other mistresses, but Madame de Pompadour was now a permanent fixture in palace life. Louis had come to appreciate her perceptive mind and her judgment, so he allowed her to act much like his executive secretary. For close to two decades she would have great influence on all important affairs of state. Because no one was appointed to office without her consent, there would be many in power who owed her political favors. She also acted as an intermediary between the ministers and the king, often manipulating the information that he received.

At this particular dinner party, Frederick was enjoying the conversation about the French court. Using his often cynical and cutting wit, he gestured to Biche, who was sitting beside him. "This is my Madame de Pompadour," he said. "She sleeps in my bed and breathes her advice in my ear. The only difference between my Pompadour and that of Louis is that he has conferred upon her the title of Marquise, while I have conferred upon mine the title Biche." The group laughed heartily since Biche is the French word for "bitch," which even then had the dual meaning of a female dog and a lewd and wanton woman.

Word of this incident made its way back to Madame de Pompadour, and she was enraged by what she took as a humiliating insult. In revenge, she set her mind to turning Louis XV against Frederick and Prussia. She succeeded in doing this, and largely because of her influence France sided with its traditional enemy, Austria. With the powerful coalition of Austria, Russia, and France against a Prussia that had only England as its ally, Maria Theresa launched the Seven Years' War. At first Prussia did quite well, with victories at Rossbach and Leuthen in 1757. However, as the war dragged on Frederick lost a major battle at Kunersdorf, and Maria Theresa's troops actually managed to occupy Berlin in 1760. In that dark period, it is said that Frederick was on the verge of suicide, and his sister tried to cheer him up by scouring Europe for some magnificent Italian greyhounds to add to his collection. It at least had the effect of easing his depression enough so that suicidal comments disappeared from his letters.

It would be fate, however, that saved Prussia. Empress Elizabeth of Russia, who disliked Frederick, died and was replaced by Peter III, who admired him. Peter was quick to pull Russia out of the war, ending Maria Theresa's hopes of recovering Silesia. Wanting to avoid further wars of this sort, Frederick signed a treaty with Russia to guarantee peace for the time.

Biche was with Frederick all during the war and went out with him even when combat was threatened. Sometimes she would run beside his horse, barking excitedly but never abandoning him, no matter what the circumstances. At other times he would let the dog sit in front of him on the horse's saddle. Once Frederick got too far ahead of his group and suddenly noticed an approaching troop of Hungarian dragoons, who had been assigned to the Austrian army. He and his escort quickly hid beneath a wooden bridge. The king kept Biche with him, holding her in his arms. She had always been a very vocal dog, but Frederick knew that this time even a single bark would risk capture or worse. He whispered in her ear, "We must be silent, my lady, or we will be dead." Obediently, Biche remained totally still as the enemy soldiers passed by. Once they were out of sight, Frederick returned to his worried generals and declared that Biche was a hero and his greatest friend.

During the battle of Soor in 1745, Biche caused Frederick great mental anguish. The king was, as usual, risking his safety by going too far forward, and the dog was, as usual, running free near him even though the battle was beginning. During one surge of enemy activity, an Austrian soldier saw the little dog and grabbed her. The little silver plate on her collar identified her as Frederick's dog, so she was immediately brought to the commander of the Austrian forces, General Radaski. Radaski knew of Frederick's fondness for all of his dogs, although he probably did not know that this was the dog that was partly responsible for bringing France into the war on his side. He thought that as the property of the king, however, the dog would make a wonderful trophy and conversation piece. With that in mind, he gave Biche to his wife as a gift.

Frederick was distraught. He raged around the camp, speaking of the "kidnapping of a member of the royal family." He reminded his commanders that this was not merely his friend and a pet, but a Prussian hero who had saved the life of the king that day under the bridge. He therefore charged his longtime friend, General Friedrich Rudolf Rothenburg, with negotiating for her release.

In addition to being a respected military leader, Rothenburg had the advantage of being the nephew of the former French ambassador to Prussia, so he had many political connections on both sides of the conflict. After much protracted discussion, Rothenburg managed to persuade the Austrian general to release Biche as part of a formal prisoner exchange. The king did not know the specific date and time of the transaction, so when Rothenburg brought the dog back to the palace it was a complete surprise. As the general walked into the wing at Sans Souci where the king's living apartment was, Biche recognized where she was and leaped out of his arms. She immediately scampered into Frederick's room, where he was sitting and writing some letters. The athletic little dog then leaped up onto his desk and placed her paws around the royal neck and began to lick his face. Frederick burst out "Biche! My love! My friend! My hero!" and tears ran down his face. He wrapped his arms around the dog and, clutching her close to his chest, ran through the halls to announce that all was well again and his family was once more intact.

When Biche became ill in 1752, Frederick showed a tenderness and sympathy that had no parallel in his dealings with his fellow men. He called in no fewer than ten doctors to care for her. Watching this scene the British ambassador, Sir James Harris, was struck by the contradiction of a king who would "pay as much care to a sick greyhound as a fond mother could to a favorite child," yet be so cold and unfeeling about humans—even to the point of ignoring his own brother's illness by continuing to indicate his displeasure with him over minor offenses.

Unfortunately, Biche died despite the medical attention given to her. The depth of Frederick's grief was expressed in a letter to his sister, Wilhelmina:

> I have had a domestic loss which has completely upset my philosophy. I confide all of my frailties in you; I have lost Biche and her death has reawakened in me the loss of all my friends. . . . I was ashamed that a dog could so deeply affect my soul; but the sedentary life that I lead and faithfulness of this poor creature had so strongly attached me to her, her suffering so moved me, that, I confess, I am sad and afflicted. Does one have to be hard? Must one be insensitive? I believe that anyone capable

of indifference to a faithful animal is unable to be grateful towards an equal, and that, if one must choose, it is best to be too sensitive than too hard.

After Biche's death, Frederick attempted to learn some veterinary and medical skills and later personally attended to the nursing of his dogs when they became ill. Interestingly, it was in that same year that he found himself confined to his bed due to an attack of gout. He needed some form of medical treatment and had no option but to send for a doctor. The man that he selected, a Dr. Cuttenius, appears to have had only one redeeming feature: Among all of the palace physicians, he alone had refused to prescribe for Biche when she lay dying. In Frederick's mind, this absolved him from responsibility for his favorite's death.

After the war Frederick attempted to be a bit more sensitive to the plight of the citizens of Prussia, if not to individuals in his own life. He set about trying to rebuild the economy of the country that had been badly hurt by the long years of war. He subsidized and encouraged many traditional industries, including metalworking and textile manufacturers, as well as some new enterprises, such as the manufacturing of porcelain wares, silk, and tobacco. He brought in experts to show how to apply such modern agricultural techniques as scientific methods of cattle breeding, crop rotation, and the planting of soil-enriching clover and fodder crops. Farmers were also introduced to inexpensive foods such as turnips and potatoes. He also had the swamps in the Oder and Vistula river valleys drained and initiated reforestation projects. He loosened immigration regulations, an action that allowed him to settle approximately three hundred thousand immigrant farmers in sparsely populated areas. Although he could not completely abolish the practice of serfdom, he did manage to improve the lot of peasants somewhat. He also encouraged the arts, music, and the sciences. Perhaps Frederick's greatest achievement was his attempt to set up a system of universal primary education throughout the nation.

Although Frederick did continue his formal dinner parties and palace concerts, most of the later years of his life were spent in relative solitude. As he worked for long hours on matters of state, usually his only company was his group of dogs. Each morning, the ritual was the same: He would set out accompanied by only two mounted footmen, each with one of his favorite dogs riding on the saddle in front of him. Halfway down the avenue Frederick would raise his staff above his head, which was the sign for the footmen to dismount with the dogs. The dogs would begin barking immediately and typically ran forward to be next to the king, who would address them by saying, "Well, Alcmene, well Diana, let us see who will be the lady of honor today?" As if this were a command to perform, both dogs would begin barking even louder and then try to leap into the royal saddle. When one achieved this, Frederick would announce the outcome. "Alcmene has won! Yes, Alcmene is the court lady today, and Diana the companion." The tradition was that the "lady" stayed with the king all day. He would play with her, take her when he went walking or met visitors, and give her bonbons and choice morsels of chicken, while the companion would wait her turn and take what was left.

In his later years Alcmene replaced the much-loved Biche as Frederick's preferred companion, but he had many others that he was fond of as well. Phillys, Thisbe, Pan, Diana, Amoretto, Superbo, Pax, and Lulu were among the eleven dogs that were important enough to Frederick to be buried on the palace grounds of Sans Souci. A simple sandstone marker bearing the animal's name marked each one. The rites of passage were important for Frederick; he personally laid each of these favorites in their graves.

He did not take the loss of his dogs well. As Alcmene grew older, Frederick wrote to his brother, Henry, "I have a domestic sorrow; my poor dog is about to die and, to console myself, I tell myself that if death does not spare crowned heads poor Alcmene cannot expect a different fate." Nonetheless, Alcmene's death came even earlier than he had expected, and Frederick was away at the time on military maneuvers. Not knowing what to do, the palace staff thought that it was appropriate to bury her immediately. When the king found out about this he ordered that the dog be exhumed, and he immediately returned. Then with some personal words that he said in too low a tone for any to hear, he placed her casket in the open grave. He then stood up, gazed at the nearby mausoleum that overlooked the graves of his dogs, and announced, "Don't feel lonely, my Alcmene. I shall rest there and we shall be in each other's sight for the rest of eternity."

Frederick had ordered that his body would be laid to rest in a crypt, near his dogs. The last dog that slept beside him was also to be interred next to the king. This was the dog that was the object of the very last words that he spoke. As he lay on his deathbed, Frederick noticed that his current favorite dog was lying on the floor. Italian greyhounds have very little fat and are susceptible to being easily chilled, and she was shivering. He gestured to his valet, pointing at the dog, and said "Throw a quilt over her." He then had a fit of coughing and died.

Despite the instructions about his interment, it was not seen as fit to bury a king in a palace garden. Instead Frederick was entombed beside his father in the Garrison church in Potsdam. There he lay from 1786 to until 1945, when it was feared that the advancing Russian army might desecrate his remains. For that reason, he was exhumed and concealed in a salt mine near Bernterode. At the end of World War II he was transferred to St. Elizabeth's church in Marburg, and in 1952 to Hohenzollern castle near Stuttgart. Only in 1991 were the royal remains finally returned to Sans Souci. There he was laid to rest beside his last dog—whose name we do not know, since Frederick was not alive to have it engraved on her resting place and no one else bothered to record it for posterity. Finally, more than two centuries after his death, Frederick fulfilled his promise to Alcmene, and he now lies in clear sight of his canine "family."

In some respects Frederick the Great summarized his own attitude toward his companions, and the world in general, in this much-quoted statement: "The more I see of men, the better I like my dog."

CHAPTER SIX

THE CONQUISTADOR'S DOGS

W

HEN CHRISTOPHER COLUMBUS discovered the Americas, he opened up a new era of political, military, and economic history. What most people do not know is that dogs played a vital role in the European conquest of the New World. Unfortunately it is also one of the most brutal chapters in man's long association with dogs, so perhaps we have not so much forgotten this history as pushed it out of our collective memory.

Although there are some gaps and a lot of myths surrounding the life of Columbus, there is general agreement among most scholars that Cristoforo Colombo was born in Genoa, Italy, in 1451. His father was a wool weaver and was also involved in local politics. He often took Christopher with him, and the boy quickly learned how to interact with people who had power and authority. Christopher and his brother, Bartolomeo, were educated together, learning to read and write in the craft guild school and then going on to study cartography, weather prediction, and basic navigation together. For a while Christopher was a clerk in a bookstore, a job that gave him a chance to read extensively about geography and the exploits of travelers who had visited Africa and the Orient. It also gave him a taste for travel, and the idea that there were many riches and rewards to be won in far-flung lands.

Although in that era sons were generally expected to follow their fathers in the family business, times were changing. Genoa had been a major commercial center, trading in textiles, foods, gold, wood, ship supplies, some imported spices, oriental luxury items, and above all sugar. However, there was considerable conflict throughout the Mediterranean region based upon religious lines, as Islamic and Christian powers fought for converts and territory. Constantinople fell under Muslim control when Columbus was only two years of age. With the resulting loss of the Aegean markets, Genoa adopted the modern-seeming solution of exporting knowledge. Soon cities like Lisbon, Seville, Barcelona, and Cadiz were importing a large number of Genoese marine experts, particularly seafarers and shipbuilders. In addition, Genoa was willing to supply merchants, bankers, and others with the financial expertise needed to make these new nautical enterprises successful. Thus it was not surprising when Columbus decided to look to the sea as a source of livelihood. He apparently worked as a common seaman for a while and then, as his navigational and cartographic abilities became apparent, rose in the ranks to become a junior officer.

A turning point in his career seems to be his service on a privateer ship commissioned by René d'Anjou, the French pretender to the throne of Naples. This ship set out to make a surprise attack on a large Spanish galleon sailing off the coast of North Africa. All sailors on such expeditions were entitled to a share of the booty, and as an officer, Columbus's share was enough to give him the financial means to begin to pursue his own ambitions. He would still continue to sail in various capacities on other ships but would eventually rise to command a ship himself. During these years he continued to learn more about the weather, ocean currents, and navigation, and he also became impressed with the exotic treasures that could be found in some remote places, that could be later sold for great profit.

One of the great myths surrounding Columbus is that he was trying to prove that the world was round by sailing west and arriving in the Orient. This was not true, since the theory that the earth was spherical in shape had been around since Greek and Roman times. It was then that the first cosmographers suggested there was only one large body of water and one large continent on the surface of the Earth. On one shore of the great ocean was Europe, and on the far shore was Asia. If this theory was correct, then instead of the long and dangerous overland trip eastward from Europe to China, one could sail west to get to the Asian countries. What these early geographers could not agree upon were the distances involved. For instance, on Ptolemy's map of the known world during Roman times, he drew the outline of the ocean surrounding the known lands, then marked the regions toward the middle as being "unnavigable" because the extent of the sea was supposedly unlimited. While Columbus was willing to accept the general outline of the world that Ptolemy drew, he rejected the idea of an endless ocean. Chance would soon provide evidence to support his intuition.

Columbus moved to Portugal because it was ruled by Prince Henry (later to be known as Prince Henry the Navigator). With Henry's encouragement, the Portuguese had become active explorers and were conducting trade all along the African coast. While he was there, Columbus married Felipa Perestrello e Moniz, whose family belonged to the Portuguese nobility. Although the family was relatively poor, they still had direct connections to the Portuguese court and the king, and Columbus used these to gain access to an important collection of papers. Once the property of the governor of one of the islands Portugal controlled in the Atlantic Ocean, the collection contained a treasure trove of information, including charts with details of ocean currents. It also held records of personal interviews with sailors described as found drifting in sea currents from the west, suggesting that there were lands in that direction. Columbus began a correspondence with the aged cosmographer-physician Paolo del Pozzo Toscanelli of Florence, who concluded (in part based on the information provided by Columbus) that one could reach the Orient by sea if you sailed west only a little more than three thousand miles.

Columbus was strongly motivated to explore to the west. There was a lot of glory and wealth to be gained not only by the person who opened up a quicker trade route to the Orient, but also by the nation that sponsored him. It was already known that Asia was a source of precious spices and rich textiles, and there were also tales of great stores of gold and jewels to be found there. Perhaps even more attractive was the possibility of achieving great power, since many believed that the people who occupied these lands were not very advanced. Colonization by the presumably more sophisticated and technologically superior Europeans could provide cheap labor and perhaps ready and expendable foot soldiers to defend the homeland.

Finally, there was the issue of religion. This was a time of religious tension, and Columbus was a devout Catholic. Pope Pius II had written extensively about the need to convert the heathen multitudes of the world to an understanding of Christ, with the continuing guidance (and control) of the church.

Columbus's faith was stirred by this, and it gave a new meaning to the knowledge that his given name, Christopher, meant "Christ bearer." He concluded that he was not only searching for wealth but also had a divine mission to accomplish. In 1500, Columbus would think back on his quest and write,

> With a hand that could be felt, the Lord opened my mind to the fact that it [the voyage west to Asia] would be possible . . . and he opened my will to desire to accomplish that project. . . . The Lord purposed that there should be something miraculous in this matter of the voyage to the Indies. . . . God made me the messenger of the new heaven.

Columbus often noted that there were words in the Bible that were guiding him and may have been written for his own particular benefit, as a sort of prophesy. In particular he cited a passage in Isaiah (60:9):

> For the islands wait for me, and the ships of the sea in the beginning: that I may bring thy sons from afar, their silver and their gold with them, to the name of the Lord thy God.

One could see how he would be attracted to this passage, since he viewed his own quest for far-off lands as a task done for both gold and God.

Columbus's first task was to find a royal sponsor. For an explorer in the fifteenth century, royal sponsorship was a necessity, since only a monarch could assert sovereignty, give legal legitimacy to the discoveries, and conduct diplomatic relations. A monarch was also needed if one were to colonize the land, since the new colony would have to be protected and defended, and laws had to be imposed to maintain order and oversee the exploitation of riches and the distribution of rewards. Private individuals, even those of wealth and power, such as prominent merchants or bankers would fall short of the resources to do this. To launch and sustain new explorations and discoveries, you needed not only an economic foundation, but also a strong political and military base.

Columbus first sought royal patronage in Portugal, hoping to take advantage of his wife's family connections and the Portuguese history of exploration in the tradition of Prince Henry the Navigator. The king passed Columbus's proposal on to his Council of Geographical Affairs, who thought that Columbus was underestimating the distances involved and overestimating the rewards to be won. Columbus then carried the proposal on to France, England, and finally Spain. Although the Spanish queen, Isabella, was interested in the idea of a westward crossing, she was preoccupied by a war with Muslims in the Castile region of the country. So she and King Ferdinand asked Columbus to present his Atlantic project to a committee of experts called to hear the case. The so-called Wise Men of Salamanca reached the conclusion "that the claims and promises of Captain Columbus are vain and worthy of rejection. . . . The Western Sea is infinite and unnavigable. The Antipodes [by which were meant the lands on the other side of the earth toward which Columbus was to sail] are not liveable, and his ideas are impracticable."

Columbus did not give up, however, and tried again in 1491. This time, events were more fortuitous. Ferdinand and Isabella had just won the battle of Granada and had expelled the Muslims from Spain. With the return of relative peace to their country, they could attend to other matters. Without the draining costs of military actions, they allowed themselves to be convinced that the cost of Columbus's expedition were small, and there was the potential for large rewards. The story about Queen Isabella selling her jewels to finance the fleet is simply a myth; the royal financial advisors indicated that the monarch could require the city of Palos to pay back a debt to the crown by providing two of the ships that were needed. In addition, there was already an agreement in place providing Italian financial backing for part of the expenses. This meant that the crown had to put up very little money from their treasury.

In September of 1492, Columbus set sail on what he felt was to be a trip to the Orient. Contrary to the myth that his crew was made up largely of convicts taken from prison, in fact they were mostly experienced seamen recruited by the Pinzon brothers, who owned one of the ships and served as officers. There were a few government officials, but there were no priests, no soldiers, no settlers, and no dogs. This was a small-scale voyage of exploration and discovery, nothing more. The ships were quite tiny, no longer than a tennis court, and less than thirty feet wide. Columbus, who was a tall man, could not even stand fully upright in his little compartment. There were only ninety men—forty on the Santa María, twenty-six on the Pinta, and twenty-four on the Niña. The decks were crowded with supplies to last a year, and Columbus did not anticipate any need for dogs.

Although the first voyage took a month, it was relatively uneventful. Landing at San Salvador, the Europeans saw people "as naked as their mother bore them" and many fruits and green trees. Columbus and his captains went ashore in an armed launch but were warmly greeted by the natives. When he unfurled the royal banner and declared that these obviously inhabited lands now belonged to the Catholic sovereigns, the natives appeared to offer no resistance to Spanish domination. In his own words, Columbus concluded, "I recognized that they were people who would be better freed [from the bondage of their pagan religion and uncivilized lifestyle] and converted to our Holy Faith by love than by force." He also encountered some native dogs in the New World; however, these did not bark and seemed only to be raised as food. Unimpressed, Columbus did not include them among the curiosities that he brought back to exhibit in Spain.

When he explored Cuba and some of the other islands, Columbus encountered a few problems. The Santa María ran aground and was wrecked beyond repair. He considered that only a minor problem, however, since it provided him with lumber that he could use for building a fort and also surplus crewmen to start a first colony. He left a small group of men with instructions to treat the natives well and not to "injure" the women. Their job there was to explore for gold, and to seek a place for a permanent settlement. He assured the local chief, Guacanagari, that their intentions were peaceful, and then gave the new colony the name "La Navidad."

The second voyage started in 1493, and it would be quite different. It was massive, consisting of seventeen ships, twelve hundred men and boys (including sailors, soldiers, colonists, priests, officials, and gentlemen of the court), horses, and twenty dogs. The dogs were the idea of Don Juan Rodriguez de Fonseca, archdeacon of Seville and the personal chaplain to the king and queen. Don Juan had been put in charge of determining the supplies and equipment necessary for the voyage. In his mind, these mastiffs and greyhounds were classed as weapons, along with muskets and sabers.

The Spanish military had recently learned to appreciate the effectiveness of dogs against men with little or no armor. When Spain took the Canary Islands away from Portugal, they were resisted by intelligent, brave, and proud natives called Guanches, whom the Portuguese had never been able to subdue. The governor effectively used large war dogs to wreak havoc, resulting in the loss of many native lives. When the military saw how useful the dogs had been in that campaign, they decided to employ dogs in their struggle with the Moors of Granada. The lightly armored Muslim fighters were no match for the mastiffs of that era, which could weigh 250 pounds and stand nearly three feet high at the shoulder. Their massive jaws could crush bones even through leather armor. The greyhounds of that period, meanwhile, could be over one hundred pounds in weight and could stand thirty inches at the shoulder. These lighter dogs could outrun any man, and their slashing attack could easily disembowel a person in a matter of seconds. Several of the men who had served as dog masters at Granada and helped to disperse the Moors would be among the crew of Columbus's second voyage.

Fonseca wanted dogs on this voyage because he anticipated difficulties ahead. Both the king and the queen had indicated that they wanted kind treatment of the Indians and, of course, their speedy conversion to Christianity. The monarchs also wanted the land to be settled, communities and trade centers organized, and materials and valuables collected for shipment back to Spain. Fonseca recognized that these two aims were basically incompatible and some compromises would have to be made between the evangelical and the material aims of this voyage. To meet the royal expectation of large profits, the colonists would eventually have to rely on enforced labor and perhaps even enslavement of the natives. Although the Indians might truly be as peaceful as Columbus described them, it seemed unlikely that the demands of this new regime for manual laborers would be readily accepted. Furthermore, the anticipated taking of resources and valuables, as well as the seizing of land, would likely need to be backed up by force. Since these natives had no armor and only light weapons, dogs would be a formidable form of coercion. The twenty dogs that Columbus took with him, and the others that followed, would eventually blaze a bloody trail across the New World.

One of the first things that Columbus did upon his return to the Americas was to go to the site of the colony that he had established. All of the personnel on the ships were eager to land; they wanted to start looking for gold and building new settlements. As they approached La Navidad, they fired a cannon to announce their arrival. However, there was no response—no one returned the salute, and no flags were waved. As the site came into view, the voyagers were horrified to discover that the entire population of La Navidad had been massacred, and the fort had been burned to the ground. When they searched for traces of their countrymen, they discovered a mass grave in which several Spaniards had been buried. They also found that the village of Columbus's good friend, Chief Guacanagarí, had been destroyed. Although the full details of what happened may never be known, stories told around the countryside were that the settlers had become greedy, making demands for valuables and food. In addition, they had raped some Indian women and acted cruelly toward other natives. In response the Indians razed the settlement. More importantly, they became hostile toward Europeans and began to spread the word among the other tribes. It was becoming clear that Fonseca was right about the need for dogs.

The very first military conflict between Indians and Europeans would also mark the first incident where a dog served a military purpose in the New World. In May 1494, Columbus approached the shore of Jamaica at what would become Puerto Bueno. He could see a gathering of natives, painted in various colors and carrying weapons. The fleet needed wood and water, and Columbus was still angry and looking for revenge for the destruction of La Navidad. He also felt that perhaps a demonstration of Spanish military strength might just frighten the natives enough to cause them to avoid any further hostilities. Three ships approached the shore. Soldiers fired their crossbows and then waded ashore, slashing at the natives with their swords while others continued to fire bolts. The Indians were surprised at the ferocity of the onslaught; however, when one of the massive war dogs was released their response was absolute terror. They fled from the raging animal that bit at their naked skin and did them great harm. The admiral then came ashore and claimed the island in the name of the Spanish throne. Columbus would write in his journal that this incident proved one dog was worth ten soldiers when fighting the Indians. Some time later he would revise that estimate to say one dog was worth fifty men in such combat.

The pattern for conquest had now been set. Weapons would be used to actually take and hold territory, while dogs would be used to worry and terrify the natives. Thus when Columbus took an expedition into the interior of Hispaniola (the island in the West Indies that contains both Haiti and the Dominican Republic), he met any show of resistance by unleashing his dogs and allowing them to pursue the Indians. The dogs killed many of the natives, and those who survived to be captured were sent to the slave market in Seville.

Among those held at bay by the dogs until they were captured by the Spanish soldiers was an Indian chief named Guatiguana and two of his companions. Scheduled to be hanged the following morning, they managed to gnaw through the thongs used to bind them, and escaped. Guatiguana was now bent on eliminating all of the Spaniards in his territory, and he began to organize a large-scale resistance. First the Indians tried to weaken the invaders by planting no more maize and removing all of their livestock from the region. Columbus, angered by the starvation tactics and the gathering of a hostile force, decided to act before the chief could mount an attack. Because many of his men were ill and weakened by the shortage of food, he could only muster a force of around two hundred soldiers, but they were supported by twenty vicious and well-trained dogs. What would be the first pitched battle between the European invaders and the native Indian population took place at Vega Real in March 1495.

Guatiguaná's forces, numbering in the thousands, advanced upon the small band of Spaniards. Columbus had given control of the dogs to Alonso de Ojeda, a small man who combined physical courage with a personality disposed toward violence and rash cruelty. He justified his often gruesome behavior by citing the fact that he was acting to honor the Holy Virgin and always had a small portrait of her with him. Ojeda had learned the art of using war dogs in the battles against the Moors of Granada. He gathered the dogs on the far right flank and waited until the battle had reached a high level of fury. He then released all twenty mastiffs, shouting "Tómalos!" (meaning "take them" or "sic 'em"). The angry dogs swept down on the native fighters in a raging phalanx, hurling themselves at the Indians' naked bodies. They grabbed their opponents by their bellies and throats. As the stunned Indians fell to the ground, the dogs disemboweled them and ripped them to pieces. Spinning from one bloody victim to another, the dogs tore through the native ranks. One observer of the battle, Bartolomé de las Casas, reported that in less than one hour each dog had torn apart at least one hundred Indians. Recognizing that his readers might find this difficult to believe, de las Casas explained that these animals had originally been trained to hunt for wild game. In comparison, they found that the skin of their naked human opponents was far easier to tear apart than the hides of deer or boars. Furthermore, as Fonseca had surely anticipated, the dogs had now developed a taste for human flesh.

The battle of Vega Real awoke Columbus to the potential that his dogs had as weapons against the inhabitants of this new land. He would work his way through the countryside, now always accompanied by his dogs. Ultimately he would bring all of the tribal leaders in Hispaniola under his control through the threat of force and the use of his dogs to inspire fear.

Each subsequent voyage to the Americas would bring more war dogs, and ultimately virtually all of the leaders of the conquistadors would employ them as fearsome weapons. Familiar names, like Ponce de León, Balboa, Velásquez, Cortés, De Soto, Toledo, Coronado, and Pizarro, all used dogs as instruments of subjugation. The dogs were encouraged to develop a taste for Indian flesh by being allowed to feed on their victims. Soon the dogs became very proficient in tracking Indians and could tell the difference between a trail made by a European and that made by a native.

The cruelest of the Spanish leaders would use the dogs as a means of public execution. Known as "dogging," it involved setting the dogs on the chiefs or other high-ranking individuals in the various tribes. Watching their leaders being torn to shreds instilled great fear in the native population, who would ultimately submit to Spanish control rather than risk such a horrific death.

The cruelty of the conquest eventually brought out a sadistic streak in many of the soldiers. Some would release the dogs on Indians simply for the sport of watching the natives suffer and die. Sometimes they would bet on the outcome, such as where the dog would draw blood first, how or where the fatal wound would be dealt, or how long it would take for the victim to die. Although word of such barbaric behavior was brought back to Spain, little was done to stop it.

While these dogs were considered to be mere weapons and sometimes instruments of torture, some of them became famous as individuals, and their names have been preserved in the histories of the time. There was Amigo, the dog of Nuño Beltrán de Guzmán, who played a pivotal role in the conquest of Mexico. Bruto, the dog of Hernando De Soto, was a vital factor in the takeover of Florida. In fact, when Bruto died, his death was kept secret because the simple mention of his name was capable of striking terror into the natives and causing them to submit immediately. There was also Becerrillo, the dog of Juan Ponce de León, and the dog's son, Leoncico (the name means "little lion"), who belonged to Vasco Núñez de Balboa. Leoncico would evaluate each situation and respond accordingly. When he was sent to apprehend a native, he would race out and grab the man's arm in his mouth. If the Indian did not struggle but came along, he would be led safely back to Balboa. If the Indian resisted, he would be killed and torn apart immediately. Leoncico was considered to be so valuable that he was awarded the rank of a corporal, including the pay and entitlement to share any goods or gold obtained as booty.

When one considers the bloody history of dogs during the conquest of the Americas, there is almost an automatic emotional response. One feels ashamed of the behavior of the dogs, and wonders how we could ever consider these vicious creatures to be our friends and companions. However, it is important to remember that dogs are born with courage, intelligence, and a sense of loyalty—not with a code of morality. Their human masters trained their own concept of right and wrong into these dogs; in the hands of hardened soldiers, they were changed into lethal weapons. Remember that in a murder trial it is not the weapon used to kill but the individual wielding that weapon who is called to justice. The conquistadors who ordered the dogs are thus responsible for the savagery, whereas the dogs were merely responding out of a sense of loyalty, and their actions were performed with courage.

Despite the cruelty of that time, there was one incident in which a dog caused the invaders to question the morality of their actions, at least for a short time. This involved Becerrillo, the dog of Juan Ponce de León. He was a large dog (his name means "little bull calf"), who also looked quite fearsome due to his scars from so many battles. Since Ponce de León had many duties as governor of Puerto Rico, the dog was often entrusted to Captain Diego de Salazar, an intimidating and ruthless man who was often deliberately employed to strike terror into natives so that they would accept Spanish rule. Becerrillo was frequently the instrument used to create that terror. Salazar often ordered Becerrillo to tear apart Indians who showed any defiance to their conquerors, and this was done publicly as an object lesson to others in the community.

In battle, this dog was devastating. For example, when the natives decided to band together to kill all of the Christians, they sent a chief, Guarionex, to lead a surprise attack against the village where Salazar and his troops were staying. In the middle of the night, the raiders began setting the straw-thatched huts on fire. Becerrillo began to bark frantically, waking the troops. Salazar leaped out of bed with a shout, and naked except for his sword and shield, he rushed into battle with Becerrillo at his side. The clubs and darts of the Indians were no match for the Spanish blades and firearms, and their own naked bodies were no match for Becerrillo's teeth. Although the battle only raged for about a half hour, at the end even the Spaniards were surprised to find that the casualties included thirty-three natives killed by Becerrillo's savage fangs. Over the next several months, Salazar and Becerrillo went in pursuit of Guarionex and the other surviving raiders. The Indians came to fear this beast to the extent that they would more readily stand and fight a hundred Christians without him than ten with him.

On one particular occasion, not far from Ponce de León's capitol at Caparra, Salazar and Becerrillo had just broken the resistance of a group of natives. When the struggle was over, the troops had nothing to do while they waited for the arrival of the governor, who was expected in a few hours. Salazar decided to relieve the tedium with a bit of brutal entertainment. Calling over an old Indian woman, he gave her a piece of folded paper and told her to carry the message down the road to the governor. She was told that if she did not do this, she would be cast to the dogs. The old woman was frightened, but also hopeful that perhaps this errand might somehow lead to some freedom and respite for her people. She had not gone far toward the road when Salazar laughed and unleashed Becerrillo with the attack command, "Tómala!" (take her). The great dog dashed toward her as expected, and the amused soldiers waited for Becerrillo to tear her to pieces and then gorge himself on her flesh, as he had done with so many other Indians before.

The unfortunate woman saw the huge dog rushing toward her with his fangs bared. She dropped to her knees and cast her eyes down and then softly, in her own language, uttered a humble plea. "Please, my Lord Dog," observers heard her say, "I am on my way to take this letter to Christians. I beg you, my Lord Dog, please do not hurt me."

Who knows what went through the mind of Becerrillo. Those who saw the event claimed that the dog displayed almost human intelligence and compassion. Perhaps it is the fact that the woman had assumed such a humble and non-threatening posture, or perhaps it was the soft tones of her quiet words that soothed the dog and demonstrated that she was not hostile. He stared at the woman's face as she gingerly held the sheet of paper with both hands in front of her chest—to show him that what she said was true, or maybe to hide behind it as if it were a shield. Becerrillo sniffed at her, nudging her with his nose, and then sniffed at her hands and the paper. This fearless killer then turned away from the terrified woman, lifted a leg, and sprayed urine on her. He then walked to the side and watched as she shakily rose to return to the soldiers who had planned to have her killed.

Since Salazar and the assembled troops knew Becerrillo so well, and had so often seen him with his mouth dripping from the blood of his victims, this seemed like an impossible outcome. In their minds this only could have come about through some form of divine intervention. The vicious pranksters had been put to shame by the charity and mercy of a hound. Doubtless they felt humiliated by this incident. A short time later, Ponce de León arrived and was told the story.

The governor shook his head in astonishment. "Free her," he commanded, "and send her safely back to her people. Then let us leave this place for now. I will not permit the compassion and forgiveness of a dog to outshine that of a true Christian."

CHAPTER SEVEN

THE DOGS OF THE
SCOTTISH WRITER

W HILE IT IS EASY to think of dogs as companions, guardians, and even weapons, it is difficult to imagine that dogs have played any role in literature—other than as the subject of novels, such as *Lassie Come Home, The Call of the Wild,* or *The Hound of the Baskervilles.* However, they have often played a role in our literary and cultural history by stimulating and inspiring writers.

When one thinks about knights and armor, for many of us what comes to mind is that classic scene at the tournament where the young knight Ivanhoe lies wounded, and all seems lost. Then, out of nowhere, the knight in black armor appears to challenge the Norman champions of the evil Prince John and save the honor of the oppressed Saxons. This stirring scene from *Ivanhoe* has been recreated many times in films and on television. It may be hard to believe that the writing of this classic book—as well as a number of other classics, such as *Rob Roy, Quentin Durward,* and *The Talisman*—might have anything to do with dogs. The truth of the matter is that these books, and the entire writing style that we call the historical novel, were born in part because of a love of dogs. The critical human figure in this story is Sir Walter Scott.

Walter Scott was born in Edinburgh in 1771. When he was quite young, Scott suffered from a serious illness (probably polio) that left him lame in his right leg. It was thought that his condition might improve if he spent some time in the country, so he was sent to his grandfather's farm in the Scottish border region to convalesce. It was during this time that Scott learned his relaxed and comfortable way with both dogs and people.

Scott's grandfather kept cattle and sheep, and was an avid horseman. This meant that the farm was filled with working dogs, such as collies to herd the sheep and terriers to keep the rats and other vermin under control. There were also a few greyhounds and tracking hounds that were used for the occasional hunt. The shepherds and farmhands allowed the boy to wander where he wanted and would often carry Scott on their backs over some of the rougher stretches of ground. He would talk with them and watch them work, and they soon fell into a comfortable relationship. Because of these early experiences he developed a set of social skills that allowed him to have a relaxed rapport with people at all levels in society. This ability would serve him in good stead for the rest of his life, both as a lawyer and when he was collecting stories and ballads from the countryside. He was also very comfortable around animals and was fond of them. He learned the names of all of the dogs on the farm, and even came to know most of the sheep and lambs by their markings as well. When his uncle gave him a pony, he quickly learned to ride. Often he would imitate his elders, pretending to hunt while galloping around the countryside with dogs barking and circling him and his small horse.

Scott was mostly entrusted to the care of his grandmother and his aunt Jane, and they also spent many hours reading to him. Often the young boy would bring a dog into the room and would rest against it while the ladies read. Sometimes, when he was using the dog as a pillow, he could listen to epic poems and classic tales in one ear while the rhythm of the dog's heartbeat filled the other, providing a meter of its own. Since he was the only child in the house, he was pampered and became what he later referred to as a "spoiled brat." From these early years, Scott developed a love for the stories and history of the Scottish border that his elderly relatives were so fond of. Because they could not read to him all of the time, his aunt taught him how to read when he was quite young as a way to have him fill his time when he was alone. Despite his youth he learned quickly, and soon he became a voracious reader of anything that had a plot and a story, including history, drama, fairy tales, romances, and epic poetry.

When Scott grew to school age, he was returned to his parents' home. Although he was now one of six children in the house, his physical infirmity prompted special treatment, and he became his mother's favorite child. At this time he was sleeping in his mother's dressing room, which was a small room off the main bedroom. This room had several special features, not the least of which was a set of bookshelves that contained some of Shakespeare's plays as well as other classical works. The room also had a separate door, which allowed him to hide a dog in the room with him. He would later write: "nor can I easily forget the rapture with which I sat up in my shirt reading by the light of the fire in her apartment until the bustle of the family rising from supper was detected by the sharp ears of my little yellow terrier. His warning told me it was time to creep back to my bed, where I was supposed to have been safely deposited since nine o'clock."

Scott's family was well educated and highly cultured for that time. His father was a lawyer, and his mother was the daughter of a professor of medicine. In the end his personality would show evidence of the rational attitudes of his parents as well as the romantic traditions of his Scottish heritage that he heard described in the poetry and stories. He continued to be an avid reader, soon stretching his scope of interest to include literature of all kinds; however, he had a particular fondness for the heroic ballads and legends of Scotland that he had first encountered at his grandfather's farm.

Scott's two older brothers had both gone into occupations worthy of gentlemen at the time—one became an officer in the navy, and the other an officer in the army. His two youngest brothers showed little promise, so his father decided that Walter would follow in his profession and study law. After completing his education at Edinburgh, Scott was apprenticed to his father's law practice for the next five years.

When Scott began his own law practice, he showed that he was better at the more literary aspects of the law. For instance, he was very good at writing informations, which contain the formal accusation and description of the crime used by the prosecuting official (as distinguished from the formal charges handed up by a grand jury). He did manage to create a law practice of his own, although most of his clients were poor prisoners, which brought him little in the way of fees. When he worked his circuit at Jedburgh he found that his clients were mostly local poachers and sheep stealers. Unfortunately for his clients, although his defense arguments were often amusing and literary, they were also often unsuccessful. For example, he once was asked to defend a minister who was accused of "toying with a sweetie-wife" and of singing doubtful songs while intoxicated.

Scott's arguments to the court focused on word meanings as he tried to draw a distinction between being occasionally drunk and being a habitual drunkard. He lost his case even though the judge, the prosecuting attorney, and the unfortunate minister all admitted that the arguments were fascinating and enlightening.

One of his early cases influenced the choice of some of the dogs that Scott would have around him in later years. In this case he was called upon to defend a burglar, which he did successfully this time, even though this housebreaker was in fact guilty—not only of the crime for which he was charged, but several others. Based upon his experience as a criminal, his client gave Scott the following bit of wisdom: "Always keep a terrier that barks, rather than a large dog, which you think may serve as a more formidable guard, but may spend most of its time sleeping. Size doesn't matter, just the sound." Scott took his advice and always made sure that his collection of dogs contained a few terriers, which are vigilant little dogs, always ready to begin barking at the first sign of someone approaching the house.

Although Scott's love was literature, he still had high hopes for his legal career, including the possibility of rising to the position of judge at some time. His ability to make friends gave him many contacts and ultimately he was appointed to the post of sheriff of the county of Selkirk. This was a good start, and gave him a secure income for the rest of his life. A few years later he also secured an appointment as clerk to the Court of Session in Edinburgh, which provided additional income and prestige. Scott's rise in the legal profession, however, soon stalled because his interests in literature continually diverted him from the law. He spent much time reading works in Italian, Spanish, French, German, Latin, and Greek, even managing to publish a few translations and edited versions of this literature as well.

Because of his love of his Scottish heritage, Scott became what he called "a ballad collector." In this pursuit his legal office actually turned out to be a great help, since he collected many of the ballads while he was on his tours of the countryside as sheriff. His ability to get the country folk to open up and reveal this material was remarkable, because most of the people in the countryside had suspicions about officials of any sort or anyone else associated with the law. They also felt insecure around educated people and were often suspicious of people from big cities such as Edinburgh. Walter Scott was all of these, and hence exactly the person least likely to win the confidence of the people who would know the obscure ballads that he was seeking. It was here that Scott's skill with common people and his special relationship with dogs served him so well.

In the countryside there was scarcely any farm or residence without at least one dog, and most had many. A man named Robin Shortreed, who had been assigned to Scott to serve as his guide and companion on these official trips, described how dogs could often serve as Scott's passport to their master's acceptance. He tells of one occasion when they arrived at a farm where the owner had been expecting them. Although the farmer had agreed to give them lodging, he was leery about having "such-like high folk" in his home. While Shortreed went to the door, where the farmer was peeking out hesitantly, Scott jumped off his horse and immediately introduced himself to the mixed pack of terriers and hounds that had come to greet the strangers. Dogs of all kinds seemed to have an affinity for Scott, and he tended to forget the humans nearby when he had four-footed things to greet and play with. The farmer, observing this, shook his head and opened the door with a smile. He turned to Shortreed and whispered, "Well, Robin, the devil have me if I'm fearful of him now. He's just a child like ourselves, I think. A man who is so hearty with dogs is one a farmer can understand and talk to himself."

In this instance, as in many others, Scott gained a hearty and sincere invitation to spend the night after he finished his play with the dogs. He left the next day with a few special remembered ballads and tales that were given to him during a long evening spent talking and drinking in a dim room with a pile of dogs near his chair.

Scott soon began to publish some collected ballads. The earliest were translations from other languages, but soon his interest in those border ballads bore fruit in a collection entitled *Minstrelsy of the Scottish Border*. These were not just word-for-word repetitions of the ballads that he had heard, but attempts to restore those versions (which often had been weakened through many retellings) back to their original compositions. This effort sometimes resulted in powerful poems that had a sophisticated Romantic flavor. Later he would take some of the themes and story structure from the ballads that he collected and create new, full-length narrative poems (such as *The Lady of the Lake*) that could stand by themselves as completely original contributions to literature. All of this made Scott very famous as a poet, and he was actually offered the post of poet laureate of England, which he declined.

Not only did Scott's literary reputation increase, but so did his income, as the string of popular publications continued. This allowed him to eventually purchase his dream home, an estate in Abbotsford. The manor provided the space and setting for Lady Scott to exercise her passion for entertaining guests, and it provided room for the couple's growing family. However, just behind his family in importance to Scott was the retinue of dogs that attended him all of his life. For instance, Scott's workspace was always arranged so that his dogs would be with him. He once commented to a friend that he found it nearly impossible to write unless there was a dog at his feet.

There were several dogs in the house at that time, including a pair of greyhounds, Douglas and Percy, who used to hunt with Scott and were quite good at getting hares. These were restless souls, and although they would often rest near his writing table, Scott found it convenient to leave the window of his study open so that the dogs could go and come as they desired.

A much more reliable writing companion was Camp, a bull terrier. Scott described him as being "of great strength, very handsome, extremely sagacious and affectionate towards the human species but somewhat ferocious towards his own." Camp would rarely move out of the study when Scott worked at his desk, but would look up attentively at him when he was spoken to. This was quite frequently, since Scott had a habit of speaking to the dogs as if they were human. Perhaps because of this constant exposure to human language, Camp became quite clever at interpreting what was said to him. Thus in later years, when he had hurt his back and could no longer run with his master as the latter went riding and hunting, the old dog would lie waiting for a hint as to the road by which Scott would return. If someone from the household said to him, "Camp, my good fellow, the sheriff's coming home by the ford," the dog would get up and painfully make his way toward the river. If they said, "The sheriff is coming by the hill," the dog would turn and go in the other direction to await his master.

An example of how Scott interacted with his dogs was described by Washington Irving, the American author best known for stories like *Rip Van Winkle* and *The Legend of Sleepy Hollow,* who visited Scott one day. "In our walk he would frequently pause in conversation to notice his dogs and speak to them as if they were rational companions, and indeed there appears to be a vast deal of rationality that these faithful attendants of man derived from their close intimacy with him."

At a later date, one of his greyhounds, Bran, was given the honor of sitting with Scott for a portrait painted by Francis Grant. During one of the sittings, the dog decided that the session had lasted long enough, so he stood up and poked his nose into the hand in which Scott held his pen.

"You see, Mr. Grant, Bran thinks it is time we went to the hills," said Scott. When the artist asked him to hold the pose a little longer so that he could finish painting the hand, Sir Walter turned to the dog with a careful explanation.

"Bran, my good man, do you see that gentleman? He is painting my picture, and he wants us to bide a wee bit till he has finished this hand, so just lie down for a while, and then we'll go to the hill."

The dog had watched attentively and seemed to understand, because he obediently curled himself up again on the rug. Scott explained to the artist, "Depend upon it, if people would speak slowly and with emphasis to their dogs they would understand a great deal more than we give them credit for."

When the well-loved Camp became ill, Scott became his devoted nurse. When the dog wouldn't take his food, Sir Walter fed him milk by the spoonful until he recovered. A few years later Camp died in Edinburgh. Scott buried him in the garden, within sight of Scott's seat at his writing table. The entire family stood around the grave in tears. Sir Walter was supposed to attend a fairly formal dinner engagement that evening, but he excused himself "on account of the death of a dear old friend."

In order to gain more control over his written work, Scott became a partner in a publishing company owned by James Ballantyne and his irresponsible brother, John. At first this arrangement was very successful, but this very success contributed to Scott's financial downfall. He was eager to own an estate and to act the part of "a bountiful laird," so in purchasing Abbotsford he spent anticipated income, rather than waiting until the money was actually in hand. He and his publishers engaged in some complex financial arrangements, meeting almost every new expense with bills discounted on work still to be done. In essence, these bills were just written promises to pay at a future date. While this form of payment was an accepted practice, pressure from the banks eventually led creditors to demand actual immediate payment in cash. Thus Scott and his associates found themselves looking at the prospect of bankruptcy.

Although his children were provided for because of trusts set up when the earnings were good, Scott was now looking at the likelihood that he would lose his country home and everything else. He now faced the pain and the shame of returning to his Abbotsford estate broken and penniless, and this seemed too much for him. Yet at this moment of grave personal crisis, to what does he turn his mind? He thinks of his dogs. In his journal, he wrote:

> I was to have gone there on Saturday in joy and prosperity to receive my friends—my dogs will wait for me in vain—it is foolish—but the thoughts of parting from these dumb creatures have moved me more than any painful reflections I have put down—poor things, I must get them kind masters. There may be yet those who, loving me, may love my dog because it has been mine. I must end this or I shall lose the tone of mind with which men should meet distress. I find my dogs' feet on my knees—I hear them whining and seeking me everywhere—this is nonsense but it is what they would do could they know how things are.

The Scottish judge Lord Henry Thomas Cockburn reports that within a few days of learning of his calamity, Scott returned to his duties at court. On his arrival there, some friends offered to give him money to help pay off his debt. With a modest and determined manner he declined, since he had already assumed personal responsibility for both his and the Ballantynes' liabilities. "No! This right hand shall work it all off. . . . Neither my family nor my dogs shall want for a home."

Scott's only asset was himself, so he determined that he would write whatever material would be most profitable. These would be novels, instead of ballads and poetry. Just as in our times, novels were well read, but in comparison to poetry or histories they were considered to be unworthy of serious consideration. In other words, all novels at that time had much the reputation that romance novels, such as those popularized by Harlequin Press, have today. They make money, but are not considered worthy of review. For example, in the first twelve years of its existence, the *Edinburgh Review* (the leading source of literary criticism) had reviews of only ten novels, and these were accompanied by apologies explaining why they were being reviewed. Meanwhile, every issue devoted at least one article to verse, even if the poets were quite forgettable.

Scott's first novel was based on the not too distant past. It involved an episode of Scottish history that still aroused national passions in Scott's time, namely, the Jacobite Rebellion of 1745. He called the book *Waverley,* and it was a saga of the manners and loyalties of a vanished Scottish Highland society. The text seemed so alive because Scott was a born storyteller who knew how to place a large cast of characters in an exciting and turbulent historical setting. Scott was a true master of dialog, and he wrote comfortably using both the common expressions of the Scottish countryside and the polished courtesies of knights and nobility. He also had a good grasp of the structure of Scottish society because his experience as a sheriff, law clerk, and attorney had exposed him to many different people in all walks and stations of life. This allowed Scott to write sympathetically and accurately about the whole range of the population: beggars, farmers, the middle classes, and professionals on up to the nobility. This attention to ordinary people marked a departure from previous historical novels, which were mainly focused on royalty. Combining his flair for picturesque and exciting incidents with his descriptions of ordinary and eccentric people, he was able to produce an engrossing picture of the fierce political and religious conflicts that disrupted Scottish life during the seventeenth and eighteenth centuries. Readers of *Waverley* had the feeling that they were present during these events and were seeing history unfold through the eyes of people that they could identify with. This was the birth of a new form of literature— the historical novel—and it was one of those rare and happy occasions in literary history when something original and powerful was immediately recognized, enjoyed, and supported by a large public audience.

The book was finished in an amazingly short time. Scott wrote it in about a month, even though he was still spending five or six hours in court five days a week. His work schedule involved getting up early in the morning and writing for at least three hours. Sometimes, when court was not in session, he would write till nearly noon.

One striking aspect of *Waverley* is that Scott's name does not appear on the book. The reason for this is that he knew that novels were not held in very high esteem, and he still had some aspirations to rise to a higher place in the legal profession. He explained it this way:

> I shall not own *Waverley;* my chief reason is that it would prevent me the pleasure of writing again. . . . In truth I am not sure it would be considered quite decorous of me, as a Clerk of Session, to write novels. Judges being monks, Clerks are a sort of lay brethren, from whom some solemnity of walk and conduct may be expected. So, whatever I may do of this kind I shall whistle it down the wind.

He even required the publishing house to post a bond of two thousand pounds to certify that they would not divulge his identity. During the fifteen years that followed, Scott produced a large number of novels. Because all were issued anonymously with only the inscription "By the author of *Waverley*," they became known collectively as the Waverley novels. The earliest works, like *Waverley, Guy Mannering, Old Mortality*, and *Rob Roy* were placed in seventeenth- and eighteenth-century Scotland. *Ivanhoe*, his most popular novel, was set in twelfth-century England, while *Quentin Durward* was set in fifteenth-century France, and *The Talisman* is set in Palestine during the Crusades.

The success of these books provided enough income so that Scott could keep his home at Abbotsford and begin to pay down the debt he owed. It meant that he could also keep dogs, and there were many of them. After the greyhounds Douglas and Percy had passed on there were additional greyhounds (Bran, Hector, and Hamlet), plus several pointers, including his favorite, Juno. After his bull terrier, Camp, died, his constant writing companion became Maida, a cross between a wolfhound and a Scottish deerhound who stood around four feet high at the shoulder and was roughly six feet in length from the tip of his nose to the base of his tail. Scott would talk to Maida as he wrote, discussing the fine points of the text that he was writing, and then proceeding on with his work as if the dog had responded with a great insight that made the task easier.

Maida was a calm comrade for Scott. He was seldom stirred to any excited outburst, except around the family cat, Hinse, who had taken to sleeping in the study at the top of the ladder Scott used to reach the books on the higher shelves. Scott ultimately developed a liking for Hinse but attempted to explain this away in his journal by noting, "My fondness for this cat may be a sign that old age is coming upon me." Maida became Scott's true soul mate, and when he died of old age, Scott had a local stonemason carve a statue of him, with an inscription:

> *Beneath the sculptured form which late you wore,*
> *Sleep soundly, Maida, at your master's door.*

Scott's next companion dog would be Nimrod, a wolfhound. Scott loved the attention that "Nym" would give as he followed his master, even for such short trips as that from the desk to a bookshelf to get a reference volume. It was a great solace to have him around, as Scott wrote in his journal: "I am happy in this place where everything looks so friendly, from old Tom [a friend who also served as caretaker of Abbotsford when he was away] to young Nym."

There were yet other dogs. There were many terriers, all long backed and short legged, and named after items on the condiment tray; thus, there was a Mustard, a Pepper, a Spice, and a Ketchup. There were the many spaniels that belonged to Lady Scott, but seemed to gravitate toward Walter as a matter of preference. There were also a number of hounds and some setters. All were always in Scott's mind. He was continually working to keep his family, his estate, and his dogs, and to free himself from the bondage imposed by his debts. He would write in his journal that if he could climb the mountain which his liberty from debt represented, he would only do so if he could bring his dogs with him.

Scott's dogs filled his heart, so it is not surprising that they began to find their way into the pages of his novels. The valiant Bevis, who plays a part in several heroic episodes in the novel *Woodstock* by saving the life and honor of its heroine, Alice, is clearly Maida. In *The Talisman,* Maida lives again as the brave Roswal, who saves the honor of his master, Kenneth, the crown prince of Scotland. While Scott had had only a few mentions of dogs in his poems, in the novels they are everywhere, often with names similar to those of his own dogs. Thus in *Waverley,* when we reach the happy ending and the Baron is set free from hiding, Scott makes a point of assuring us that Bran (a namesake of his own Bran) and Buscar (the name of one of his hounds) get the full meal that they had long wanted. The namesake of another of his dogs, Juno, appears under an accurate description of her size and coloration as the pointer in *The Antiquary.*

Perhaps the best known of Scott's literary dogs appear in the novel *Guy Mannering.* In it he describes a fictional farmer named Dandie Dinmont who kept a house full of dogs, including some terriers known as the "immortal six." The dogs were named Auld Pepper, Auld Mustard, Young Pepper, Young Mustard, Little Pepper, and Little Mustard (where Pepper and Mustard refer to the colors of the dogs, but also were names of two of Scott's own terriers). These terriers are described as short legged, long backed, and rough coated. The dogs are also described as being "gritty and plucky" animals, and among the fiercest of all terriers when aroused. Dandie Dinmont says of them in his heavy Scottish dialect, "they fear naething that ever cam' wi' a hairy skin on't."

While Dandie Dinmont was a fictional character, there was a real man who came close to the description painted by Scott. This was James Davidson of Hawick, who lived very near the spot where Scott placed the fictional Dinmont farm and kept a pack of dogs that were almost identical to those described by the author. People were soon calling him Dandie Dinmont, and coming to him to purchase dogs like those described in the novel. These dogs ultimately were given the breed name of Dandie Dinmont terriers, and versions of them can be seen in many dog shows around the world under that title.

As I noted earlier, Scott did not want people to know that he was the author of novels, which was why the books were published anonymously. Scott's ability to continue writing incognito, however, was ultimately compromised by his dogs. Given the success of his historical novels, it became a great challenge to the literary world to uncover "the author of *Waverley*." People began to look for clues in the books and compare them with other written works, and Scott was already a well-known writer based upon his ballads and poems. The literary sleuths tracking the anonymous author concluded from the novels that the man must be Scottish, interested in history and ballads, an avid reader (perhaps a bibliomaniac), a poet, a man of the law or at least one with legal training, a lover of outdoor sport, and a veritable expert and admirer of dogs. How many men would that description fit? One critic announced proudly, "Then what other hand but that of the author of 'Marmion,' the 'Lay of the Last Minstrel' and the 'Lady of the Lake' [all Scott poems and ballads] could have drawn Bevis, Roswal, Fangs, Wasp, Juno, the famous Mustard and Pepper terriers, and a dozen other dogs who bark, gambol, and fight in the pages of the anonymous novels?"

Once these sleuths had set their suspicions upon Scott, only a bit more detective work was needed. They quickly found that he owned not only dogs with the same names as many of the *Waverley* author's four-footed heroes, but also dogs of the same build, color, and description. The secret was clearly out. At the Theatrical Fund Dinner in March 1827, Lord Meadowbank made a speech in which he gathered all of the data about *Waverley*'s unknown author. Scott sat and listened, shaking his head "No" as Meadowbank repeatedly pointed to him with each successive fact. However, when Meadowbank began to list the canine evidence—the names, descriptions, and behaviors of Scott's dogs and those depicted by *Waverley*'s author—Scott broke into a broad smile. He leaned his head forward, and with arms widespread and palms up, he rose from his chair and bowed. His own dogs had helped to sniff out his best-kept secret.

There were benefits associated with the revelation that he was the author of those extremely popular historical novels. It is true that he would never rise any further in the legal profession, but this may have been due to the simple fact that he never put as much effort into his legal work as he did into his writing. He did, however, enjoy the fame and recognition that came with the attachment of his name to so many wonderful books, and he also liked the respect that people had for his writing. Unfortunately, although he still tried to work at his usual fast pace, his health was beginning to fail. His doctors recommended a trip to southern Italy in the hopes that the warm weather and relaxed lifestyle might allow him to recuperate. The last thing that he said as he prepared to leave, however, was "Be careful of my dogs!"

Scott was declining rapidly, but he did make it home from Italy, and his dogs greeted him warmly on his return. He gathered the whole pack of them around himself for comfort and settled down to rest. The dogs were still huddled near him at the end.

CHAPTER EIGHT

DOGS IN THE

OPERA HOUSE

DOGS HAVE NOT ONLY CONTRIBUTED to literature, but also to music. In the opera *Siegfried,* as the hero walks through the woods on his way to the den of the dragon, Fafner, few listeners will hear the footsteps of a dog in the orchestral music. There is no dog on the stage, nor is any mentioned in the story. There was a dog in the mind of the composer when he wrote that particular passage, however, and there were other dogs in his mind as he wrote some of his other masterpieces. Just as dogs were both solace and inspiration for Sir Walter Scott, so they were also for Richard Wilhelm Wagner.

Wagner is one of the most brilliant and controversial figures in the history of musical composition, and doubtlessly the most recognized German operatic composer in history. His most epic composition, the series of four operas which make up *The Ring of the Nibelung* (usually just referred to as the *Ring* cycle), unfolds as a single continuous story of gods, dwarves, dragons, heroes, supernatural heroines, and magic, all set in the world of German and Norse mythology. It is the *Ring* cycle that has given us our classic clichéd image of the operatic diva as a full-bosomed woman wearing plate armor and sporting a helmet with great horns on it. Wagner wrote thirteen full operas and numerous other musical compositions. His operas were new in form, and thus were often met with resistance.

Outside of his music, Wagner was even more controversial. He was extremely political, a social activist, and regarded himself as "the most German of men" (and even more grandiosely as "the German spirit"). Many labels have been given to him. He has been called an anarchist, a socialist, a nationalist, a proto-fascist, an anti-Semite, a conman, a self-centered egotist, an animal rights advocate, a vegetarian, and a wife-stealing womanizer. All of these descriptions probably have some truth to them, but even his detractors will admit that he was a genius, who, in addition to his activities as a composer and a librettist, also wrote more than 230 books and articles. These prose works cover a broad spectrum of topics, from theories of opera and music to political critiques, social commentaries and a two-volume autobiography. Even then he still had time to write thousands of letters. He is such a source of controversy and inspiration that one bibliography estimates more than fourteen thousand books and articles have been written about him to date. Few biographers, however, have noted the fact that Wagner lived a life that was full of dogs. His dogs inspired him, worried him, were the focus of much of his joy and his philosophical thinking and at least twice placed his life in jeopardy. One even rests beside him in his grave.

Wagner was born in Leipzig, Germany, in 1813. He was the ninth child of Carl Friedrich Wagner, a police actuary, and Johanna Rosine Wagner, who had an artistic bent and a desire to be an actress. At the time when Wagner's father died, Johanna had been living for months in Teplitz, Bohemia, with Ludwig Geyer, who was an actor, playwright, and portrait painter. Geyer married Wagner's mother in August 1814, and for the early years of his life Wagner was known as Richard Geyer and treated as a favorite son. There is a suspicion that Geyer was actually Wagner's natural father, since his affair with Johanna had predated the boy's birth by so long. The family soon moved to Dresden, where Wagner would complete most of his schooling. Geyer died when Wagner was only eight.

As a boy, Wagner already showed a fondness for animals in general and dogs in particular. He and his sister Cecile set themselves up as a sort of undercover rescue team for unwanted litters of puppies in their neighborhood that were about to be drowned. Several times they succeeded in saving some of the poor young beasts from their fates, and more than once they attempted to smuggle the survivors into their home. It was to little avail, as their mother would not permit them to keep any of these rescued puppies. However, recognizing the feelings of her children, when possible she would attempt to find some kind of home for these unwanted dogs.

Given the artistic and theatrical backgrounds and interests of both Geyer and Johanna, it is not surprising that the children developed an interest in the performing arts. Several of Wagner's older sisters became opera singers or actresses, and at an early age he became interested in theater and music. He was not a diligent scholar at school, but he attended as many concerts as he could and taught himself the piano and composition. He also read extensively, including the plays of Shakespeare, Goethe, and Schiller.

Wagner enrolled at Leipzig University, but he was not initially regarded as a very promising prospect. He had not completed his preparatory schooling and tended to lead a very wild social life. However, when he became interested in composing music and studied under Christian Gottlieb Müller, Wagner began to show the disciplined work style and high rate of productivity that would characterize his life. During these few years he wrote at least four piano sonatas, four overtures, and a symphony. Two of the overtures would be performed in concerts conducted by Heinrich Dorn while Wagner was still a student. He next took lessons with Christian Theodor Weinlig, a composer, theorist, organist, and cantor who was music director at the Thomaskirche. Wagner, however, was impatient with traditional methods of instruction, and subsequently much of his real schooling involved independent and careful study of the scores of the masters, notably the quartets and symphonies of Beethoven. Weinlig was so impressed by Wagner's talent that he refused all payment for his services and then arranged to have several of the young composer's pieces published. In addition, he was an important factor in arranging to give Wagner the opportunity to conduct the performances of his Overture in C major and also his Symphony in C major. These performances brought Wagner his first significant international notice.

Wagner always had the ability to get people to support his work. He impressed Weinlig and Dorn, who helped set the scene for his early musical successes, and later won patronage and assistance from the composer Franz Liszt; the king of Bavaria, Ludwig II; and the controversial political philosopher Friedrich Wilhelm Nietzsche. His success in securing backing and financial aid for his work and lifestyle was due to a number of factors. Obviously, Wagner had great talent, which was recognized and appreciated. He was also charming and sociable. When he had the funds to do so, Wagner lived a very rich and stylish life and entertained frequently. He was always ready to engage in conversation, and topics included not only music but politics, philosophy, literature and art.

He was also handsome, with a sharp sense of humor, which made him attractive to women. On the downside, Wagner had a quick temper, was subject to paranoid ideas in which he believed that he was being conspired against by various ethnic and racial groups (most specifically the Jews), and could be subject to periods of depression and insecurity. His saving grace was that he knew that these characteristics were socially unacceptable to most people. He therefore used his considerable social skills to keep these emotions and beliefs out of sight from all but his closest friends and family—at least during the early years before his fame had given him a degree of immunity from criticism.

Wagner's first attempt at writing an opera was a planned three-act work entitled *The Wedding.* Because of his considerable literary as well as musical skills, Wagner began by writing the libretto (the poetic text of the opera) himself. He would end up writing the librettos for all of his later operas as well. However, when his sister Rosalie expressed her dislike for the text of this work, he abandoned it and simply kept some of the characters' names in his first completed opera, *The Fairies.* Like many of his most famous later works, this first one was based upon folklore. It told a story about Oberon, the king of the elves and fairies. Unfortunately, Wagner was learning how difficult it is to get an opera produced, and he could not find enough investors to put his first one on stage in Leipzig.

While still faced with this stumbling block in his career, Wagner was offered the position of music director with a traveling theatrical company that was based in Magdeburg. The company was failing, and Wagner at first refused the post. He soon reversed his position, however, after meeting one of the troupe's actresses, Christine Wilhelmine Planer, whom he would call Minna. Wagner was in love for the first time.

Once having assumed this post, his debut as an opera conductor was a production of *Don Giovanni.* Meanwhile Wagner was working on the libretto and music for another opera called *Forbidden Love,* based upon Shakespeare's play *Measure for Measure.* It was written in a romantic form, reminiscent of earlier operas in the fashionable French and Italian style of the time. Although the composition was speedily completed, there were few resources in the small company, and one of the things that had to be skimped on was rehearsal time. In fact, the troupe was so ill prepared for the premiere that major roles were in effect improvised, and the performance was a disaster. There was no second performance of the work, and the company folded.

With no job, Wagner was in dire straits; however, friends would save him this time, as they would many times in the future. Minna, who was well respected as a performer, quickly got a job in the theater in Königsberg. Once she was there, she began a campaign that won the post of conductor for her lover. As soon as they were together again they married. Unfortunately, the Königsberg theater had only taken a chance on the unproven conductor because it, too, was on the verge of bankruptcy. When the company folded, another friend came to the rescue. Heinrich Dorn, who had conducted the first performances of Wagner's works while the composer was still a student, obtained for him the post of music director at the theater in Riga. Wagner performed the duties of music director by conducting opera performances and orchestral concerts based on the work of other composers. He also began composing a new opera based on *Rienzi, the Last of the Roman Tribunes,* a novel by the English writer Edward Bulwer-Lytton. Financial problems still followed Wagner, though. His income was meager, and his expenses often included items that are usually covered by the theater company, such as music scores and other items used in the performances themselves.

Probably the best thing that happened to Wagner in Riga was finding a dog named Robber. He first met the big Newfoundland in a shop that he frequented, where he always greeted the dog in an affectionate way. The dog soon attached itself to him with a passionate devotion. Robber had decided that he was going to adopt the composer, and there was nothing that Wagner could do about it. The dog followed him like a shadow, setting up camp outside of Wagner's door and staying there until the composer's affection for dogs caused him to soften his resolve and let Robber in. When Wagner went to town for a rehearsal, Robber would escort him, deviating from the path only for a few minutes to take a bath in the moat. This was one of Robber's passions and he would do this even in the winter, and even if only a small hole could be found in the ice.

Robber regularly attended rehearsals with Wagner. At one such orchestral rehearsal the dog took up a post next to the conductor's podium, maintaining his usual respectful silence. Unfortunately, he had taken a place quite close to one of the contrabass players. As the musician worked his instrument the bow pointed directly at Robber's eye, and the dog glared in his direction since it appeared to be a personal menace. Suddenly the musician gave a particularly vigorous stroke, and Robber snapped at it. The musician cried in alarm, "The dog,

Herr Kapellmeister!" To which Wagner replied, "The dog is a fine critic. He is merely telling you that playing this passage requires more delicacy."

Finances were extremely tight by now. Wagner was dreaming of going to Paris and producing *Rienzi* there, but he needed financial support for such an enterprise. He sent a copy of his overture *Hail Britannia* to Sir George T. Smart, the president of the philharmonic society in London, to try to solicit funds or at least make some contacts with potential backers for a production. In Riga he also convinced the members of his troupe to perform in a couple of benefit concerts to earn some funds for Minna and him to make the trip to Paris to continue looking for financial backers. Unfortunately, he had to personally advance the funds to cover the initial expenses for the benefit performances, which did not work out well. The time of year was wrong, the weather did not cooperate, and there were competing performances from more popular companies at the same time. In the end the benefits lost money, leaving Wagner with a sizeable debt. Riga, the capital of Latvia, was at that time part of Russia, which did not look kindly upon debtors. If the legal system concluded that he could not pay his debts, there was a real possibility that Wagner would be sent to prison. In this case, given the size of the debt that he had amassed, even exile to Siberia would not be an unusual punishment. As it was, his creditors had already begun to take action against him, having his passport seized so that he could not easily flee the country.

Wagner quickly sold his furniture and most of his household goods to obtain some money so that he and Minna, along with one and a half completed (but unpublished) operas and an exceedingly large Newfoundland dog, could all buy their escape from Russia.

Again, help came from a friend. This time it was Abraham Moller, a merchant and an avid theatergoer who agreed to smuggle the group across the Russian border. It was a tense and bizarre scene. Picture a man fleeing for his life, but shaping the nature of his escape to fit the needs of bringing along a dog—not just any dog, but a huge 160-pound dog! One bark from the big black dog while they crossed the frontier could have brought a hail of gunfire down on them from the sentries. Once in Prussia they could not travel by rail or coach because of the dog, so the only way to get to Paris would be to travel by boat to London, then make their way to France. If they were stopped by police or guards, the fact that they had no proper documents would surely have led to their arrest. Thus, to avoid attracting attention they decided to secretly haul Robber up the steep side of the vessel and hide him below decks. The dog remained silent, and the small ship, its crew of seven, and the three passengers (two human and one canine) left the dock safely.

It was not a pleasant trip. The sea was rough, and both Minna and Robber suffered greatly from seasickness. Wagner would later use what he had experienced in those rough seas to shape the music in his opera *The Flying Dutchman,* which is a story about an immortal but ill-fated sailor doomed to sail the sea forever in search of love.

Once in England there would be more problems and inconveniences. Wagner describes it this way:

> So we reached London Bridge, the unique centre of this immense, densely packed universe. After our dreadful three weeks at sea, we were at last on solid ground again, and we yielded to a state of giddiness— still used to the pitching motion of the ship—which also affected Robber. The dog whisked round every corner and threatened to lose his way every minute. So the three of us sought refuge in a cab which took us to the Horseshoe Tavern, a sailors' pub recommended to us by our captain. Here we contemplated how to conquer this monster of a town. . . . The narrow cabs then in use were meant to carry two people facing each other, so we had to lay our huge dog crosswise, his head through one window and the tail through the other.

After a short and fairly uneventful stay in London, the couple made it to Paris. The city was like most political and cultural centers of that time, in that it attracted the rich and powerful. This was good for Wagner, since the aspects of Parisian life that most interested the composer were heavily influenced by money and connections. Unfortunately, Wagner lacked both, so his ability to move in the social spheres that he felt would be most useful were limited. In the end his two years in Paris turned into a bitterly disappointing experience, all the more so since it began with great promise. After a chance meeting with the German composer Giacomo Meyerbeer, who had risen to prominence and influence in France, Wagner obtained a promise that Meyerbeer would use his considerable clout to open the doors to the operatic circles of Paris. Unfortunately, the Parisian arts establishment was a relatively closed network, and all of the doors that the older composer opened led to dead ends. Wagner and Minna ended up living with a colony of poor German artists, while he staved off starvation by writing articles on music for some magazines. He also resorted to composing a number of popular melodies, and took a job as a part-time secretary for a publisher.

The professional highlight of Wagner's stay in Paris was the completion of two operas: *Rienzi* and *The Flying Dutchman.* The personal highlights had to do with his dog Robber, who cavorted his way through the city, swimming in fountains and making friends with everyone he met. Robber actually had more local notoriety than his master. Each of these uplifting events was offset by a corresponding setback. First, Wagner could not raise the money to produce either opera, and second, his beloved dog went missing. It has never become clear as to what happened to Robber. Wagner was always a bit inattentive about his dogs' whereabouts, so the big Newfoundland could have simply wandered out in the street and met with an accident. Wagner also had more than a few enemies, since his social views were not always popular and were always expressed with great noise. Any one of those who disagreed with him could have abducted the dog, given that his ownership was well known. It is also possible that Robber simply tired of the sparse life of a starving composer and abandoned Wagner just as he had abandoned his former master, the shopkeeper in Riga. In any event, this was the final psychological blow. Wagner decided to leave Paris and return to Dresden, where he still had contacts in the musical world, plus some family, friends, and former student associates who might be willing to back one of his new operas. Robber would be immortalized in a fictional story that Wagner had published in 1841. Called *An End in Paris,* the pathos-filled tale tells of a musician's dog, much like Robber, who is left mourning beside the grave of his master.

Dresden would be good for Wagner in his time of need. He quickly found investors willing to support a production of *Rienzi,* and although it is considered to be a minor piece today, it was finely tuned to the taste of audiences of its era. When it premiered in Dresden in 1842, it was a huge success. As a result of this triumph Wagner was offered, and accepted, the position of musical co-director at the royal court in Dresden. This was the beginning of one of the more stable periods in Wagner's life. The financial security allowed him to continue to compose and to experiment with new forms of what he would call "music drama." The next year, he cemented his position with a successful production of *The Flying Dutchman.*

Material security also allowed him to build what would be his immediate family. This involved getting a puppy to replace the missing Robber. Since he and Minna were childless, this involved a conscious act of substituting dogs for children, as became clear from a letter that he wrote to his sister Cecile: "We are forced to make do with dogs since there is still absolutely no prospect of human progeny. We have another now, just six weeks old, a funny little beast; his name is Peps, or Striezel (because he looks as if he had come from the gingerbread-market). He's better than the last one, Robber." He closed this note with the sad statement, "I'd rather have a Maxel," referring to his sister's son. Wagner described the new pup as "a sort of a spaniel," and from drawings and other descriptions we can assume that he was an English toy spaniel or a Cavalier King Charles spaniel.

Peps (or Pepsel, as Wagner called him when he was in a playful mood) immediately became a vital part of the composer's life. The dog did not have the same freedom to roam that Robber had, but was expected to be near Wagner whenever he was close to home. In return, Wagner would talk to the dog all of the time. Sometimes he would get down on the ground and roll around with Peps, talking nonsensical baby talk to the little dog.

By now Wagner was beginning to establish his unique style of operatic composition, drawing exclusively on Germanic and Norse myths for his story lines. He believed that myths expressed certain eternal truths about the human condition, and that an opera based upon myths might speak directly to human emotions. The first opera of this nature was also the first that he conceived in Dresden, *Tannhaüser and the Contest of Singers on the Wartburg.* This was also the first opera that he wrote with, and some say for, Peps. The dog was required to be present when Wagner composed. A special stool was provided for him, although at times he would climb up on other pieces of furniture to obtain a better vantage point. Wagner would play on the piano, or sing passages while keeping his eyes on Peps to see how he reacted. All of this attention tended to spoil Peps a bit, and he soon felt that it was his prerogative to demand attention from anyone who came to the house.

The importance of Peps in Wagner's creative routine is told in a reminiscence by Marie, the daughter of Ferdinand Heine (a close friend who was also the costume designer for the theater). Marie was warmly accepted by Wagner and Minna and often came to call at their home. She later recalled:

I hold many friendly and interesting recollections of Wagner's brightest period in Dresden as a royal *Kapellmeister,* and we often spent cozy hours there. My horror was his beloved Peps, a white and brown speckled little monster who tyrannized over the household and probably imagined that his master could not accomplish anything without his presence. It is known that there stood next to the piano an upholstered stool, on which Peps had to lie when his master wanted to compose. If the dog was not there, the whole household was set in motion to look for him, and many a time Minna herself had to go out and fetch him from the park near the Ostra-Allee. I often made a timid and anxious detour when I had to pass Wagner's apartment, for as soon as Peps got sight of me he circled around me with such a pitiful howling that we attracted the gaze of all the passersby: hardly a desirable prominence for the schoolgirl I then was! When later I complained to his master, Wagner, highly delighted, burst into laughter and said: "'Well, my dear Marichen, he well knows the friends of the house and wants to salute them too!'"

Peps was a particularly sensitive dog. When Wagner would talk to him (as he often did) and his speech would turn into a harangue against some perceived enemy, the dog would respond to the escalating tone of his master's voice by jumping up and barking, all the while spinning around as if looking for the composer's foes. Peps also appeared to be sensitive to the emotional tone of music. As Wagner composed on the piano, or sang passages he was working on, he noticed that Peps responded differently to particular melodies or musical phrases. His reactions were predictable and seemed to be based upon particular musical keys. For instance, certain passages in E-flat major caused an occasional calm tail wag, while some passages in E major might cause him to stand up in an excited manner. This caused Wagner to consider the possibility of associating specific musical keys with particular moods or emotions in the drama. In Tannhäuser, this translated to linking the key of E-flat major with the concept of holy love and salvation, while E major is tied to the notion of sensual love and debauchery—all of which seemed consistent with Peps's reactions.

Now that Peps had made him consciously aware that it was possible to associate specific musical elements with recurring dramatic moods, Wagner went back and looked at the score of *The Flying Dutchman* and found that he had been unconsciously doing some of the same thing in that earlier work. However, now that the potential to manipulate the mood and dramatic understanding of the listener with particular sound elements had been made clear, he could elaborate on the idea to raise the emotional impact of his operatic works. He would do this in the next opera that he would compose with Peps's help, *Lohengrin*.

In *Lohengrin*, although the conventional opera components (such as arias, duets, and choruses) are still identifiable, Wagner used the hint supplied by Peps and associated individual characters not only with particular musical keys, but also with specific instruments and themes. Thus Lohengrin, who is a knight of the Holy Grail, is linked with higher-pitched string instruments and the key of A major; the evil sorceress Ortrud is associated with lower-pitched string and wind instruments and the key of F-sharp minor; Elsa, the heroine, is linked with higher-pitched woodwinds and various flat keys; and King Henry is associated with brass instruments and the key of C major. There are also particular themes that would come to be known as musical motifs. These are used to identify important characters and other aspects of the drama when these first appear, and they recur at appropriate moments in later parts of the story.

When Wagner had been in Paris, he had met the composer and conductor Franz Liszt. Liszt soon became a friend and a financial backer, and it would be Liszt who would conduct the first performance of *Lohengrin*. When Liszt came to Germany to conduct and compose, he and Wagner would get together whenever possible to talk about musical matters. Liszt recognized that both he and Peps were serving much the same advisory function for Wagner. Shortly after the two composers had spent some time together, Liszt wrote to Wagner, "God grant I may soon come to you again—Your Doppel-Peps, or 'Double extract de Peps,' or 'Double Stout Peps.'" In fact Liszt adopted the nickname "Peps" and often used it in signing notes that he had written to Wagner. It is truly strange to learn that a great composer—one who wrote some of the finest pieces ever done for piano, and completely revolutionized our concept of the sonata—was simply aspiring to be as helpful to another composer as his pet dog!

Unfortunately, Wagner's peaceful and successful life at Dresden would not last, due to his penchant for social activism. Wagner was swept up in the liberal antimonarchy movement of the time, then became embroiled in the German revolution of 1848. He wrote a number of articles advocating revolution and even took an active part in the Dresden uprising of 1849. When the uprising failed, a warrant was issued for his arrest, and he fled Germany with Minna, Peps, and a gray parrot named Papo. Banned from returning to Germany, Wagner was unable to attend the first performance of *Lohengrin,* which was conducted by his friend Franz Liszt in Weimar.

Residing in exile in Zurich, Wagner found some wealthy patrons in the form of Otto Wesendonk and his wife, Mathilde, who gave him financial support and eventually provided him with a house. With his living conditions again stable, Wagner soon returned to his usual writing routine. He was now about to undertake the composing of his most ambitious project, a set of four operas that would have the overall title of *The Ring of the Nibelung* and tell an epic mythological tale about gods, heroes, heroines, dwarves, dragons, and a magic ring. A new leather stool for Peps to rest on was purchased, and the dog served as companion and critic while he wrote the first in the series, *The Rhine Gold,* and began the music for the second opera, *The Valkyrie.* Unfortunately, before this second work was finished, Peps became ill. He took a turn for the worse only a week or so after Wagner returned from a second trip to London. The composer became quite distraught at this and tried heroically to save the dog, even to the point of rowing all the way across Lake Lucerne (where the closest veterinarian was located) for medicine.

Peps had always slept in a basket beside Wagner's bed. Each morning he would gently awaken the sleeping man by pawing at him. Peps had been the focus of much love, and was one of the few living things to whom Wagner could afford to expose his inner thoughts. The dog would often release him from his rigid attempts to maintain a respectable level of decorum, and from his need to always appear to be a genius that was in total control of his life. One day Liszt observed the way that Peps brought Wagner back to a more normal view of himself. Wagner was trying to read something relevant to the piece that he was composing when Peps came over to him and gently pawed at his leg. When that brought no response, he pawed more vigorously and began to whimper. Wagner looked at the dog over the top of his book and asked in a stern tone, "Why do you disturb the great Richard Wagner?" Then, as if amused by just how pompous that sounded, he broke into laughter, put down his book, and lifted the dog onto his lap, gently asking, "Have you come to suggest a new aria for the Rhine maidens, my Pepsel?"

But now Peps, his musical helpmate, the dog he had called the coauthor of *Tannhaüser,* was dying. Wagner was devastated. He canceled a planned trip and all of his appointments, then stayed up all night to be with the dog. He wrote a few days later that Peps showed him "a truly heart-rending love to the last, and even on the verge of death kept turning his head—or finally his pleading eyes—towards me, if I moved a few paces away. Then without a cry, without a struggle, he peacefully expired beneath our hands in the night from the 9th to 10th—the following noon the pair of us buried him in a garden by the house. I have wept without cease—I could not help it—and felt a grief and sorrow for the dear thirteen-year friend, who had always worked and walked with me, and taught me plainly that the world exists in our heart and our intuition alone." Wagner would write a number of further letters in which he asked forgiveness for weeping openly for his dog.

Meanwhile, Wagner's relationship with his wife, Minna, was deteriorating. From the beginning there had been spats and disagreements, but as his fame increased and the demands on his time became even greater, things were getting quite bad. Mathilde Wesendonk, the wife of his patron in Zurich, Otto Wesendonk, had developed a personal fondness for Wagner. She gave him another dog to replace Peps. It was the same breed as Peps, and Wagner immediately fell in love with him. The new dog was given the name Fips, and he took Peps's place on the stool next to the piano while Wagner worked. Fips went on walks with Wagner, and one fall day they were walking through a nearby park. Fips detected something, perhaps the scent of a squirrel, and began to cast around through the cover of dry autumn leaves that lay on the ground. As the dog searched the ground with quick back-and-forth swings, he scattered the leaves. Wagner laughed and observed, "You look as lost as Siegfried in the woods searching for the dragon." Then he stopped a moment and listened to sounds that the dog's feet made on the dry brown leaves as he ran from side to side sniffing. "Ah Fipsel," he said out loud, "you have composed a fine piece of music this morning. Let's go home and write it down."

When Wagner left Zurich on several extended holidays to escape the bickering with Minna and to attempt to cure himself of some of the ailments that now were affecting his sleep, stamina, and digestion, the only companion that he took with him was Fips. His stay away would last a number of weeks, so Wagner took up a residence in a summerhouse in sight of Mont Blanc. He was served alone, and Fips was his sole society; there even was some time for him to work on his new opera *Siegfried* with his new canine coauthor. Minna was suspicious of this trip, suspecting that Wagner was really away having an affair with Mathilde. When he returned she began to carefully monitor his correspondence with the younger and prettier woman, and her suspicions continued to grow. Eventually Minna had convinced herself that Wagner was having a sexual liaison with Mathilde (which probably was not true) and left Wagner for Paris. Her anger was such that she also took Fips, the dog that had been given to her husband by her hated rival. It is likely that she was hoping for some reconciliation, since she knew that a revised version of *Tannhaüser* was being mounted in Paris, and Wagner would surely come there to take part in the production.

Wagner was quite disconsolate over these events—more so at the loss of Fips than the loss of Minna, since the dog had been a much more pleasant companion than his wife in recent years. He could not understand why Minna took the dog, unless it was to hurt him and deprive him of social support. When he learned shortly thereafter that Fips had died, Wagner became convinced that Minna had poisoned the dog out of spite for him, and out of jealousy for Mathilde. This was more than he could stand, and he resolved not to even try to repair the marriage. As he recorded in his diary, "The sudden death of this lively and lovable animal acted as the final rift in a childless union which had long become impossible."

The one saving factor in his life at that point was that in 1861, just after the death of Fips, an amnesty allowed him to return to Germany. He first went on a retreat to Wiesbaden to work on the opera *The Mastersingers of Nürnberg,* but he missed his dog. In an attempt to get some canine companionship he approached his landlord's bull terrier, Leo. This was an unwise action, since Leo responded by biting the maestro's hand so badly that he could not play the piano for several weeks. Shortly after he recovered, Wagner went to Vienna.

Unfortunately, by this time he was again in financial straits. The Paris production of *Tannhaüser* had been a disaster. Controversy over Wagner's social views had caused protests that shut the production down, leaving a big monetary loss. While keeping his residence in Vienna, where he heard his opera *Lohengrin* for the first time, he traveled through Europe as a conductor. After only three years there, however, his habit of spending money on a grand scale for both personal and professional purposes (plus his tendency to borrow large sums and live at the expense of others) brought him to financial disaster. Once again, he found himself fleeing a city to avoid imprisonment for debt. And as in his flight from Riga, he had the company of a large dog, which made his travels more awkward.

The composer's new dog was named Pohl, and it was a Saint Hubert hound, which is actually a parti-colored bloodhound. The dog had been lent to him by his master, who was Wagner's Viennese landlord. The landlord noticed that Wagner seemed to have a need for canine companionship, and since the maestro was often away this lending arrangement seemed to work well. When Wagner fled the city he not only left behind an unpaid debt to the landlord, but also decided to take the dog, for which he had developed a real fondness. The two of them arrived in Stuttgart without a penny. Wagner was a fifty-one-year-old man without a future, almost at the end of his tether, with only a ninety-pound hound as a companion. He needed a miracle to save him, and he got it.

In 1863, Wagner had published the poetic text of the *The Ring of the Nibelung*. This was done to earn some money immediately, but also to present his dream project of mounting the four-opera cycle for possible backers and investors. The publication actually contained a direct plea for financial support, or any other support that the reader might be able to provide. In the foreword to the book he specifically asked if, somewhere, there was a German prince with the means and the vision to support dreams such as his. Fortunately for him, there was. When Ludwig II, the king of Bavaria, ascended the throne at the age of eighteen, he was already a fanatical admirer of Wagner's work. He had read *The Ring* and decided to answer the composer's cry for help. He invited Wagner to Munich to finish the work, paid his debts, installed him in an elegant villa, and provided him with a generous stipend. Pohl kept him company, lying near him when he worked on the opera *Parsifal* and urging him to take long walks, which seemed to help Wagner's physical and mental states.

Shortly after he was installed in Munich, Cosima von Bülow, the daughter of Wagner's friend Franz Liszt and the wife of Hans von Bülow, the brilliant pianist, composer, and music director of the Munich Court Opera, arrived to provide another form of help by joining Wagner in his villa. She had known him because of her father's friendship and had been attracted to him; now they began an affair that resulted in the birth of a child in less than a year. The openness of Wagner's relationship with a married woman was considered to be scandalous, and members of Ludwig's court directed a wave of hostility toward him. In effect, Wagner was banished from Munich, and he returned to Switzerland to reside in a house on the shore of Lake Lucerne. Pohl continued to travel with him, but the hound developed a cough and was left behind in Geneva while Wagner traveled to France to conduct some of his works. While the composer was away, Pohl died. His death was nearly at the same time that Minna, his estranged wife who had by now returned to Dresden, died. Once again Wagner was distraught, but it was because of his canine, not his conjugal, loss. He returned to Geneva and had his beloved hound exhumed. He then put a necklace (containing his name and a written tribute) on his dog's body and had him buried in an elegant casket. A marble headstone was erected over his final resting place. In contrast, Wagner never paid a visit to his former wife's grave, nor expressed any interest in doing so.

Cosima soon joined Wagner in Switzerland. They would ultimately have three illegitimate children before she dissolved her marriage to Hans von Bülow. Once divorced, she would marry Wagner in 1870. Fortunately for Wagner, his grief at the loss of Pohl would be eased, since Cosima brought with her a little fox terrier named Kos. Although supposedly Cosima's companion, Wagner immediately adopted the dog and had it with him most of the time. As was his typical manner, he developed a strong bond with the dog, and in this case it almost cost him his life. Wagner and Cosima were out walking near the railroad on their way to the post office. Kos was wandering with them, without any leash, when he saw another terrier and ran toward it. The other dog rushed at Kos, and the two of them began to fight in the middle of the track. Wagner noticed that a train was bearing down on the two small animals and ran to save Kos. He was running and shouting, none of which had any effect on the fighters. Finally Wagner reached the dogs, and grabbed Kos by the collar, swinging both the dog and himself away just in time to avoid the train by only a few feet. Wagner's last desperate maneuver saved the dog but threw both of them on the ground. When the frightened and tearful Cosima reached his side, the composer was limping but smiling at his successful rescue. Turning to Cosima, he asked "Now that I have saved his life, will he have the courtesy to compose a piece of music for me as Fipsel did?" If Kos did, Wagner never recorded that fact in his notes or diaries.

The next dog to enter Wagner's life was a black Newfoundland named Russumuck, who would be called Russ. His housemaid, Vreneli Weidmann, gave it to him after hearing him speak fondly and often about his first Newfoundland, Robber. Wagner never spoke of any musical assistance that Russ provided, but the dog was always present when the composer was working. When the children were young Russ kept constant watch over them, and he would swim behind them when they went boating. Once this probably saved the life of Wagner's daughter Eva, who tumbled from the boat only to be immediately snatched out of the water by the dog who followed their little craft.

Cosima had never lived with a dog as large as Russ. He was not always neat and well groomed, since he had a predilection to go swimming and then wander over lawns and through woods. He could accumulate a goodly amount of dirt and mud in this manner, and Cosima thought that it was best that he stay outside in the yard, rather than tracking it all through the house. Wagner was not happy with this arrangement. "If he must sleep outside, then perhaps I should too," he complained. Rather than bother the maestro any further, Cosima relented, only leaving instructions that the dog should first pass through the kitchen, where someone should make an effort to brush him out and dry him off before releasing him to the rest of the house.

Russ was extremely protective of Wagner, and sometimes his concern for the composer's safety was not welcome. He once refused to allow Wagner to enter a carriage, thus forcing the man to walk several miles home. On another occasion, Wagner took the children out to to do some ice skating. When he saw his children having fun, he decided to try it himself, renting a pair of skates and moving in a shaky manner toward the skating area. Suddenly, Russ rushed at his skates and tried pull them off. When one of the employees tried to restrain him, Russ snapped at him. The man pulled back and announced, "The dog is too faithful. You can't go skating." As the children laughed at Wagner's predicament he spread his arms in defeat, but was so unsteady on the skates that he nearly fell over. "Perhaps Russ has just saved me from my own rash and dangerous behavior," he admitted sheepishly.

The operas that made up the *Ring* cycle were nearing completion. Wagner was convinced that these productions could never be adequately performed in any existing opera houses, so he convinced Ludwig to sponsor the building of a new opera house that Wagner had designed himself. It was in the Bavarian town of Bayreuth, which would soon become the world's center for the promotion of Wagner's works and ideology. Wagner's last opera, *Parsifal,* would premier there in 1882 with the ceremony normally accorded only to a religious event. Following the composer's death, the control of the annual Bayreuth Wagner festival would pass to Cosima, and later to their children and grandchildren in a succession that continues to the present.

At the same time that the work on the Bayreuth opera house began, Ludwig provided Wagner with an elegant villa that he named Wahnfried ("freedom from illusion"). Russ became the ruling animal and Wagner's constant companion there. When Russ died just as Wagner was scheduled to go to Vienna to give a

concert, the trip was delayed for a day so that Russ could be buried. He was interred at the head of the gravesite that his master had prepared for himself in the
garden, with a headstone bearing the epitaph, "Here Lies and Watches Wagner's
Russ."

A clergyman once confronted Wagner about what he considered this dese-
cration of a churchyard. Wagner grew quite angry about this and retorted, "But
is a man to be deprived of his humbler companions in the 'world to come,' or
are they to be created afresh out of 'nothing'? The assumption that the birth of a
beast is an origination out of nothing and its death accordingly is an absolute an-
nihilation, whilst man is supposed to have equally sprung from nothing and
nevertheless is to enjoy an endless individual continuance, is an absurdity against
which my common sense revolts!"

There would be several other dogs at Wahnfried during Wagner's last
years. One was a Saint Bernard named Branke, and two others were both Newfoundlands—Mollie, who had been purchased to be Russ's mate, and a large
male named King Marke. Mollie grew ill and died not long after an unsuccessful
pregnancy. Branke and Marke, however, romped around the grounds of the villa
and were frequent visitors at the opera festival. Their antics, however, often caused
trouble for the aging and ailing Wagner. Branke killed a neighbor's cat, while both
dogs were also accused of killing chickens. Wagner thought that this was simply
exuberant behavior on the part of his dogs; he loved them both so dearly that he
could not imagine any malice was intended. The population of the village, however, became quite incensed at this wanton destruction by his pets, and actually
held demonstrations at the gate of Wahnfried and at the opera festival. Wagner
made restitution for the damages, and King Ludwig himself provided a written
guarantee that the dogs would be more closely watched and would not cause further harm. Only Marke would live long enough to see Wagner at the end.

Things were going well financially for Wagner, although his health was failing. Marke was with him all of the time when he was at the villa, but the restrictions that had been placed on him to conform with Ludwig's promise
limited where he could go, and prevented any traveling with his master. When
the family prepared to go to their winter residence in Vienna for a month or two,
Wagner stopped to speak openly to Marke, saying, "I fear I may not return again
to see you, Be faithful and brave."

While Wagner expected Marke to be faithful, there were some doubts about
his own intentions. Cosima learned that he had developed an infatuation with

Carrie Pringle, one of the flower maidens from the recent production of *Parsifal*. On February 13, 1883, after learning that the girl had been invited to visit their Viennese home, Cosima angrily confronted her husband. The heated argument that resulted was loud enough to rouse the rest of the house. A few hours later, Wagner was found dead of a heart attack, slumped over an unfinished essay, "The Eternal Feminine Quality."

When Wagner's body was returned to Wahnfried for burial, Marke, whose love was always faithful, stood by the coffin and howled lamentably. Wagner was laid to rest, as per his instructions, next to his beloved Russ. Marke could not be kept away from the gravesite and, according to Cosima, "died from grief" only a few days later. He was buried a short distance away with the epitaph, "Here Rests Wahnfried's Guardian and Friend, the Good, Beautiful Marke."

The music written by Wagner with his coauthors Peps and Fips, and under the watchful eyes of Robber, Pohl, Kos, Russ, Branke, and Marke is still played and appreciated today. Listen carefully as Siegfried walks the woods in search of the dragon, and in the music you can hear the footsteps of Wagner's dog Fips rustling in the leaves.

CHAPTER NINE

THE TALKING DOG

O NE RECENT SURVEY of the behaviors of dog owners revealed that about one out of every five of them admitted that they had, at some time, tried to communicate to their dog over the telephone when they were away from home. Some admitted to asking a family member to hold the telephone next to a dog's ear so that they could say something, while others said that they left an answering-machine message of greeting or reassurance in the hope that the dog was nearby and would hear it. Whether messages delivered to dogs over the phone make sense to the listening canine is an issue that could certainly generate a lively debate. There is little debate, however, about the fact that a dog played an important role in the life of the inventor of the telephone, Alexander Graham Bell.

One remarkable thing about Alexander Graham Bell is that although everyone thinks they know about his life and accomplishments, most people woefully underestimate his contributions to our modern way of living. While everybody knows that he invented the telephone, the truth is that Bell did a lot more. The money from his invention of the phone was important, though, because it gave him the freedom to work on other projects and produce many other significant inventions. For example, Bell invented the hydrofoil used on boats. To demonstrate its speed he had the HD-4 built, which weighed more than ten thousand pounds and reached a speed of seventy miles an hour. This was the world speed record for a nautical craft in 1919, and it would not be broken for more than a decade.

Bell also invented the iron lung, which was the first mechanical respirator and saved many lives. Another lifesaving invention was the magnetometer, which allowed physicians to accurately locate bullets or metal fragments in a patient's body long before the invention of the X-ray machine. He also improved on Thomas Edison's design of the phonograph, developing the first commercially successful version (along with the concept of the flat phonograph record to replace Edison's cylinders). In addition, Bell invented the photophone to demonstrate that light could be used to carry sound information, which in turn eventually led to the development of motion pictures with sound. He filed several patents for devices associated with flight; one, a steam-driven airplane, did prove to work, but never caught on. Another device that he created was the aileron, a movable section of an airplane wing that controls roll, and it is found on every plane in flight today. Along the way he found time to develop a strain of sheep that had a high degree of fertility and extra teats to nourish the many lambs that they produced.

In addition to inventions, Bell had time to contribute to science in other ways. He founded the journal *Science,* which became the official publication of the American Association for the Advancement of Science and continues to be one of the world's most important and respected publications containing original scientific reports. He was also a cofounder and later the president of the National Geographic Society. It was his idea to turn their rather staid journal *National Geographic* into the richly illustrated magazine that has become so familiar to us today. The pictures were important, he believed, as a form of "visual education."

One other contribution of Bell's was the invention of the audiometer, a device that allows physicians to measure the amount of hearing loss that an individual has. This apparatus is important because it reflects his lifelong interest in deafness and in the teaching of deaf people. It was in this realm of his activities that we find an interesting canine contribution to an issue that continues to occupy the minds of teachers of the deaf today.

Bell was born in Edinburgh, Scotland, in 1847, but his family soon moved to London. The teaching of speech was a family tradition, since his grandfather had been a teacher of elocution and his father, Alexander Melville Bell, was recognized as the leading authority on this subject. A. M. Bell's book, *The Standard Elocutionist,* continued to be revised long after his death and actually went through nearly two hundred editions in English. The senior Bell also made a significant contribution by developing a form of phonetic notation that he called "visible speech." The importance of this system is that the symbols used represented an analysis of the shape and movements of the lips and the position of the tongue in the mouth. This meant that someone who knew how to read these notations and had learned to move their mouth to assume the proper positions could produce any sound that was indicated, even meaningless sounds with no linguistic uses. Alexander and his brothers were trained in this system and were used by their father to demonstrate its effectiveness. During the demonstrations the boys would leave the room and the audience would recite passages, combinations of sounds (such as kissing or chuckling), or even non-English words from languages ranging from French to Gaelic. Their father would write the sounds in his visible-speech alphabet, and the boys would then return and accurately produce a copy of them. One observer described the scene by saying, "I well remember our keen interest, and by and by, astonishment, as the lads . . . reproduced the sounds faithfully; but like the ghost of its former self in its detachment from the stretching and body twisting with which it had originally been combined."

It was through his mother, Eliza Bell, that Alexander Graham Bell's interest in teaching language to the deaf began. Alexander was very close to his mother. She was a good pianist, and the boy shared this talent with her. When he was twelve, however, his mother began to lose her hearing. Although other people resorted to shouting into a rubber ear tube to communicate with her, Alexander found that he could still talk to her in a low voice if he kept his face close to hers and articulated slowly. It became quite clear to him that she was learning how to read his lips, at least to some degree. He also found that by having her practice proper elocution, using the patterns of mouth movements from his father's visible-speech system, she could maintain clearly understandable speech. It thus dawned upon young Alexander that his father's analysis of lip and tongue positions might help to teach speech to the deaf. His father was skeptical, however, and nothing further came of this for several years, during which Alexander went off to become a teacher of music and elocution.

Bell did not know it at the time, but he was beginning to shape his own stance at the heart of a controversy. There were, and are today, two rather extreme views on the education of the deaf. The first says that the deaf should be taught common language skills so that they can interact with, and become integrated into, society at large. Thus, for instance, deaf persons living in a society where a particular language is spoken should learn to read lips, so that they can understand the language that is being spoken around them. They should also learn to speak this language as clearly as possible, so those around them can understand them without special skills. Bell claimed, "The great object of the education of the deaf is to enable them to communicate readily and easily with hearing persons, or rather to render intercommunication between the deaf and the hearing easy and certain. That is what is meant by 'restoring the deaf to society.'" This viewpoint is now known as oralism, since it emphasizes the development of oral language skills in deaf individuals.

Opposed to the oralist view are the advocates of sign language. Since the signs are made with the hands, this viewpoint is often called manualism. Sign language for the deaf was first popularized in France during the eighteenth century by Abbey Charles Michel de l'Epée, who founded the first public school for deaf children in Paris. His reasons for emphasizing signs had to do with his Catholic religion. He thought that by teaching deaf children to communicate in some form, they could take vows in some way that could be understood by the priests and God, and in this way save their souls. Since this was a residential school, and the children were immersed continuously in this deaf culture, they learned to sign well and fluently. The school became a manualist environment, and de l'Epée soon came to believe that sign language was the natural way deaf people communicated their ideas.

Edward Miner Gallaudet in the United States adopted de l'Epée's ideas wholeheartedly. Like Bell, he was influenced by his father. Thomas Hopkins Gallaudet was a teacher of the deaf who went to Paris and learned the methods being taught there, including sign language. He then brought the manualist theories back to America, eventually establishing the first free public school for the deaf in the United States (now the American School for the Deaf in Hartford, Connecticut). Gallaudet was also similar to Bell in being influenced by his deaf mother. His mother, however, never learned to speak well and could only communicate by signs. Gallaudet often referred to the sign language of the deaf as "the language offered to them by nature" and felt that there was nothing arbitrary in the signs, since they were the spontaneous and natural expression of the deaf mind. E. M. Gallaudet would go on to found the first institution of higher education for the deaf, which is now Gallaudet University in Washington, D.C.

Bell felt that the views of the manualists were not valid in any way. "The proposition that the sign language is the only language that is natural to congenitally deaf children is like the proposition that the English language is the only language that is natural to hearing children. It is natural only in the same sense that English is natural to an American child. It is the language of the people by whom he is surrounded."

It was inevitable that these two views—and their two main proponents—would come into conflict. Ultimately there would be public debates, hostile exchanges in magazines and journals, and even heated legislative committee hearings before the U.S. Congress and Senate. In some respects this battle tended to polarize the views of many, and this polarization can still be seen today in the debate over what is now called "deaf culture," with some advocates claiming that deaf students should be taught only sign language, and the other side claiming that exclusive teaching of sign language will condemn deaf people to limited lives behind the walls of communication that signing builds between the deaf and the hearing majority.

Why was Bell so set in his oralist views, in the face of arguments by Gallaudet that some congenitally deaf people simply can't learn how to make coherent linguistic sounds? To put it simply, Bell felt that the manualist view was wrong because of a dog.

Bell's relationship with animals was always a bit ambiguous. Later in his life, in his Canadian home in Cape Breton, Nova Scotia, he would have many animals—horses, bobcats, eagles, snakes, sheep, and of course dogs. According to his daughter, Daisy, her father loved "any and all animals. But Father didn't love enough to take any responsibility about them, and he always knew that Mother would."

Bell's love of dogs was often a problem, especially during the early years of his marriage to Mabel Hubbard when money was tight and she was worried that he was about to squander some of their sparse funds on an expensive dog. She did understand that Bell needed the companionship of a dog, since he was used to working odd hours and being by himself. During the years that he was a teacher of the deaf, Bell would work a full day, then spend much of the night developing his inventions. Sometimes, later in his life, he would feel the need for isolation to deal with a difficult technical problem. At those times he would leave their Washington, D.C., home and go to their Canadian home to work for extended periods of time. Mabel always knew that he expected to be away for a while when he insisted on taking one of his dogs with him as company.

Bell had a good understanding of the psychological value of dogs, and the feeling of security that they provided. Once while he was away Mabel wrote to him about their dog Becky disturbing the house because she saw "ghosts." Apparently the dog woke up in the middle of the night and "she disturbed me very much by running wildly around, barking furiously and leaping up on me. I tried to quiet her, no use, she kept on barking and barking and running towards my room. I got up, found it was 12 [midnight] and everyone gone to bed. What could be the matter? Horrible memories of thieves discovered by dogs barking came to my mind. I followed Bec. She ran into my room and O horrors! barked violently all around the bed. Thoroughly scared."

Bell replied like someone who had a good understanding of both dogs and people, and gave her some reassuring advice.

What a suspicious old thing my little wife is to be sure! Thieves, burglars and ghosts too—come into her mind when I am away. Quite flattering to me. I did not feel before that I was such an important personage in the house and now—if I go away—the whole household is disturbed by that miserable little yelping animal that so constantly jars my nerves. I have learned by experience to take no heed of her barking—she does not yet recognize her friends from her enemies. Still I have never liked to check her noise, for it is a safeguard to have her around and her indiscriminate barking may be of use to you if you observe it. It means "Someone is around." But I am afraid she barks so much that you have ceased to take notice. She even greets me with a growl and yelp when I go down to bed—but this rarely seems to disturb you. Now the two dogs are just what you want. Take them both to bed and let them lie down where you can feel them if they bark.

"Bow-wow" goes Bec—but staid old Yo keeps curled up and does not so much as move her tail all night—don't be disturbed—It's only Nellie or Miss Palmer or Elsie or Daisy.

But if Yo joins in you may suspect a strange step. She will not bark by herself except for an unusual noise—although sometimes she joins in a chorus with Bec.

Take care of my little dog for me won't you. Let her have a basket somewhere filled with hay.

Bell's understanding and his way with dogs influenced a crucial experiment that would eventually lead to his support for the oralist position on deaf training. At the time of this incident, Bell was around twenty years of age. He had not yet taught any deaf people and had only recently come to the conclusion that his father's analysis of mouth and tongue movements (which formed the basis for visible speech) could be used as an aide to teaching the deaf to speak. The manualists argued against this, claiming that since deaf persons cannot hear the sounds that they make, they will not have enough information to know whether they have made the right sound. Furthermore, the manualists did not believe that there was a way for the deaf to learn to properly shape a sound in the first place.

For Bell, the answer was simple: All that you needed to do was to teach the deaf person to emit a continuous sound on cue. The nature of that sound was really not very important, because you could then shape the tone (by moving the tongue and lips) into any word that you wanted. The resulting words might not be as cleanly articulated as an elocutionist might like, but they could still be understandable to a person who knew the language.

To test his theory, Bell decided to use someone more obviously difficult to train to speak than a profoundly deaf person—his pet dog, a Skye terrier. Skye terriers are small, low to the ground, and longhaired. One story about the origin of this breed has it that there was a ship that sank off the shore of the Scottish Hebrides, and some Maltese dogs survived and bred with the local terrier population to produce the Skye. They can be very stubborn, tough, and independent dogs, so even though Bell describes him as a "very intelligent" Skye terrier, he was clearly taking on a rough task. This shaggy black animal was to be taught how to speak.

At the beginning of his experiment, Bell reported, "I found little difficulty in teaching the dog to growl at command." He did this by limiting the dog's food supply so that food became a very powerful reward. After a while, the dog would happily growl for his food.

Next the dog was taught to sit up on his hind legs and growl continuously until Bell signaled that it was time for him to stop. For each instance of this behavior, he was rewarded with a bit of food. The purpose behind having the dog sit upright was so that Bell could easily manipulate the dog's mouth.

Based upon his father's research, Bell knew how to shape the dog's lips so that by opening and closing them a number of times in succession while the dog emitted his continuous growl, he could shape the sounds "ma, ma, ma." To make the sounds wordlike, the dog had to be taught to stop growling the moment Bell released his mouth. This was easy since the dog learned to stop growling in anticipation of the expected food treat, and that reward was never withheld. After a little practice, Bell was able to make the dog say the word "Mama." Not only was the word perfectly distinct, but it was clearly pronounced in the English way, with the accent on the second syllable.

The second sound that the dog had to make was a little more difficult to shape. Bell began by placing his thumb under the dog's lower jaw, between the bones, and then pushing up a number of times in succession. This made the dog pronounce the syllables "ga, ga, ga." Now some of that finger dexterity that Bell had developed in his years of playing piano with his mother came into play; he was beginning to use the dog's mouth as a sort of musical instrument. By pushing up his thumb once and then constricting the dog's muzzle twice in succession, he managed to produce the string of sounds "ga, ma, ma." With enough practice Bell was able to shape this to a reasonable approximation of the word "Grandmama," although the actual sounds produced were "ga-ma-ma." For this linguistic breakthrough the dog got a double reward, and Bell reports that as a result "the dog became quite fond of his articulation lessons."

Bell did encounter some breed-based limitations. Since the Skye terrier is a small dog, its mouth is also small. Ultimately the dog's mouth proved to be too small to allow Bell to manipulate other parts of his tongue. This meant that he had to content himself chiefly with effects that could be made by manipulating the lips. However, Bell was not discouraged. By careful manipulation of the muzzle, he managed to get the dog to make a sound that passed for "ah." Next, he found a way to finish off the "ah" sound with a final "oo." This gave Bell a diphthong vowel sound that passed for "ow," as in the word *now*.

All of this was moving along fairly swiftly, and the dog was nearing the peak of his linguistic education. Bell's ultimate goal was reached when the dog was able to say in a distinct and intelligible manner the complete sentence, "How are you, Grandmama?" (In truth, the actual sounds pronounced were the sequence "ow ah oo, ga-ma-ma.")

The fame of Bell's dog spread among his father's friends. Soon a string of visitors came to the house for the express purpose of seeing this dog sit up on his hind legs and, with a little assistance from Bell's hand, growl forth the words, "How are you, Grandmama?"

The dog was so successful that the local rumormongers began to spread tales about his speaking ability. With each retelling the dog's linguistic skills grew greater, and soon Bell began to hear reports about things the dog was supposed to have said that were totally unwarranted by the facts. These tall tales would later come back to haunt Bell, since some people assumed that the claims of a speaking ability for the dog—which clearly were beyond any credibility—must have originated with Bell himself. Bell, however, knew he had merely demonstrated that the dog could be taught to make sounds for a food reward, and by manipulation of the dog's mouth these sounds could be shaped into intelligible language. He concluded his report of the experiment by noting, "I made many attempts, though without success, to cause him to produce the effects without manipulation. He took a bread-and-butter interest in the experiments, but was never able, alone, to do anything but growl."

To Bell, this experiment was conclusive. If a dog could learn to emit continuous sounds on cue, then obviously so could a deaf person. The advantage that deaf humans had, however, was the ability to consciously modify and control the shape and movements of their lips and the placement of their tongue. Furthermore, it was his father's visible-speech system that could help the deaf to learn these mouth movements.

Bell's chance to test the theory that he had worked out on his dog came when Susanna Hull, the director of a small school for deaf children in South Kensington, London, offered Bell the opportunity to work with the students in her school. One must remember that Bell was approaching this task from a completely theoretical stance, since he had absolutely no experience or prior knowledge of teaching deaf children. In May 1868 he began working with two deaf pupils and, according to his detailed journal notes, was almost immediately successful. After just one lesson the students were making sounds that were entirely new to them, and by the fifth lesson Bill reported that they were uttering complete and intelligible sentences.

On the basis of his study with his dog and the success that he had in teaching deaf children, Bell was able to write, "It is not generally known that the experimental stage has passed and that all deaf-mutes can be taught intelligible speech." Although Bell felt that the case had clearly been made for the oralist viewpoint, Gallaudet remained unconvinced and continued to be an advocate of the manualist tradition. The controversy continued to rage, and the fight goes on even today. The modern view, however, is actually more of a compromise, with most programs for the deaf teaching both speech skills and signing, although various programs tend to emphasize one or the other to a greater degree. It appears that now the battle lines have more to do with the relative importance given to each of these skills, while recognizing that both are useful.

Strange as it seems, had Bell never attempted his experiment with his dog, and had he never begun teaching deaf people, it is likely that he never would have invented the telephone. The connection came about after Bell had moved to Boston and opened a school for teaching deaf children. At this time he was leading a double life. During the day he taught deaf children and trained teachers of the deaf; at night—often well into the small hours of the morning—he worked on scientific and technological problems. Two of the deaf students to whom he successfully taught speech skills were George Sanders and Mabel Hubbard. Both had wealthy fathers who were so impressed with Bell that they decided to financially assist his scientific pursuits. This allowed Bell to purchase the needed apparatus and to hire Thomas Watson, a clever young repair mechanic and model maker. Since Bell's strength was in the design realm and he was never very good with his hands, it would be Watson who actually built the first telephone, and who heard the first electrical sound transmission over a wire on March 10, 1876. History, however, has not recorded the date when the first attempt was made by a lonesome pet owner to communicate with his or her dog over a phone line.

In one of those twists of fate, a half century after Bell's death dogs would play a role in allowing the deaf people whose welfare Bell cared about so deeply to more effectively use his most important invention. The telephone can be an important communication channel for people with hearing impairments. If the individual is not totally deaf, and has reasonable speaking ability, one strategy is simply to amplify the volume of sound to allow communication. And recently computer keyboards, monitors, and printers have been attached to phone lines to permit interactive and real-time conversations through written words rather than sounds. A problem that remains, however, is how the deaf person will know that someone is calling if he or she can't hear the phone ring. A flashing light to indicate that a caller is on the line works only if the deaf person is in the room with the phone and, even then, only if the individual is looking in the proper direction.

The solution to this problem, and to the whole issue of assisting deaf people to detect important sound signals in their home and work environments, presented itself in 1974. Agnes McGrath was a dog trainer at a kennel near White Bear Lake, Minnesota. One day a deaf woman asked if McGrath could train a *hearing assistance dog* for her. The woman explained that she had had a dog that naturally provided this service. Whenever the dog heard the phone ring or the doorbell chime, it would tug or nudge her to get her attention. It would then run back and forth between its mistress and the sound source. Unfortunately this remarkable dog had died of old age. McGrath conducted a pilot project to see if training could produce hearing assistance dogs, and a few years later the first formal program to produce such dogs began at the American Humane Association in Denver. There are now about a dozen training programs. Typically the dogs are trained to respond to common but important sounds, not just the ringing of the telephone, but also an alarm clock; doorbell or knocker; smoke alarm; baby's cry; and the subtle sounds of a doorknob twisting or a window being raised or breaking, the threatening sounds of an intruder. However, most hearing assistance dogs, after alerting their companions that the telephone has rung, do not bother to check if the incoming message is a greeting intended for themselves.

CHAPTER TEN

THE DOG ON THE

THERAPIST'S COUCH

A FEW YEARS AGO I SAW A MIRACLE, or at least it seemed like a miraculous case of psychological healing at the time. A friend of mine had enrolled her golden retriever, Sandy, in a pet-assisted therapy program. Sandy had been certified to be a visitation dog, which meant that Frieda could bring her into hospitals and old age homes to visit the patients. For many patients, the arrival of a dog is a wonderful event that helps fight the depression and loneliness of being separated from one's family. In some cases pets are actually used as part of psychotherapy, with a lot of success. In this instance, we found ourselves standing outside a hospital room while a nurse explained the situation.

"This is a sad case," she said. "Her name is Eva, and she is in her middle sixties. A month ago she was in a bad car accident where the vehicle that she was in was hit by a very large truck. She sustained some bad bruising and some internal injuries, which are healing, but her husband and her only son, along with his wife and their young baby, were all killed in that catastrophe. When she learned what had happened to her family, she just shut out the world. She hasn't spoken to anyone since then, barely looks at the hospital staff, and often has to be assisted even to eat. The doctors say that there is nothing physical causing this problem. The psychologist says that it is some kind of traumatic stress reaction.

We are told that she likes dogs, so he suggested that we include her on the schedule when a pet-therapy dog next visited."

The nurse didn't look very hopeful about all of this as she quietly opened the door to reveal a small gray-haired woman in a flannel nightgown, lying in bed and vacantly staring at nothing. She didn't move, or even glance our way, and for a moment it crossed my mind that she might have died. We walked over to the bed with Sandy out in front.

Frieda introduced the dog, saying, "Hi there. I've brought you a visitor. Her name is Cassandra, but we all call her Sandy." There was no response from Eva, not even a flick of her eyes.

The big yellow dog had reached the bed and gently pressed her nose against the woman's hand. Sandy gave a tentative lick, then rubbed her head gently against the unmoving fingers. Next she reared up, so that her front paws were resting gently on the bed, and looked at the woman's face. She gave a bit of a hopeful whimper and then laid her big head down on Eva's chest.

Nothing happened for several moments, and then Eva's eyes moved to look at the dog. A frail hand slowly moved to the dog's head and gently stroked it, then ran fingers along her ear. The tiny woman's eyes were filled with tears, and a soft voice slowly spoke the first words that anyone had heard from her in more than four weeks: "You're just like my Goldie. She had ears just like yours, and she would try to climb into bed whenever Ralph wasn't there."

Both of her hands were now resting on the head of the big blond dog, and the woman was looking directly into her dark eyes as she said, "Goldie always knew when I was sad, too."

It was the breakthrough that was needed. Sandy came back almost every day for a couple of weeks. Eva, however, was now speaking and beginning to respond to psychotherapy that would help her cope with her stress. She would eventually go home, accompanied by a toy spaniel puppy that had been purchased for her by her brother, and together they would begin a new life. That miraculous first step toward her cure however, might never have taken place if it had not been for another dog. This was a longhaired reddish-brown beast who liked to lie next to the desk of a psychologist during therapy sessions held at 19 Berggasse in Vienna, some seventy years earlier.

If you ask the average person to identify some historically important psychologists, for nine out of ten people the first or second name they produce will be Sigmund Freud. It can be said that Freud redefined human beings by shifting the explanation of our actions away from simple physiological mechanisms and toward psychological mechanisms. His theories dominated the first half of the twentieth century. While some aspects of his psychodynamic theories have been challenged and even abandoned, many of the concepts that he introduced are still considered to be valid today. His notion of the unconscious, the idea of repressed memories, the demonstration of psychological defense mechanisms, or the proposal that early childhood experiences have both a subtle and wide-reaching influence on later adult psychological adjustment, are still accepted psychological concepts.

Freud's fondness for dogs developed during the last two decades of his life. It sustained him and kept him happy and functioning during a very difficult period. Furthermore, the legacy of his relationship with his dogs resulted in the formation of a new form of psychotherapy (namely pet-assisted therapy) that has very little relationship to the psychoanalytic system that Freud is identified with. However, there also is an incident involving a dog, which influenced Freud's psychoanalytic thinking as well.

Freud was born in 1856 in the small town of Freiberg, which was then in Moravia, a province of Austria (but now is known as Příbor and is part of the Czech Republic). His father, Jakob, was a wool merchant who earned just enough to keep the family going. At the age of forty, after the death of his second wife, Jakob married twenty-year-old Amalie, who gave birth to Sigmund shortly after. Amalie was bright and lively, and Sigmund was much closer to her than he was to his rather stern and distant father. Sigmund was part of a large family; there had been two sons by a previous marriage, and two more sons and five daughters would follow him. Because of economic pressures on Jakob's large family, and the fear generated by anti-Semitic rioting in Freiberg, his father moved the family first to Leipzig and then shortly after to Vienna, where Sigmund would remain for most of his life.

It might be said that the goal of the typical Viennese Jewish family of this era was to have at least one of their sons earn the title of doctor. The objective proof of this comes from the fact that while Jews made up only four percent of the Viennese population of this era, forty-eight percent of the medical students in the region were Jewish. Sigmund was the brightest of the sons and always at the top of his classes, so he was encouraged as the one most likely to succeed in that career. By the age of eight he was reading Shakespeare. He was broadly educated and knew Greek, Latin, French, and German history and literature as well. Initially Sigmund was leaning toward a career in law, but after developing an interest in science, neurology, and medicine he became a medical student at the University of Vienna.

Sometime in his third year at the university, Freud began some research on the physiology of the central nervous system. This was done in the physiological laboratory supervised by German physician Ernst Wilhelm von Brücke. Brücke was part of the new generation of scientists who were moving away from the notion that thought and actions were due to some form of metaphysical or holy life-giving spirit. They would come to be called "biological reductionists" and were proposing the then-radical notion that "No forces other than the common physical-chemical ones are active within the organism." This concept had a strong influence on Freud's thinking, and he would spend many years trying to "reduce" personality to simple neurological and physical processes. He would eventually abandon this notion when he was faced with certain psychological problems that could only be explained by a person's early history, not their physiology, and required a psychological cure rather than a physical-chemical one.

Freud's search for knowledge often became obsessive. He was so engrossed in the neurological research that he ended up neglecting some of the courses that were required to complete his medical degree. His research was productive, however, and he had even developed a new way to stain cells in the brain so that they could be studied more easily. Nonetheless, the delays that this caused also meant that he remained in medical school three years longer than was normally required to qualify as a physician. In 1881, after completing a year of compulsory military service, he received his medical degree and immediately returned to the university to continue his experimental work. He held the post of demonstrator in the physiological laboratory, which paid only a modest salary but did provide him with research facilities. These allowed him to make some significant discoveries about a section of the brain known as the medulla (just at the top of the spinal cord).

Unfortunately, there were few faculty positions available at the time, and the fact that Freud was Jewish did not help. He had been courting Martha Bernays, and it was unlikely that he would ever be financially secure enough to marry her and support a family unless he found a better-paying position. Brücke urged him to abandon the physiological research and to get some practical experience so that he could open an office and begin practicing medicine. Freud was reluctant to do this, but it eventually became clear to him that this was the best route to financial stability. As a result he spent the next three years at the General Hospital of Vienna, where he devoted himself successively to psychiatry, dermatology and nervous diseases. His clear competence and knowledge in both theory and therapy eventually won him an appointment as a lecturer in neuropathology at the University of Vienna.

Since Freud was now back at the university, he could apply for one of the few government research grants that were then available. Despite strong competition from two other applicants, he managed to win one of these with Brücke's support. The grant would allow him to spend four months in Paris to learn some new techniques from the neurologist Jean-Martin Charcot, who was the director of the clinic at one of France's most respected mental hospitals. Charcot was studying the psychological problem called hysteria. This is a type of mental disorder in which strong emotional conflicts express themselves in some striking symptoms. In one of the most common forms, known as conversion hysteria, people might show physical symptoms, including muscular paralysis, blindness, deafness, nausea, headaches, dizziness, fainting or tremors. When examined, however, there were never any organic causes for these difficulties. In dissociative hysteria, the symptoms were more likely to be mental and emotional, with intense emotional swings and a loss of the sense of self-identity. The word *hysteria* comes from the Greek word for uterus. The ancient theory was that somehow the womb "wandered" and became transplanted in various inappropriate places in the body, thus causing the intense emotional and strange physical symptoms. Obviously, if the cause of the problem involved the womb, this could only be a disease found in women, and any man who showed similar symptoms was thought to be malingering or faking the disease.

At that time, Charcot was suggesting that the problem was not physical at all, but psychological in nature. He was suggesting a form of therapy that employed hypnosis, and trying to popularize this treatment by giving regular lectures and demonstrations for medical professionals and the public. Charcot was able to show that he could remove, and even produce, hysterical symptoms under hypnotism. His theory was that hysteria resulted from a combination of psychological trauma and inborn vulnerability. Charcot would ultimately come to believe that vulnerability to hysteria was the same thing as hypnotizability, which meant that a person had to be neurotic or at least have neurotic tendencies in order to be hypnotized.

During his stay with Charcot, Freud came to accept his view that hysteria was a psychological rather than a physical problem. He also learned that there were cases of male hysteria, and that some of the symptoms of hysteria could be removed by hypnosis. Freud went on to study with other people to try to perfect his techniques, but he was becoming very dissatisfied with hypnosis because some patients were simply not hypnotizable. Even more important, he noticed that the success of the hypnotic treatment seemed to depend on the personal relationship between the therapist and the patient. If, for any reason, the relationship weakened or was disturbed, any previous good results that had been obtained using hypnotism would instantaneously disappear, and the symptoms would return.

Freud came to the conclusion that the real cause of hysteria was the patient's attempt to repress painful memories. Pushed out of consciousness, these emotions built up in intensity and had to find a way to express themselves, which they did via the hysterical symptoms. According to this notion, therapy involved getting to the memory of the original painful incident and making it conscious. Once it was conscious, the emotions would vent themselves naturally, and the neurotic symptoms—having nothing to sustain them—would disappear. The therapist's task was to question, guide the thought processes, and work insistently to uncover the problem, making it known to the person consciously and in this way curing him or her.

The confirmation of Freud's emerging theory would come from a patient whom he referred to using the pseudonym Anna O. This case demonstrated both the nature of hysteria and the path to its cure, and coincidently centered on an incident that involved a dog. The physician Josef Breuer, who had been treating this patient initially, started a partnership with Freud and would also be the coauthor of his book on hysteria.

Anna was twenty-one years of age when she came for treatment, and had been spending most of her time nursing her ailing father. This was difficult and unrewarding work, and she was continually cleaning up after him and making sure that the environment around him was uncontaminated. This gave her a bit of an obsession with cleanliness. The emotional strain was intense, so had this occurred today we would understand why she was beginning to show psychological symptoms associated with stress.

When her father eventually died, Anna had a crisis and it was at this point that she sought medical help. She developed some speech difficulties and began to have involuntary spasms. She also suffered from a loss of feeling in her hands and feet, and had the feeling that her vision was narrowing down to a small tunnel of sight. Despite a full medical examination, however, no physical causes for any of these problems could be found. As if this weren't enough, she had dramatic mood swings and even attempted suicide. This was a clear case of hysteria.

Freud became involved when Anna developed a new set of symptoms. It was the summer, and Vienna was undergoing a period of extreme hot weather. Anna was very thirsty, but for the last few weeks she had been unable to drink any fluids. She would lift a glass of water to her mouth, but as soon as it touched her lips she would push it away with an expression of fear and disgust. The only way that she had been able to physically survive up to that point was by eating watery fruits, such as melons, to relieve her thirst. The therapy session that Freud set up involved a sort of free association in which the patient would be allowed to say whatever came into her mind. As she began to zero in on a problem area, the therapist would guide her toward what appeared to be the crucial issues and events. As her focus became narrower, an observer would get the impression that the patient had entered a state of self-hypnosis, as she unsystematically explored the problem in her mind and sorted through repressed memories.

During this period of association, Anna began to grumble about her English "lady-companion" who was supposed to help care for the household, but whom Anna did not particularly like. In her focused state Anna described an incident regarding a little dog the lady kept in her room. Anna, with her obsessive cleanliness, did not like the dog, which she described as a horrid and dirty creature. One day, Anna had gone into the Englishwoman's room and, while she watched, the dog began to drink out of a glass on a low table. The lady did not seem to notice the event, and Anna, who did not want to be impolite, said nothing. A few moments later, the woman lifted the glass and drank from it herself. As Anna described the scene, her emotions seemed to break out of their repressed state, and she began to express real anger and disgust at the entire situation. When she had vented her feelings, she asked for something to drink. She consumed a large quantity of water without any difficulty, and this set of symptoms simply vanished and never appeared again.

Freud would later write of this incident as follows: "With your permission, I should like to pause a moment over this event. Never before had anyone removed a hysterical symptom by such a method or had thus gained so deep an insight into its causation. It could not fail to prove a momentous discovery if the expectation were confirmed that others of the patient's symptoms—perhaps the

majority of them—had arisen and could be removed in this same manner." Such
deep and intense emotional pain in Anna, and such a wondrous insight on the
part of Freud—all due to the impoliteness of a dog!

Obviously, in the case of Anna O., the dog was just a stimulus for an emotional event. It should be clear that Freud's insight could have just as easily been
obtained from other situations that had no canine involvement. As Freud grew
older, however, dogs began to have a particular importance in his life, and his activities with dogs would eventually lead to an alternative to psychoanalysis.

As a boy Freud never owned a dog, nor did he keep one for most of his early
adult life, perhaps because his small home was already crowded with six growing
children. It was only in the last quarter of his life that dogs became important to
him, and his love of dogs is ultimately traceable to two women. The first was his
daughter Anna, the youngest of his children. As a child she was lively, with a reputation for mischief. As Freud wrote to his friend Wilhelm Fliess, "Anna has become downright beautiful through naughtiness." This spunky child was later
trained to be a teacher, and then began studying psychoanalysis. She combined
these two interests in a series of studies of the psychology of children. Ultimately
Anna would become an influential child analyst who made a number of theoretical contributions. She eventually became director of the Vienna Psychoanalytical Training Institute, and then after she and her father took up residence in
England, she started the Hampstead Clinic (later renamed the Anna Freud Center). She wrote numerous books on a psychoanalytic approach to child psychology, and did significant research on children whose lives were disrupted by
World War II, including child survivors of Nazi concentration camps.

Shortly after World War I, Sigmund learned that he had cancer of the jaw,
probably due to his heavy cigar smoking. This cancer resulted in chronic and continuous pain, and he would eventually undergo thirty-three operations before he
succumbed to the disease. Despite his condition, however, he refused to take
painkillers, since their numbing and narcotic effects would have made him unable
to think clearly. Instead he continued his research and his writing until the last few
months of his life. Freud often mused about the fact that he had had two addictions
in his life. Early in his career he had done research on the effects of cocaine, and he
became addicted to it. He was able to cure himself of his drug addiction, but he was
never able to cure his addiction to tobacco, and it would eventually kill him.

From the time that cancer was detected in Sigmund, Anna became his nurse
and major source of support. When he had to go to Berlin for operations, she al-

ways accompanied him. She organized his care, made sure that the conditions and reference materials were available for him to continue his work, and looked after the quality of his life even as she pursued her own career. This was necessary because Sigmund's wife, Martha, although caring and supportive, was not well organized and did not understand the demands of his professional life. Martha also lacked the strong personality needed to get Sigmund to agree to do what was needed. Anna and a series of dogs would provide Sigmund with continuous companionship, a chance to express his affection, and an outlet for the sense of humor that he maintained throughout his life.

The first dog in Sigmund's life actually was acquired as a companion for Anna, who was then living with her parents. Anna liked to take walks in the evening, but the streets of Vienna were not considered safe for a woman walking by herself, especially a Jewish woman during that anti-Semitic era. So a big German shepherd named Wolf was purchased to accompany her; his size, and his wariness of strangers, made her feel much safer.

While both Sigmund and Anna appreciated Wolf's protectiveness, it could sometimes be troublesome. For example, once when Ernest Jones, the founder of the British Psychoanalytical Association and later Freud's definitive biographer, visited their home, Wolf bit him. Freud said later, "I had to punish him for that, but did so very reluctantly, for he—Jones—deserved it." The event must have been a bit traumatic for Jones, since several years later Freud wrote to him reassuringly, "The prospect of your visit to Vienna at Easter makes me both feel joyful and melancholy. I know that as a result of the restrictions of age I shall only be able to fulfill the duties of hospitality very inadequately. Our Wolf, too, who once behaved with such unfriendliness toward you, is now an old man, in his doggy way as old as me."

There was once when Wolf failed in his protective function, but ended up showing great intelligence. One morning while Anna was out walking Wolf, some nearby soldiers were exercising and fired a salvo of blanks into the air. This so startled Wolf that, much to Anna's distress, he disappeared like a streak of lightning. Since Anna knew how devoted he was to her, she was certain that he would return, but when she searched the area calling his name, she could not find him. In a very distressed state of mind she returned home, only to be greeted by Wolf. He had taken a taxi home!

According to the taxi driver, Wolf had jumped into the cab and then courteously, but firmly, resisted all efforts to remove him. All the while he kept raising his nose sufficiently high to allow the cab driver to read the name and address on the medallion that was hanging from his collar. Wolf apparently must have thought that the driver was very stupid not to understand what he meant when he displayed the clearly written text "Professor Freud, Berggasse 19."

Meanwhile, back at the Freud home there was considerable concern over Anna's lateness. While Wolf's arrival was welcome, they feared that something might have happened to his mistress. Nonetheless, Wolf's fare had to be paid, so Freud asked the cost. The cab driver shrugged and replied, "Herr Professor, for this passenger I have not switched on the taxi's meter." He left with a smile, however, at the generous fare that Sigmund gave him for bringing back his wayward dog.

Despite his tendency to be cantankerous at times, Wolf filled many of Sigmund's needs. Freud had a strong sense of family, and loved his children and his grandchildren. When one of his grandchildren, Heinerle, died, Freud was despondent, and it was then that he turned to Wolf for companionship. He would later muse about this: "How is it that these little beings [children] are so delightful? For we have learnt all sorts of things about them that do not correspond to our ideals and must regard them as little animals, but of course animals too seem delightful to us and far more attractive than complicated, multistoried adults. I am experiencing this now with our Wolf who has almost replaced the lost Heinerle."

While Anna may have provided the motivation for the first dog in Sigmund's home, another woman determined the breed of dog that would come to dominate Freud's life. This woman was Princess Marie Bonaparte, a direct descendant of Lucian Bonaparte, one of Napoleon's younger brothers. She was married to Prince George of Greece, who was the younger brother of Constantine I, the king of Greece. Through these family ties she was also related to the royal families of Denmark, Russia, and England. Marie originally came to Freud for treatment but later went on to become a psychoanalyst herself, and a leading figure in the international psychoanalytic movement. One of her main interests was criminal psychopathology, and she wrote extensively about the minds of murderers and other criminals. Over time, a close and enduring friendship developed between Freud and Marie. There was a real compatibility of temperaments between the two; both were intelligent, inflexibly dedicated to scientific truth, sincere, and kind, with a social consciousness and a sense of morality. They would also develop another bond—namely, a love of dogs.

Marie Bonaparte loved Chow Chows. These are compact, powerful dogs of ancient Chinese origin whose characteristic appearance is one of scowling independence. They generally have a thick, coarse coat that may be of any solid color. They have large, broad heads that they carry high, a short muzzle, a broad, black nose and deep-set eyes. One unique characteristic of the breed is its blue-black tongue, framed by a black-lined mouth. A Chow's chest is broad and deep, and its tail curls over the back. When full grown, it is about twenty inches tall, at the shoulder, and has an average weight of around fifty pounds. Marie felt that the temperament of the Chow (good with family members, and accepting but a bit aloof around strangers), along with their medium size, made them a breed that would be more compatible with Freud than the German shepherd, Wolf. Besides, since she bred Chows, it also allowed her to bestow upon Freud a dog from her own kennels as a gift. The dog's name was Lun Yug, and she quickly became a cherished family member.

Unfortunately, Lun Yug was run over in the street at a young age. Freud was devastated, and although Anna wanted to replace the dog immediately Sigmund could not face it. He had to work through his grief over a period of several months before he was ready for another. Lun Yug's successor, her sister Jofi, soon became everyone's darling and was Sigmund's constant companion. Anna would later set up a breeding program of her own with Marie Bonaparte's help, and long after her father's death there was still a Hampstead line of Chow Chows.

It is difficult to know whether Freud simply had a predisposition to love dogs, or whether they fulfilled a need that could not be otherwise expressed in his life. This was an era of great formality; open and playful affection could only be expressed toward young children (and even then with some restraint) or to dogs. Judging from some of the home movies that we have, Freud loved playing and clowning with his dogs. They also helped him to deal with difficult moments in his life. For example, Freud hated birthdays, perhaps because they were a sign of his aging and mortality. However, Anna managed to get him to celebrate them through the dogs. At each of his birthdays, the family would gather around the table, where there was a birthday cake. Each of the dogs (now there were three, Jofi, Lun, and Tattoun) were seated in chairs and they, as well as Sigmund himself, would all be wearing paper party hats. Hanging around the neck of one of the dogs would be an envelope containing a poem, which was composed by Anna but signed in the name of one of the dogs. Sigmund would always read the poem out loud, with great dramatic flourishes, then thank the dog in whose name it was signed and offer the dog the first slice of birthday cake.

Before we go any further, I should note that the record of Freud's dogs is a bit confusing at times. The reason for this is that the names of these Chows are often spelled in various ways by different people in the family and by friends, and in addition the Freud family tended to recycle the names when they acquired new dogs. Thus there are a number of Luns (named after their first dog), a few Tattouns (named after a favorite of Marie Bonaparte), and several generations of dogs named Jofi. At least two dogs named Jofi were important in Freud's last years.

Freud knew that his cancer was probably fatal, and it certainly was painful. It frightened him, although he never expressed it. As Sigmund's condition worsened, Marie Bonaparte was dealing with a similar medical problem in one of her most loved dogs, Topsy. Just like Freud, Topsy was suffering from cancer of the mouth and jaw, and was in fact undergoing many of the same types of medical treatment. Marie attempted to deal with her psychological pain by writing a book about Topsy's life and her condition—not a frivolous or maudlin story, but a thoughtful meditation on sickness, love, and death. It was ultimately published as *Topsy: The Golden-haired Chow.* Freud read a copy of the manuscript and was so moved by it that he offered to translate it from the original French into German. He spent much of the last year of his life working on the book, and it was clear that he could see the parallel between Topsy's situation and his own. The similarities were unavoidable in such passages as "The verdict on Topsy has been delivered: there is a lympho-sarcoma beneath her lip which is once again beginning to swell, a tumour which will grow, spread, proliferate, burst open, and kill her. In a few months she has been condemned to die the most terrible of all deaths." This passage could well have been a paraphrase of the report that Freud's doctor, Max Shur, had given him about his own condition.

Translating *Topsy* helped Freud work through his feelings about his own situation and to achieve some peace of mind. After the Nazis took over Austria and his personal situation became dangerous, Freud and his family were forced to flee. The Nazis were already publicly burning his books, declaring psychoanalysis to be a subversive Jewish plot. One of Freud's sisters and her family were taken to a concentration camp and were never heard from again. Anna had also been arrested and detained once. Now, through the efforts of Marie Bonaparte, Ernest Jones, and others, Freud's immediate family managed to get the needed exit papers and they fled to England, carrying with them virtually nothing of value except his beloved Jofi. Probably one of the most distressing aspects of his arrival in England was the fact that Jofi now had to undergo the mandatory six-month quarantine. For this reason, Anna and Marie Bonaparte quickly found him another dog (named Lun, again recycling the name of their first dog) to serve as a companion until Jofi was released.

Freud's major source of comfort during those last days was his dogs, which he had next to him and on his bed all of the time. Unfortunately, his condition was worsening, and a putrid secondary infection ate a hole through his cheek. The smell was awful, and his dogs would not approach close enough for him to touch them. This was simply too much for the great psychologist. He reminded his Dr. Shur of a pact that they had made, saying, "Now it is nothing but torture—no comfort—and makes no sense any more." Shur kept his promise, and on September 23, 1939, he gave Freud an overdose of morphine that allowed the analyst to die in his sleep.

While the story of this groundbreaking psychologist and the comfort that his dogs provided during his time of pain is interesting in itself, it becomes much more significant when we find that Freud's closeness to his dogs left a lasting legacy. He would often have one of the dogs (usually Jofi) in his office with him even while he engaged in psychotherapy sessions, explaining that the dog's response was a good indicator of the patient's state of mind. If the patient was anxious and under stress, Jofi would move away from her normal place next to the desk and lie farther away than usual. If the person were particularly depressed the dog would lie quite close to the couch, where the patient might be able to touch her if he or she reached out a hand.

Freud's oldest son, Ernst, claimed that there was another reason why Freud liked having the dog near him during a therapy session. This was because when Jofi was in the room he never had to look at his watch to determine when the hour's treatment should end. Without fail, roughly fifty minutes after the session began, Jofi would stand up, yawn, and move toward the office door. Ernst said that his father claimed that she was never late in announcing the end of a session, "although father did admit that she was capable of an error of perhaps a minute at the expense of the patient."

A dog in the room during therapy was not only a comfort to the psychoanalyst, but Freud began to notice that the presence of the dog seemed to help patients during their sessions. This difference was most marked when Freud was dealing with children or adolescents, who seemed more willing to talk openly (especially about painful issues) when the dog was in the room. The presence of the dog seemed to make adults feel more comfortable as well. In addition, during psychoanalysis, when the patient is getting near to uncovering the source of his or her problem there is often a resistance phase—as if the person were trying to hold back the psychological pain and deep emotions that exposing their repressed trauma might cause. During resistance the patient might become hostile, stop actively participating in therapy, or obviously withhold information. Freud's impression was that this resistance was much less vigorous when the dog was in the room.

When he began to observe the effects that the dog had on therapy sessions, Freud speculated a bit as to the cause. In a psychoanalytic session the patient is asked to free-associate, simply saying whatever comes into his or her mind. To facilitate this, the patient is asked to stretch out on a couch and relax, as the therapist sits behind him or her, out of the line of sight. This arrangement keeps the patient from watching the facial expressions of the therapist, which might be interpreted as disapproval or some other emotion. The idea is to let patients freely follow their own patterns of association while they work their way toward the problem, rather than taking any indirect guidance from the therapist's responses. In contrast to the therapist, the dog is quite clearly in view, usually lying calmly and quietly nearby. Since the dog appears to be unmoved by anything that the patient says, Freud concluded that this gives the patient a sense of safety and acceptance. Even when the patient describes very painful or embarrassing moments, the dog doesn't react, except perhaps with a calm glance in the patient's direction. This gives the patient some confidence that all is well and anything can be expressed in this place, which is a reassuring feeling. Freud recorded this information in his notes, and it would eventually encourage the systematic use of dogs in therapy.

At various other times in history, animals have been used as part of a therapeutic program. For example, the Quakers established York Retreat in England, where mentally ill and handicapped people were rehabilitated by trying to have them live as normal a life as possible. They were taught to care for themselves and also to care for small animals (such as rabbits and poultry) in the hope that this would also teach them self-control. Such attempts were rather informal, however, and not based upon any research findings or even any deep theoretical reasoning.

The first formal presentation of what would become known as animal-assisted or pet-assisted therapy came in the 1960s from a child psychologist, Boris Levinson, at Yeshiva University. He was working with a very disturbed child, and found by chance that when he had his dog Jingles with him, the therapy sessions were much more productive. Furthermore, other children who had difficulty communicating seemed more at ease and actually made real attempts at conversation when the dog was present. Levinson gathered data from a number of such cases and then presented a scientific paper describing his results at a meeting of the American Psychological Association. He was distressed to find that many of his colleagues treated his work as a laughing matter. Some even asked him what percentage of the therapy fees he paid to the dog.

It is at this point in time, some fifteen years after his death, that Freud's influence was felt in a new venue. Just by chance, several new biographies of Freud's life had recently been released, and translations of many of his letters were just being published. Finally some new insight into Freud's life was coming from books published by people who knew him, and some even described his interactions with his household full of dogs. From these sources came the information that Freud, during therapy sessions when Jofi was present, had observed very much the same phenomena that Levinson described. When Levinson and others learned about this, it seemed like a form of certification. With evidence that Freud was willing to entertain the usefulness of animal helpers in psychotherapy, the laughter stopped and some serious work began. Psychiatrists Sam and Elizabeth Corson opened the first pet-assisted therapy program at a psychiatric unit at Ohio State University in 1977. Soon the psychologist Alan Beck and the psychiatrist Aaron Katcher were providing solid scientific data showing how animals in a therapeutic situation can reduce stress, improve treatment outcomes, and generally improve mental health. The number of pet-assisted therapy programs grew from less than twenty in 1980 to more than a thousand by the year 2000. These not only include dogs who are brought into the psychotherapist's office as part of treatment, but also visitation programs where dogs are brought into hospitals and homes for the elderly. There are also some rehabilitation programs where the dogs are brought in as companions to build morale and confidence. This is the unintended legacy of that reddish-brown chow chow lying at the feet of the founder of psychoanalysis.

Freud never stopped speculating about why dogs can have such a positive effect on a person's psychological state. In some letters to Marie Bonaparte written in 1936, he speculated, "Dogs love their friends and bite their enemies, quite unlike people, who are incapable of pure love and always have to mix love and hate in their object relations." He then went on to say, "It really explains why one can love an animal like Topsy or Jofi with such an extraordinary intensity: affection without ambivalence, and the simplicity of a life free from the almost unbearable conflicts of civilization, the beauty of an existence complete in itself. And yet, despite all divergence in the organic development, there is that feeling of an intimate affinity, of an undisputed solidarity. Often when stroking Jofi, I have caught myself humming a melody which, unmusical as I am, I can't help recognizing as the aria from *Don Giovanni:* 'A bond of friendship unites us both . . .'"

CHAPTER ELEVEN

FOR THE LOVE OF DOGS AND OTHER BEASTS

THROUGHOUT HISTORY, dogs have served as a testing ground for the ethical beliefs of mankind. As the domestic animal that we have lived with the longest, and one who shares our homes and our intimacies, the dog has often brought into sharp focus the difficulties and contradictions associated with our views of morality, humanity, responsibility, decency, justice, and even the ideas of a soul and immortality. Historically, there have been two opposing views concerning our treatment of animals in general and dogs in particular. Is the dog to be treated as a fellow being, with a right to be protected from abuse and an entitlement of freedom of action similar to those enjoyed by humans, or is it merely a biological machine that deserves no more humanitarian concern than any other machine—one to be kept or disposed of like any other material property?

Among scientists and philosophers, you will find some who are convinced that dogs cannot really think or reason. According to them, all of the behaviors that your dog engages in occur without planning or insight. These experts still believe the theories of the French philosopher Descartes, who would have described your dog as just some kind of machine, filled with the biological equivalent of gears, pulleys, and computer chips. It doesn't think any more than your desktop computer does, Descartes would say, but it can be programmed to do certain things and to respond to changes in the world around it.

If the dog is merely a machine that does not possess a soul or consciousness as humans do, then we owe dogs no special treatment. What we do with or to them has no moral consequences, any more than what we do with or to our automobile. Certainly, no sane person would think of starting a Society for the Prevention of Cruelty to Cadillacs, with moral or criminal sanctions against anyone who willfully dents a fender or breaks off a radio antenna.

An equal number of scientists and philosophers, however, feel that dogs are capable of reasoning and have the same kinds of mental processes and emotions that people do, although perhaps somewhat simpler in nature. For them, dogs are almost equivalent to four-footed children in fur coats. Many cultures, including the Ainus of Japan, the Kalang of Java, and the Niasese of Sumatra, have stories that claim dogs are really the ancestors of humans. In some Tibetan monasteries, a dog is brought into the room of a dying priest; the monks believe that the dog will serve as a temporary home for the soul of the holy man until he can be reincarnated in a new human body. Some religious sects go even farther, believing that dogs are actually people who will be restored to human form in the afterlife.

Certainly most ordinary people believe that their pet dog has feelings, is capable of being happy, sad, angry, or frightened. If someone killed or tore a leg off your dog, you certainly would be much more upset than if they tore a wheel off your car or smashed your bicycle, even though the bicycle may have cost considerably more to purchase than your dog. Thus it is not surprising what happened when one newspaper article reported the case of Else Brown, a widow aged sixty-seven years. Her dog, Tilly, was killed by a neighbor in a drunken act of aggression. The court ruled that this was not an assault, but just a crime against property that would be treated like simple vandalism—the equivalent of breaking a window. Thus Tilly's murderer was simply given a fine equal to the cost of the dog, which was just a pitiful few dollars since she had been adopted from an animal shelter. The fact that Tilly was Else's only life companion did not count in the eyes of the law, since that had no dollar value.

Needless to say, the people in Else's community were outraged. Radio call-in shows were swamped by angry people complaining bitterly that the man who killed Tilly was a murderer, and he should be punished as such. Monetary contributions and sympathy cards were sent to Else, and someone even provided a new puppy for her to share her life with. Clearly, in the minds of the vast majority of these people, dogs are living, thinking, and feeling creatures, to whom we owe a moral obligation.

As people have begun to accept the idea that dogs are beings capable of thought and emotion, who deserve ethical treatment, this change in attitudes has actually altered the course of the history of our society. For the most part the changes have been beneficial, at least for dogs and other animals who find themselves cradled in the protective care of humane societies. However, history teaches us that no major events are ever all good or all bad. Some attempts toward the humane treatment of dogs have had very dire consequences for dogs (at least in the short run) and sometimes have proven disastrous for people caught in the flow of events that had been started for compassionate reasons. On the other hand, through the attempts to help dogs, human lives have also been saved, and much misery has been prevented.

In Britain, the beginning of the animal welfare movement is usually credited to Richard Martin, a big, sociable Irishman noted for his quick temper. He was born in 1754, the son of Robert Martin, a member of an established and wealthy family. When his mother died, his father remarried—this time to Mary Lynch, whose family was also prosperous, and their combined resources provided Martin with a good education, including a law degree from Cambridge. A world tour gave him a broader knowledge of life, and by the end of the 1770s, Martin's education and his family's influence helped to make him a member of parliament from Galway and also a colonel in the Galway Volunteers.

No one is quite sure why and when Martin developed a passion for the protection of animals. He owned an enormous estate, encompassing more than two hundred thousand acres, and a good portion of this was kept in a wild state so that he could hunt. He kept a large pack of dogs of various types for the hunt, and several were allowed in the house and treated as companion dogs. Some people have suggested that his fondness for dogs came about because of his poor relationship with his wife, Elizabeth. His parliamentary, military, and business duties kept him away from home quite a bit, and it was widely rumored that at least one of the couple's several children was the result of a liaison between Elizabeth and the tutor hired to educate Martin's sons. With her husband away attending to his various responsibilities, Elizabeth continued her indiscreet behavior, and when a scandalous affair with a Mr. Petrie of Paris became public, their divorce was inevitable. Martin did remarry so that the children would have a caretaker, but some historians suggest that during this difficult period of his life, his only steady companions were the several dogs that traveled with him.

Perhaps this association with dogs during a time when he needed their social support convinced Martin that dogs and other animals have rich mental and emotional lives. If that is true, then they can feel pain, love, and abandonment, as humans do. Martin reasoned that in the same way that it would be immoral to allow a human being to suffer from physical or emotional pain because of the abusive behaviors of another person, it was likewise immoral to permit such suffering when the victim was a dog or another animal.

The strength of his passion for dogs, combined with his easily inflamed temper, resulted in a series of confrontations over the apparent abuse of these animals. In 1783 he ended up in a duel with "Fighting" Fitzgerald, a local landlord who had shot a friend's dog. This earned him the title of "Trigger Dick," which he lived up to by his involvement in several other duels over the mistreatment of animals. It also earned him the friendship of the Prince of Wales, who would later become King George IV. Apparently both men shared many ideals, and they were often seen conversing together in Parliament.

Martin decided to attempt to get Parliament to formally establish a legal requirement for the ethical treatment of animals. Therefore he proposed a bill in the House of Commons designed to make cruelty to animals punishable by law. The other parliamentarians did not appreciate his ideas. They greeted his speeches with ridicule, interrupting him with catcalls, laughs, and whistles. When called upon to respond to the issues that he was raising, they instead abused him personally. They mocked his Irish brogue, they challenged his personal integrity, and they even publicly tried to question his sanity.

When his first animal welfare resolution was defeated, Martin did not give up. He immediately brought in another. When that bill was amended to the point that it no longer accomplished anything meaningful, he presented Parliament with yet another—and this cycle went on for several years.

His breakthrough actually came as a result of his short temper. During another one of his many speeches on the issue of cruelty to animals, a member of the opposition began to taunt him. The politician laughed at Martin and scoffed, "You don't even know what cruelty really is!"

This time Martin did not try to control his temper. "I do so, sir. If you will step outside of this chamber, I shall explain it to you."

The two men stepped out of the chambers and then left the Parliament building. At the top of the stairs, the rotund politician paused and laughed again. "You were about to give me your explanation?"

Martin glared at him. Suddenly he lifted the ornate walking stick that he carried and swung it twice, knocking the opposition member to the ground. "That is a little of what is meant by cruelty, sir. Would you like a little bit more of it?"

"No," moaned the politician as he rose from the ground. "I have had more than enough."

"Well, sir," said Martin, "a poor dog or a horse is not able to say that he has had enough, or too much, and therefore wants protection."

The opposition member stared at Martin. He swayed slightly, then placed a hand on Martin's shoulder to steady himself. "I understand now. It has been a painful act of learning, but because of it I will support your act."

This particular member of Parliament was as good as his word. With a show of support from the opposing party and the implied support of King George IV, the bill was taken more seriously, and in 1822 the first animal welfare act was passed. It was limited in scope, but further versions would strengthen it over time. For his efforts in passing this law, the king gave Martin the nickname of "Humanity Martin," which would stick with him for the rest of his life.

Two years later, a number of people gathered with Martin at the Old Slaughter's Coffee House in London. At that gathering, they founded the Society for the Prevention of Cruelty to Animals to enforce the new animal welfare act. Reverend Arthur Broome, a moderately prosperous London vicar, employed at his own expense a gentleman named Mr. Wheeler, who together with an assistant managed to bring sixty-three offenders before the courts in the first year of the society's existence. Although at first plagued by financial problems, public support began to appear in the form of donations and, most importantly, an increased willingness to give evidence against animal abusers. In 1835 the society's prospects improved further when the Duchess of Kent, and her daughter, Princess Victoria, became patrons. By 1840 the princess was now Queen Victoria, and she honored the society with the prefix "Royal." This assured continued support, and by the next year there were five inspectors traveling throughout the countryside, responding to complaints and bringing offenders before the courts.

No one can doubt that the Royal Society for the Prevention of Cruelty to

Animals has done wonderful things for the welfare of animals over its years of service. When it first began its activities, however, it had two immediate goals. The achievement of the first of these ultimately cost the integrity of a dog breed, while the achievement of the second may have cost the lives of what some people have estimated to be up to a quarter of a million dogs.

The very first goal that the RSPCA set for itself was the abolition of the fighting-dog sports. One of the several RSPCA members and supporters in Parliament, a Quaker named Pease, managed to introduce the first effective bill to outlaw these blood sports, specifically naming bullbaiting and dogfighting. It passed in both the House of Commons and the House of Lords, although the dogfighting component of the law proved to be difficult to enforce. Unlike baiting, dogfighting does not require a sizable arena, so it is often not easy to detect when a group has gathered to engage in this activity. (The sad fact is that a clandestine dogfighting circuit continues today.) The baiting sports did disappear, however, and doubtless this has saved the lives of many dogs and prevented the pain and suffering of many more. There has been only one casualty in this campaign, and that was the bulldog.

The original bulldog was a marvel of early genetic engineering. It was designed with wide shoulders and legs set well to the side to allow the dog to crouch low to the ground, thereby avoiding the bull's horns when it charged. The head and forequarters were well developed, allowing the dog to spring up and lock its jaws onto the bull as the latter raced by. Once the dog had latched on, the lighter hindquarters allowed it to be shaken violently without suffering any spinal injuries. If the bulldog was lucky enough to grab the nose (the preferred target), its ribcage was strongly built and padded so that if the bull banged the dog against the ground in an attempt to dislodge it, the dog could take the brunt of the blow.

The bulldog's head was perhaps the most specialized part of its body. It was large and broad to provide for a wide opening, and for the attachment of the large muscles needed to lock the jaws closed. The lower jaw was undershot (longer than the upper jaw), which permitted the dog to hang onto whatever it bit with a surprising tenaciousness. Even if the bulldog was knocked out during the fight, its jaws, once locked in a grip, remained locked. Most other dog breeds fought by biting and tearing and then moving swiftly away; the bulldog was designed for a unique type of bite-and-hold fighting. It had a short snout and nostrils that pointed upward to allow breathing while retaining its grip on an opponent. The original bulldogs had a bit of terrier in them, which made them swift and agile as well.

With the end of bullbaiting, the bulldog's continued existence fell to breeders who were only interested in a particular appearance and did not care about function. Thus they began to breed dogs that showed the bulldog characteristics in the most exaggerated forms—huge heads, extremely broad chests and wide-set legs, markedly back-sloping foreheads, and a prominently undershot jaw. The size and shape of the head is now so distorted that most modern bulldogs must be born via cesarean section, and puppies must often be bottle-fed by hand, since the size and shape of their heads make it difficult for them to nurse normally. The flattened, sloping face leads to all sorts of breathing difficulties as well. The *Encyclopedia of Dogs* in 1970 described the breed this way: "It is the result of a long process of selection, at the end of which stands a breed whose principal traits consist of pronounced anomalies!" The one thing that the breeders did do well with was the dog's temperament. This newer, nonfunctional version of the bulldog does have a remarkably sweet disposition—which perhaps is its one solace, given the often short life it leads due to its physical problems.

There have been several attempts to reestablish the original bulldog physical characteristics in the American bulldog and the Old English bulldog. The physical specimens that have been produced in these new breeds are clearly healthier and stronger than their recent predecessors, and certainly look more like the early paintings that we have of bulldogs. Unfortunately, these reconstituted breeds have a temperament much closer to the original as well. Thus breeders' attempts to restore the breed seem to lose that gentle and accepting nature that had been the best development of the bulldog's recent history.

While the disappearance or distortion of a dog breed might not be considered tragic, the second original aim of the RSPCA—its long and vigorous campaign to abolish the use of dogs for transport—did lead to some immediate and fatal consequences for thousands of dogs. In the nineteenth century, affluent people sometimes used dog-drawn carts simply for pleasure. In 1820, *The Sportsman's Repository* (a popular magazine that carried stories relating to hunting, racing, and other pastimes) carried one story about a sporting dog owner who "exhibited a carriage drawn by six dogs. These were the largest and most powerful which we have ever witnessed." The story went on to describe the speed that the dogs could maintain, and the pleasures of darting around the countryside in a small and easily maneuvered dog cart. In another story from that same year, readers learned about a Mr. Chabert who "arrived in the Metropolis [London] from Bath with his great Siberian Wolf dog, which he now offers to the public for the sum of two hundred pounds. He has had a gig [a light two-wheeled carriage] purposely constructed in which, he says, this dog can draw him thirty miles a day." At that time, two hundred pounds was not a sum that could be afforded by average working people, since it could easily represent more than a year's wages.

The use of draft dogs, however, was usually involved with more menial labor. There was a long and honored tradition, for example, associated with using dogs to haul supplies. Dogs had earned a special place in English history when they saved Robert, William the Conqueror's son, and his forces during the First Crusade, when the final push toward the siege of Jerusalem was in progress. Most of Robert's horses and mules had died due to lack of food, harsh conditions, and several enemy raids and ambushes. In desperation, he resorted to the use of dogs as transport. This allowed him to successfully carry his weapons, supplies, and siege equipment (and, of course, the flock of priests and all of their religious paraphernalia) to the wall of the holy city in time to permit his troops to take part in the final victory of that campaign.

The use of dogs as draft animals to pull small carts was an extremely convenient method of transport, especially in larger cities. To begin with, side streets in the old cities were narrow and often crowded, making a horse- or mule-driven cart simply too large to be easily controlled and moved. In some cities, such as Bristol, wine cellars honeycombed the ground under the streets, and heavy carts drawn by horses might have broken through. Another advantage of draft dogs was that they served as guards when their masters were making door-to-door deliveries, as milk, cloth, vegetable, meat, and wine merchants did. If the merchant entered the building while making a delivery, there was always the possibility that someone would snatch some of his wares while he was inside. Therefore, the traces of the dog pulling the cart were arranged so that they could be slacked to give the dog enough freedom to guard the cart from potential thieves, while not giving the animal enough freedom to run away. For poor people, dogcarts were the only practical means of transporting merchandise. They could not afford a horse or mule, and obviously would not have the space to keep them. However, a dog could be kept inside a small dwelling with the family and could be sustained on table scraps.

However, the life of a working dog could be hard. The RSPCA could certainly find instances where cart dogs were overworked, not attended to properly, and abused. For example, under the provisions of the animal welfare legislation, in 1836 a man was brought before the Lambeth Police Court for cruelty to his cart dogs. The magistrate verified that the man's three dogs were half starved and covered with sores. He found the owner guilty of abuse and sentenced him to fourteen days in prison. The dogs were confiscated and good homes were found for two, while the third was in such bad condition that it had to be destroyed. Other dog cart owners were prosecuted for forcing their dogs to continue to pull although their feet had been cut by sharp flints in the road, or for overworking their dogs or whipping them until they bled. In these instances, the RSPCA was clearly doing a service to dogs.

If it had stopped at the point of going after dog abusers, the RSPCA could have avoided a tragedy that affected the economic life of many people and ended the lives of many dogs. In its fervor to end the "forced labor" and "slavery" of cart dogs, though, the RSPCA sought to have any use of dogs for transport banned. This was a case of overzealousness, since many people who kept dogs for transport were good masters.

Most rational people know that a dog will work better if it is healthy, adequately nourished, given enough rest, and psychologically at ease. For this reason, the vast majority of transport dogs were cared for as well as the circumstances of the owner would permit. If the dog was a bit on the thin side, this was often because the family had little food and even the children would be thin as well. The dog's share of whatever was available was not withheld, if only because the family's livelihood depended upon the labor of the dog, making it too precious a resource to neglect. In addition, most cart dogs actually lived inside of the small homes of the poor and thus became companion dogs as well. There were many advantages to keeping the dog inside. First it could serve as watch dog, warning the family of the approach of strangers. In the winter, the dog's higher body temperature (usually 101 degrees Fahrenheit) could serve as a foot or bed warmer, and several dogs in the room could actually help to heat a small space. In addition, these dogs provided social support to people who often had little time for friends and seldom received much comfort or love.

There was a lot of opposition to a ban of cart dogs. One minister of Parliament named Barclay argued that it would be "an uncalled for, an unnecessary violation of the rights of a large class of humble traders by whom dogs were used. The parties using them for purposes of draught were generally knife-grinders and hawkers of various small wares through the country and in towns; the aid of dogs was found very useful to bakers, butchers, and other traders. The prohibition of this aid from dogs is not justified on the plea that so employing them was cruel." However, despite this protest, in 1839 England passed the first Dog Cart Nuisance Law, which prohibited the use of cart dogs within fifteen miles of London's busy Charing Cross station.

Flushed with this first success, the RSPCA began to push for a total ban of draft dogs. Their own documents tell of the arguments against their aims, noting that "the costermongers [vegetable merchants] of [London] have got up a petition to Parliament stating that their kindness to their dogs is well known, and that their trade will be knocked up under the New Police Act, as they can not afford to keep horses." The society dismissed these arguments, continuing its crusade for a ban and even widening its campaign to "release dogs from cruel servitude," so that it now included a heavy tax for anyone using dogs for any form of service. The notion was that this would discourage all use of dogs for work, thus "freeing" many dogs from what the society viewed as cruel labor.

Unfortunately, the RSPCA members not only ignored the impact of their actions on humans, they also did not ask the question of what would happen to all of the dogs whose sustenance currently depended upon their usefulness to the people who owned them. An editorial writer in the *Times* in 1843 did anticipate the possible dire consequences. He suggested that if the RSPCA activists had their way thousands of dogs would likely die horrible deaths due to abandonment:

> What is to become of the canine labor which is to be thus suddenly displaced from its legitimate channel? Are out-of-work mastiffs to crowd our crossings and hang disconsolately about the corners of our butcher's shops, like coachmen thrown out of employ by the railroads? Or is the more frightful alternative [*meaning the actual killing of cart dogs*] to be adopted? Why condemn to dissolute idleness or indiscriminate extinction whole generations of respectable quadrupeds? . . . Will the Thames itself contain the puppies, submerged in it under this new stimulus to canine infanticide?

The advocates of the RSPCA, however, continued to invoke images of over-worked dogs whose abuse served no purpose other than the pleasure of their cruel owners. In Parliament, Lord Brougham argued that "nothing could be more shocking or disgusting than to see the practice of great, heavy men being drawn by dogs. . . . Indeed, I have seen, near the place where their Lordships assemble, all sorts of articles drawn by small dogs who could scarcely get on."

Such graphic descriptions began to gain the movement to ban cart dogs a much wider degree of support. In the end, however, the public would be swayed by a completely false, but terrifying assertion that was also publicized by Lord Brougham—namely, the claim that overworking dogs by hitching them to carts was the true cause of rabies. When Brougham made this argument in Parliament, the general population became truly frightened. There were demands that the committee working on the provisions of the new law banning cart dogs should look into this. It did so by calling a number of witnesses, most of whom were members or supporters of the RSPCA, whose testimony would be called ludicrous by today's standards. Some argued that the increased number of cart dogs in use in the cities *caused* the "somewhat more frequent occurrence of the disease in recent years." Some argued that one of the main symptoms of the disease was viciousness on the part of the dogs, and there had been many reports of people who had been growled at or snapped at when approaching too close to a cart; this behavior must be due to the beginning symptoms of rabies. Others noted that a major symptom of rabies in dogs was a frothing or foaming at the mouth, then went on to say that everyone who has seen dogs pulling carts—especially when the carts are heavy or the dogs are maintaining a swift pace—has probably noted the frothing and drooling in these cart dogs. This was then claimed as proof that the very act of using a dog to pull a cart caused its increased susceptibility to rabies.

As silly as these claims appear, the committee accepted them, concluding that a connection between cart dogs and rabies had been proven by "medical science." At that time the bite of a rabid dog almost invariably led to a painful and an ugly death, whether the bite victim was another dog or a human being. It is thus not surprising that a frightened public rallied its support for banning cart dogs and placing restrictions on all service dogs via a dog tax. No thought was given to the human consequences. Some significant groups of people who did not use dogs just for carrying goods would be affected. For example, many handicapped people used dogs to transport them, while there were many blind people who were led around by their spaniels. Other groups who were unexpectedly affected by these laws were shepherds and truffle-hunters who were dependent upon the services of their dogs.

The results for dogs was as bad as had been predicted by the *Times* editorialist. There was a massive and sickening drop in the dog population of England. With great sorrow many people simply abandoned their former working dogs. Even worse was a set of dreadful massacres of dogs that began to sweep the country. In Birmingham, more than a thousand dogs were slaughtered in a period of one week. In Liverpool, a similar number of dogs were destroyed in only a few days. In Cambridge, the streets were so littered with the bodies of dogs that had been hung or bludgeoned to death that the City Council called upon the magistrates to dispose of them before they became a threat to public health. The High Constable of London reported having to arrange for the burial of more than four hundred dead dogs in his first sweep through the city. During the first weeks of the ban, more than twenty thousand dogs were destroyed in and around the city. The fear of the editor came true, and the river Thames was inundated with the bodies of the canine victims of the RSPCA's "successful" animal welfare campaign. Overall, estimates are that during the first year of the ban on dog transport and the imposition of the dog tax on service dogs, between 150,000 and 250,000 dogs were freed from their "slavery" by being put to death, while countless others were simply abandoned to their own resources.

The human toll exacted by this act was also high. Many families that had depended upon the dogcart to earn a meager living now found themselves virtually destitute. In the six months following the imposition of the dogcart law and the dog tax, there was a large increase in the number of children that were abandoned, given to state homes, or left with church organizations simply because their families had lost their source of income when they lost the services of their dog. In some cases, desperate merchants, tinkers, and knife sharpeners simply hitched their children to the same traces that the dogs had worn, forcing them to haul the carts through the streets. At that time there was no set of laws that prevented a parent or guardian from using a child's labor in this way, meaning that children would now endure the long hours and hard toil from which the RSPCA had just liberated dogs.

There is an interesting appendix to this episode in animal welfare. With the rise in the number of abandoned dogs, many of the same people who had supported the RSPCA's efforts began to become uncomfortable and wanted to ease the pain of the surviving canines. Two such people, a Mrs. Tealby and her friend, Mrs. Major, were out walking one evening when they came across an abandoned dog that was starving. As an act of kindness, they took him home and bedded him down in the kitchen. With such a graphic example in front of her (one that illustrated the fate of many abandoned dogs), Mrs. Tealby began her own crusade. With the help of her brother, the Reverend Edward Bates, she tried to found a private refuge for dogs. This proved to be rather more expensive than the pair had expected, so they tried to appeal to the public's sense of charity through the newspapers. The result was a set of scathing editorials in the *Times*, suggesting that the people who were trying to organize such a home for abandoned dogs had clearly taken leave of their senses. Suggestions were made that if they must help something, why not provide a shelter for starving and homeless children? Despite these negative comments there was enough of a public response to allow Mrs. Tealby and her associates to set up a Temporary Home for Lost Dogs. Obviously, given the scope of the problem this home could only handle a fraction of the abandoned dogs that had been turned out of their homes and were now wandering the streets. However, it did at least bring the problem to the attention of the public by pointing out the need for such services. It thus became the model for all of the dog refuge homes that would follow in the many years to come.

   While these early efforts to promote canine welfare in England may have had some dire consequences for dogs in the short run, there have been other attempts to promote the well-being of dogs that have had a direct impact on the welfare of human beings, as you will see in the next chapter.

CHAPTER TWELVE

THE DOG SHOGUN

IT IS IMPOSSIBLE to untangle the strands that link the welfare and pro
tection of dogs with the welfare and protection of people. Sometimes individuals with a moral mission to protect dogs and other animals affect
human lives as much or more than the lives of dogs. Sometimes the actions of
the advocates of animal welfare have a positive outcome, but sometimes they
have devastating negative consequences for people. Let's look at one extreme example of this.

The Japanese calendar shares a characteristic with the Chinese calendar, in
that a different animal represents each year over a cycle of twelve years. These animals are derived from the names given to the various constellations in the oriental zodiac, so it is not surprising to find that this aspect of the calendar has
been used as a form of astrology. Not only does the animal associated with a year
predict what kind of success and trouble to expect for the next twelve months,
but it supposedly also predicts the personality of people born in that particular
year. Each person is supposed to reflect certain characteristics of the animal
whose sign the year of their birth falls under. One of these signs is the dog. The
years 1910, 1922, 1934, 1946, 1958, 1970, 1982, 1994, 2006, 2018, 2030, 2042, and
2054 are each a Year of the Dog.

According to the folk traditions, people born in a Year of the Dog will be
honest, have a sense of commitment and duty, work hard, and often champion
moral causes. They have an intense dislike for what they feel is unjust or cruel.
People born in this year also have a high level of self-esteem and are quite opin-

ionated and uncompromising. They can be selfish, eccentric, and obstinate, and are not above using harsh means to get their way.

On February 23 in the Year of the Dog 1646, a man was born who seems to have embodied all of these aspects. Tokugawa Tsunayoshi, born in Edo (the old name for Tokyo), Japan, was the fifth of the fifteen Tokugawa shoguns, whose rule began in 1600 and would last for 268 years. Tsunayoshi would be the most controversial of all of the Tokugawa rulers, and his so-called Laws of Compassion would be called by some Japanese historians "the worst laws in the feudal history of mankind." These laws were originally drawn up for the protection of dogs, so they would also earn Tsunayoshi the nickname of *Inu Kubo* ("Dog Shogun").

The Tokugawa regime depended quite heavily upon the separation of the agricultural classes of people from the warriors or *samurai*. Under the Tokugawas, the samurai were given cultural as well as military duties in return for certain property rights and income based upon the taxes collected by the government; thus most of the high officials, scholars, and aristocracy were samurai. It seems that Tsunayoshi was a reformer at heart, and his goal was to humanize his people. He felt that they needed such reform because the samurai continued their harsh military practices and traditions, even though their new offices and positions no longer required the services of a warrior. He believed that the constant exposure of the population to some of the callous and barbaric samurai actions of those with high government offices had hardened both the aristocracy and the common people, and that the general population had become abusive in many of their practices and lacking in kindness and tolerance.

Once Tsunayoshi had become shogun, he attempted to infuse the spirit of Buddhist compassion and the idea of Taoist charity and benevolence into the people. In the beginning, this involved a number of praiseworthy actions. For example, he passed laws to protect abandoned children and appointed officials to ensure that children would be adequately provided for if their parents were unable to do so. To prevent the common practice of killing unwanted children, pregnant women and children under the age of seven had to be registered. As a general welfare measure, he ordered officials to provide beggars and outcasts with food and shelter. Sick travelers, who in the past had been turned out into the street when they could no longer afford their board or if they were considered to have an infectious disease, were now also protected by the state. In another unprecedented action, Tsunayoshi improved the conditions of prison inmates by mandating better housing, several baths per month, and warm clothing during the winter months. Noting that street gangs were terrorizing the population with robberies and murder, he ordered a very effective crackdown on these criminal activities.

Tsunayoshi's later laws to protect animals started as wise edicts, but became increasingly stringent over time. Soon the penalties for harming a dog or a cat could include banishment or even death. These animal welfare laws were apparently based upon the shogun's religious beliefs. After the death of his only son, Tsunayoshi consulted a Buddhist priest named Ryuko, who told him, "When a person does not have an heir, it is always due to the fact that they have done much killing in their previous lives. Therefore the best thing to do for a person who desires an heir is to show great love for all living things and not to kill. If Your Highness truly wants an heir, why not stop all taking of life? Furthermore, since Your Highness was born in the Year of the Dog and under the astral sign that is related to the common dog, it would be good if dogs were to be cherished and protected most." Tsunayoshi's mother claimed that she could see the truth in these comments, and thus the "Laws of Compassion for All Living Things" came to pass.

How important was this issue for Tsunayoshi? The animal welfare laws accounted for more than ten percent of all of the miscellaneous imperial orders issued during his regime. Although these laws were designed to protect all animals, by the far the largest number of regulations had to do with dogs, which were a highly regarded species at that time. The breeding of pedigreed dogs was entrusted to the samurai and noble classes. These animals were used for hunting, particularly with the aid of hawks, and as guards and companions. In addition, many dogs were bred for fighting, since dogfights were a favorite sport. Dogs were also highly valued as gifts and were often given to high officials to win their favor.

Unfortunately, the rearing of dogs in an urban environment did present some problems for the general population. Some of the feudal lords (or *daimyo*) often housed several hundred dogs in their mansions in the city of Edo. It appears that most of the stray dogs in the city were unwanted animals from these kennels. Once they were loose, they scavenged for food, fouled the sidewalks, fought each other, impeded street traffic, and occasionally attacked homeless people, especially children. Under these circumstances, it is not surprising that these stray dogs would often be maimed or killed with considerable cruelty by annoyed townsfolk. There are reports that the mutilated or dead bodies of dogs in Edo often presented a gruesome sight for visitors, and were a health hazard for everyone.

Obviously the samurai, living in their walled residences, would be less bothered by this state of affairs than the common people whose homes were more accessible to packs of marauding dogs, even though it was practices of the samurai that were most responsible for the problem. It was the warrior lords who were strongly affected by the shogun's edicts that dogs not be abandoned in the streets, since they would be subject to penalties if a dog was traced back to their particular house. Furthermore, the shogun specified that homeless dogs should not be killed on sight, and that masterless dogs should be fed and not abused. Finally, Tsunayoshi demanded that dogs should be treated according to "the fundamental principles of humanity."

Perhaps it is not surprising that his suddenly imposed set of humanitarian laws did not have the desired effect that Tsunayoshi intended. Dogs were still being surreptitiously turned out in the streets when the *daimyo* kennels no longer felt that they were of value. The officials tended to turn a blind eye toward these practices, since the offenders were fellow samurai. This in turn angered the shogun, who temporarily dismissed some officials for their "misunderstanding" of his wishes. It also caused him to increase public control by requiring owners to register each of their dogs, recording the color of the dog's fur and other details that might allow it to be identified. Once this registry (or *Kazukesho*) had been established, individuals became responsible for the care of all of their registered dogs. At specified intervals, these dogs had to be produced so that officials could confirm that they were still alive and being well cared for.

One of the most publicized violations occurred in 1702, involving one of the shogun's own veterinarians. This man was highly respected by the royal family, but apparently one day a neighbor's dog came into his yard and killed one of his favorite ducks. Caught up in a fit of rage, he crucified the dog on the neighbor's fence. Because of the man's high position and samurai family, this case went all the way to the Supreme Court or (*kyojosho*), which investigated and ordered the man to commit ritual suicide (*seppuku*). A special proclamation was issued announcing this sentence, and at the same time reminding the public that high-ranking as well as ordinary citizens were required to observe the Laws of Compassion.

The net to capture those who were abusing dogs was spread farther. A German doctor, Engelbert Kaempfer, was traveling through Japan at that time and noted, "We went by the place where public orders and proclamations are put up, not far from castle's moat, where a new proclamation along with twenty Shuits of silver had been posted. These were to be given as a reward to anybody that could discover those involved in the recent murder of a dog. Many a poor man hath been severely punished in the country, under the present Emperor's reign, purely for the sake of dogs."

If a dog simply disappeared, or was not presented to the registry at the scheduled time to prove that it was well kept, its owner could be punished simply on the suspicion of negligence or foul play. Some of the more compassionate common people stopped their practice of feeding strays, worried that this might suggest that they owned the dogs and thus make them responsible for their care in the future.

Anyone who injured, killed, or abused a dog, or even ignored a dog that was in need, was now subject to severe penalties, including banishment or even death. The number of people who were caught up and punished for maltreating dogs will never be known, since careful records were not generally kept of the arrest and prosecution of common people. For those people who had no connection with nobility, though, officials were quick to administer penalties for any form of perceived abuse. From what records we do have, we know that in one month alone in 1687 at least three hundred common people were reported put to death, and it is estimated that more than two thousand people suffered the death penalty for violation of the animal welfare regulations just in that year.

More specific records exist for the many samurai and other members of the aristocracy (or their retainers) who did not escape punishment. In the same year 1687 alone, we have the following cases involving the nobles:

- A member of a *daimyo*'s guard killed a dog that had bitten him and was forced to commit ritual suicide or *seppuku*.
- The head of the shogun's kitchens was exiled for drowning a dog.
- The personal bodyguard of one feudal lord was forced to commit *seppuku* for killing a growling dog that he felt was a danger to his master.
- The stable master of one *daimyo* mansion was banished for killing a dog that was annoying the horses.
- A scholar had his royal stipend confiscated for beating a dog.

- A priest of the Asakusa temple was suspended from office for drowning a dog.
- A samurai was placed under house arrest for mistreating dogs.

There are many other accounts from this period of people who were imprisoned or executed for crimes, actual or alleged, against dogs.

Unfortunately, although the laws were designed for the moral purpose of ending the practice of harming, killing, or abandoning dogs, the results were not what Tsunayoshi had intended. Instead, his Laws of Compassion had triggered an increase in the number of stray dogs roaming the streets of Edo in search of food. Packs of dogs were becoming a nuisance and sometimes were a danger, especially since people felt that they could not beat off threatening dogs without placing their own lives in jeopardy.

By 1695, fifteen years into his reign, the shogun felt that he had to intervene for public safety. Because of his proclamations requiring compassionate treatment of dogs, he was left with few choices. He could not require that the strays be exterminated, since this would suggest that he had been wrong in his initial prohibition of the killing of dogs. So, to protect the public from marauding packs of dogs, he had no alternative other than to house the animals in public kennels. The greatest financial burden that this incurred fell upon the samurai, who were instructed to build the kennels. The upkeep of the dogs was based upon a special tax, called the *inu-buchi* or "dog ration," based upon the size of each house's frontage. Obviously, the wealthy samurai had larger houses and thus paid greater taxes then the common people. As might have been predicted, soon fewer stray dogs were dying due to starvation and injury, so the number of dogs in the city rose dramatically. Within two years, more than forty thousand dogs were housed in the public kennels. Because these dogs were provided with a generous diet and there were now so many of them, the dog tax was quite large and burdensome.

Many of the samurai of the time were becoming very angry at this situation. Supported by taxes themselves, now they were forced to pay taxes to support dogs. To many, this suggested that dogs had been accorded the same status and respect that the samurai were entitled to. In fact, it was even a crime to insult or chastise a dog, unless there was clear proof of the dog's wrongdoing, and then any form of criticism could only come from its registered owner or the public kennel master. One samurai vented his anger by publicly crucifying a dog, then posting a proclamation next to the corpse claiming that the dog had taken advantage of the shogun's authority. He maintained that the dog had behaved insolently and without respect to his human superiors and was now receiving a just punishment. The shogun was outraged. An order for the samurai's arrest was issued, and he tried to flee the city. He was captured near the city gates, and after a trial was ordered to commit *seppuku*.

As the enforcement of the Laws of Compassion became stricter, the general population actually started to be afraid of dogs in the same way that they were afraid of all high-ranking officials who had the power to beat, imprison or even kill any commoner who did not show appropriate respect and deference. They began to treat any dogs that they encountered as if they were high-ranking nobles. Not only were dogs no longer beaten or abused, but they began to be addressed as *O-inu-sama* ("Most Honorable and Revered Dog"), a form of address typically reserved for deities or human dignitaries of the highest importance.

Here we have a situation where an honest desire to make people act in a more kindly manner, and to improve animal welfare, had gone dreadfully awry. Now, for the sake of dogs, the welfare of people was put in jeopardy. The full impact of the Laws of Compassion on the humans in the district can only be crudely estimated. Over the thirty-year reign of Tsunayoshi, the lowest estimate of those put to death or exiled is sixty thousand people, while some estimates suggest that it may have been as high as two hundred thousand. Some idea of the scope is provided by the samurai politician and historian Arai Hakuseki. When Tsunayoshi died in 1709, Hakuseki approached the shogun's son and successor, Ienobu. He asked that Ienobu grant an amnesty for all those currently being held in prison for violation of these animal welfare laws:

> If one looks at what happened recently under the previous shogun, one finds that those enforcing the law spared no efforts to use unwarranted cruelty. For the sake of a single bird or beast, the death penalty was inflicted. Even relatives were given capital punishment or deported and exiled. People's lives were in danger. Their fathers and mothers, sisters and brothers, wives and children were separated from them, dispersed, and died. Nobody knows even roughly to how many hundreds of thousands of people this happened. If a nationwide amnesty is not

declared at this point, how can we meet people's hopes that life is returning to normal?

Hakuseki then specifically asked for the pardon of the 8,831 people that he believed were currently being held in prison because of violation of the Laws of
Compassion.

The sixth Tokugawa shogun, Ienobu, found himself in a difficult position.
Tsunayoshi had specifically asked him to continue these laws as a son's act of love
for his father. Ienobu wanted to stop the suffering caused by these laws, but felt
that he could not go against the expressed wishes of his predecessor without
bringing disgrace upon his memory. He therefore delayed the funeral of
Tsunayoshi, so that it would appear that repeal of the Laws of Compassion was
the last wish of the dying shogun. Ienobu then stood before Tsunayoshi's coffin
and pleaded that in the interest of good government, he should be forgiven for
his disobedience. Then he had all those who had been instructed by Tsunayoshi
to uphold these laws stand before the coffin as well, forcing them to agree to this
repeal. Since the funeral rites had not yet taken place, it appeared that the rever-
sal was Tsunayoshi's final edict.

Ienobu did not fully repeal the laws against animal abuse, but rather soft-
ened them, at least in terms of their enforcement. He argued that the spirit of the
Laws of Compassion was correct, but that penalties had been too harsh. He
noted that punishments varied from reign to reign, and during his tenure the
abuse of dogs and other animals would be dealt with as a misdemeanor and not
a major crime.

Even though the people had suffered a great deal from the Laws of Compassion, some seemed to maintain a level of pragmatism and even humor that
helped them survive this overzealously humanitarian regime. During the height
of that fantastic era, dogs were treated as if they were nobility, and accorded the
same respect and honors. This included a proper and respectful burial in a place
of honor, such as high up on a mountain. Two men from Edo found themselves
trudging up a mountain for just such a purpose. Each carried the body of a dog
that had recently died and was to be buried. The day was warm, and the weight
of the dogs began to wear them down. One of them began to grow quite angry
at the situation and began to grumble to the other.

"Tsunayoshi and his crazy laws. Why should we work so hard to honor a
dog? Given our position in life, we are not entitled to this same respect. Yet here

we are, hauling these heavy carcasses up this hill. And all of this is just because of his stupid beliefs about what it means to be born in the Year of the Dog."

His companion grunted an acknowledgment. "You may be right, but if I were you I would hold my tongue and be quiet. Instead of swearing and cursing Tsunayoshi, you should be thanking the gods. Imagine what our burden would be like if he had been born in the Year of the Horse!"

CHAPTER THIRTEEN

THE DOG LAW AND THE MARY ELLEN CASE

T HE STORIES ABOUT the shogun Tokugawa Tsunayoshi and the early
years of the Royal Society for the Prevention of Cruelty to Animals
show that efforts to improve the welfare of dogs and other animals often have unforeseen consequences. Sometimes, despite the noble motivations of
animal welfare advocates, the very actions designed to improve the welfare of
dogs have led to the death of hundreds of thousands of them, while at other
times they have resulted in misery or even death for thousands of humans. Most
often, however, the efforts to protect dogs have succeeded, and sometimes these
improvements have actually been reflected in unexpected benefits for humans.
One famous case of this sort would reach its climax in a New York City courtroom in 1874.

The main figure in this history is Henry Bergh, who was born in 1813, the
son of a prominent shipbuilder. For the first fifty years of his life he showed little interest in the plight of dogs or other animals. His father's wealth provided
him with investments that supported a very comfortable lifestyle, and a steady
income to cover any expenses that he might have. His intelligence allowed him
to do well in school, and he was given a proper education emphasizing law, literature, and politics. After he completed his university studies he traveled

through Europe with no particular goal in mind; he spent most of his time sight-seeing and writing a little poetry now and then. When he returned, he became an active patron of the theater. This widened his network of social contacts to include not only actors and theater production personnel, but also local and state politicians, businessmen, and others who shared his interest in theater (or who simply liked the social aspects of large public gatherings). Given this background, it is not surprising that Bergh became extremely fashion conscious. He was almost always found wearing well-tailored suits, spats, and a tall hat, which emphasized the height of his thin body and made him appear to be more imposing. As final touches he wore a wide, well-trimmed moustache and carried a walking stick with an ornate head. When he was excited and trying to emphasize a point, he would often wave this stick in what could appear to be a threatening manner. Although he had been encouraged to follow the legal profession, he did so in a desultory fashion. He put much more time and effort into his theatrical interests and had some modest success in writing plays. Since his wealth did not require him to have a full-time career, he took advantage of this by spending about half of each year in expensive and fashionable resorts in America and in Europe. The rest of his time was spent in his home, which was New York City.

Bergh's indulgent, self-directed lifestyle changed in 1863. Abraham Lincoln had just become president of the United States, and he announced a number of diplomatic appointments. In one of these, he named Bergh the new secretary of the American legation to Russia in Saint Petersburg. It must be understood that this was a purely political gesture, as Lincoln had received support from a number of powerful people in New York, and they had suggested Bergh for this position. At this point in time Bergh was known to be an affluent dilettante who was intelligent, had good social skills, knew something about the arts, and would make a presentable representative of the United States at formal occasions. This meant that he was a safe appointment. In addition, his personal wealth made it unlikely that he would be requesting additional funding from the government for entertainment and other expenses. Bergh was generally viewed as being only mildly political in his interests, although he had given support both to Lincoln's Republican Party and to the antislavery movement in general. There was not the vaguest hint at that time that he might be interested in animal welfare.

Bergh would later describe the incident that changed his life. It happened that one afternoon he was walking down a street in Saint Petersburg after leaving his office at the legation. Suddenly he heard a cry of pain. He looked down the street and saw a *droshky*—a low four-wheeled open carriage, with a bench running down the center. Passengers sit on the bench with their feet hanging over the side, resting on a bar near the ground. Although droshkies provided cheap transportation in the city, they were not the safest of vehicles. Given the open nature of the cart, and the bouncing of the wagon due to rutted condition of the streets, it was not unheard of for passengers to be unexpectedly jolted out of their seats and onto the roadway. If an unfortunate passenger happened to fall near a wheel, it was possible to suffer major injuries.

The shrill cries Bergh heard that morning led him to the conclusion that a woman or a child had fallen from the droshky and had been badly hurt. Quickly, he ran down the street to see if he could be of any assistance. However, as he came around to the front of the vehicle he was surprised to see that the sounds were actually coming from a horse, which was being viciously beaten by its angry driver. "Even though I could see that it was only a horse being cruelly whipped, I still heard the cries as if they were the suffering of a tortured human. This burned like a brand in my soul and when the driver ceased his punishing, I gazed at that dumb brute, whose skin was covered with cuts from the whip. As I looked at his dark brown face I could see the tracks of tears that had been running down his cheeks. These were the same tears that would signal anguish in a tormented and injured child."

The image of this tortured animal would live with him for the rest of his life. Bergh would later admit, "I was never specially interested in animals—though I always had a natural feeling of tenderness for creatures that suffer. What struck me most forcibly, was that mankind derived immense benefits from these creatures and gave them in return, not the least protection." The event caused Bergh to think about the implications of this animal abuse, and it was obviously still on his mind when he began his trip home from Russia. On his way, he stopped in London for a week or so. Since many members of the British Parliament and other prominent people in the arts and theatrical community were also patrons of the Royal Society for the Prevention of Cruelty to Animals, he learned from them about their activities. He also spoke to some officials of the RSPCA about the nature of the legislation that they had managed to get passed.

He thus returned to New York fully committed as a crusader for the cause of animal welfare, and primed for political action.

Now Bergh's skills as both a dramatist and a diplomat, plus all of his social and political contacts, were called into play to try to gain the passage of laws, regulations, and special programs to help the lot of animals. He began his crusade in his home city, New York, where he began speaking out on behalf of the "average dog on the street," and for cats, horses, and farm animals as well. He felt that the goal of protecting the "mute servants of mankind" was shared by people from all walks of life and all social classes. Following each speech or public appearance, Bergh would ask for signatures on his Declaration of the Rights of Animals. This was a document that outlined his proposals to safeguard animals from cruel and inhumane treatment and was designed to bring pressure to bear on politicians. His efforts resulted in a petition endorsed by tens of thousands of people, and it had the desired effect. First the New York state legislature passed several laws to prevent animal abuse, and then, on April 10, 1866, it granted Bergh a charter to establish the American Society for the Prevention of Cruelty to Animals. Bergh capitalized on the momentum of the current events and, only nine days after its charter had been granted, the ASPCA gained the legal right to enforce the new anticruelty laws that the legislature had passed.

Although it was abuse toward a horse that began Bergh's interest in animal welfare, dogs were one of his first concerns when the legislation came into force. Just as in the case of the RSPCA, he was interested in stopping the sport of dogfighting and the use of dogs to pull carts. He was also particularly offended by another form of "slavery" that dogs were subjected to. This concerned the plight of turnspit dogs.

At that time, the traditional method of roasting poultry and joints of meat was on a horizontal metal spit stretched across an open kitchen fire. The spit had to be continuously rotated to cook the meat evenly, and this required tedious hours of slow turning. Many kitchens, especially in large homes, inns, and pubs, featured permanently installed dog-powered treadmills whose center was connected to the hearth spit; these looked much like larger versions of the suspended wheels that are provided in some hamster cages. The usual design had two sides, each of which looked like a wagon wheel with four broad wooden spokes, and these were fixed to either side of a flat wooden rim that served as the running track. Most turnspit dogs had a distinctive shape, with a long body and short legs. They were also fairly heavily built, which was necessary because they were often called upon to turn roasts and hams that could be thirty or more pounds in weight. Johannes Caius, the royal physician and dog expert, described them as a separate breed in 1576. He also noted that they turned the spits "by a small wheel, walking round it and making it turn evenly in such a manner that no cook or servant could do it more cleverly."

The life of a turnspit dog was not pleasant. The lucky ones worked in pairs, with one dog trading places with its mate every couple of hours. While they were in the wheel and exposed to the heat radiating from the sides of the cooking fire, these dogs had no access to water and often became quite dehydrated. For dogs that were considered lazy, the cook might put a hot coal into the wheel to make the dog move its feet more quickly.

Rotating spits were not the only place where such dogs were used as motive power. There were many other uses for the dog wheel, such as in driving fruit presses, butter churns, water pumps, and grain mills. There is even a patent on file for a sewing machine that was to be powered by a dog in a wheel. Regardless of what the generated motion was used for, it was obviously not a pleasant task for the dogs. This is shown by a story that begins with one of the less onerous tasks that turnspit dogs had. When these dogs were not needed in the kitchen, one or more of them would frequently be taken to church, where they would serve as foot warmers during the religious services. The story is told that one Sunday, the Bishop of Gloucester was giving a service in Bath Abbey. Drawing his text from the tenth chapter of the Book of Ezekiel, he turned to the congregation and shouted, "It was then that Ezekiel saw the wheel." At the mention of the word *wheel,* the turnspit's dreaded work place, one witness reported that a number of dogs "clapped their tails between their legs and ran out of the church."

Bergh was horrified by some of the ways in which turnspit dogs were being abused. For example, in 1874 he looked into the window of a New York saloon and saw a turnspit dog toiling in great discomfort on a wheel connected to a cider press. Bergh described the situation as follows: "The underside of [the dog's] collar had chafed a raw sore. . . . He panted and frequently tried to stop, but [he] was so tied that he had to keep on running or choke." Invoking the powers given to the ASPCA under law, he had the saloon owner arrested. The accused was convicted but insisted on appealing the judgment all the way to the state supreme court. Ultimately his conviction was upheld and he had to pay a fine of twenty-five dollars, which was a sizable sum of money at that time.

Bergh became notorious in the New York City press. He was frequently found storming into saloons where turnspit dogs were being used on cider and fruit presses, making accusations about animal abuse and threatening legal action. When the saloonkeepers protested Bergh would shout them down, and if they made counterthreats he would wave his silver-headed walking stick like a war club until the bar manager backed down. Bergh would later recall that these bar owners "could not see how it was any of [my] business how they worked their cider mill. What was a dog for anyhow if he wasn't put to something? Was he only fit to be patted on his head?"

Bergh's activities often resulted in noisy confrontations and disruption of the normal flow of activities. The newspapers kept an eye on his actions and that of other prominent members of the ASPCA, since they were often the basis for interesting stories. However, the press coverage that he received was not always very kind. *The New York Times,* for example, labeled Bergh "The Great Meddler" because of his continuous interference in the affairs of other people in order to rescue animals from mistreatment.

It was during this campaign against the use of dogs in treadmills that Bergh began to realize there was a clear relationship between animal abuse and child abuse. On two occasions, Bergh returned to businesses where the owners had been accused of abusing turnspit dogs. In both cases he was simply checking to make sure that the owners had not returned to their former practices. Bergh was astounded to find that although the dogs were no longer being used, Negro children had replaced them in the wheels.

It had only been around ten years earlier that slavery had been abolished in the United States. While it was in existence, black slaves had been used to turn sugar presses and mills, and in some cases were often driven to the point of exhaustion. Child labor was also still an established practice in the nineteenth century. Children were especially useful workers, because their wages could be kept low. Sometimes children were working merely for food and board, making their lot quite similar to that of the now-freed slaves they were often replacing. Children could also be used in tasks where the risk of being maimed or injured was high, with less risk of legal action than if an adult were involved in a mishap. The fact that it seemed natural to interchange dogs and children in these tedious and potentially debilitating occupations, such as turning spits and fruit press mills, incensed Bergh. In his mind, it confirmed his belief that the menial employment of children in such work was simply another form of slavery. Bergh consulted his lawyers to see if anything could be done to prevent the use of children in lieu of dogs. He was informed, however, that these children were working to fulfill contracts signed by their parents, and unless deliberate abuse (such as whipping or otherwise harming the child) could be shown, the legal system would not step in to break a legitimate covenant.

It must be understood that the case of the children in the saloon treadmills was not uncommon. In most major cities of that era, children were often forced into sweatshop jobs where they worked long hours and received only pitifully low wages. Others had to beg, steal, and scavenge in order to survive, and many had to live and sleep—and sometimes die—on the dirty streets. There were few laws to protect children at that time. If someone beat or assaulted a child, they could be arrested; however, no action could be taken if the individual committing the assault was the child's parent or legal guardian, especially if the abuse occurred within the child's home.

Bergh was now firmly convinced that there was an association between child abuse and animal abuse. Although he could not do anything about the two cases of "turnspit children" replacing the labor formerly provided by dogs, he still worried about them, sadly noting, "Men will be just toward men when they are charitable toward animals."

At that time, the agencies responsible for orphaned or abandoned children had a system that amounted to indentured service on the part of the child. The process of indenture is not familiar to many people today, but it has a long history. Basically it was a form of contract labor where a person borrowed money and then agreed to pay off the debt by working for a specified length of time. In this case, money was not lent—rather, in exchange for the care of the child, the foster parents obtained the full service of that child as if it were their own. The foster parents would annually be given a small stipend and only had to present the child once a year at the agency's office to verify that he or she was still alive and in their care. Many people became foster parents simply to gain access to cheap child labor. The foster children then served as house servants, worked in mills, or restaurants, and other settings where the required work was mere drudgery and did not require high levels of skill. For many children, their foster parents simply were taking advantage of the situation and the child was essentially being sold into slavery for the price of room and board. The advantage to the state was that it could point to the fact that the children were being cared for in homes, no additional group residential institutions were needed, and the cost to the government was minimal. The political gain was that even if their living conditions were not optimal, these children were at least off the streets and out of sight, and thus they did not become much of a social issue.

The case of one such child, though, did come to light in 1873. Mary Ellen was the child of Irish immigrants. It appears that her father was killed during the Civil War at the battle of Cold Harbor, Virginia, in 1864, the same year that Mary Ellen was born. Her mother was unable to care for her while she worked, so she made arrangements to pay for her daughter to stay with a woman known as Mary Score. After a few months the payments stopped coming, and Score simply got rid of the child by placing her with New York City's Department of Charities, claiming that she had no idea where the mother was. Some time later, when she was eighteen months of age, Mary Ellen was taken out of the group home and turned over to a foster caregiver named Mary Connolly.

Several years later, Margaret Bingham, a landlord in a poor tenement neighborhood in New York, became upset because of what appeared to be a terrible case of child abuse. The Connollys had been renting an apartment from her for about four years. Soon after they took up residence, Bingham began to notice how cruelly they treated Mary Ellen. The child was frequently beaten, often with a leather strap, and her cries of pain and terror could be heard echoing through the building. She had also been slashed by scissors and burned by an iron at various times when Mary Connolly had grown angry with her. The bruises and scars from these assaults were clearly visible on the child's body.

Mary Ellen was also not adequately fed or clothed. Neighbors complained that she was often out in the cold with only the flimsiest of clothes, and she was visibly malnourished. Mary Ellen was also often locked in a closet, then left unattended for long hours while the Connollys went about their business.

Margaret Bingham was concerned for the child's welfare, as were several of the tenants in her building. Each time Bingham tried to intervene, however, she was confronted by an angry Mary Connolly, who said that Bingham had no right to meddle with the way in which she reared her child—and if she continued to interfere, Connolly would take legal action to prevent her from doing so. The door would then be slammed in her face, and a few moments later Bingham could hear Connolly shouting at Mary Ellen that she was nothing but a troublemaker, and the muffled sounds of slaps and the crying of a child would be heard in the hall.

The situation was so distressing that Bingham finally resorted to a threat: The beatings and mistreatment of Mary Ellen would have to stop, or the family would be evicted. Unfortunately her plan did not work, since the Connollys simply moved out of the building to another tenement a short distance away. From conversations with the manager of that building, Bingham learned that the abuse of the child was continuing. In desperation, she sent for Etta Wheeler, a caseworker for a Methodist charitable assistance organization. She was well known locally for her efforts in assisting neighborhood people who were ill, destitute, or simply down on their luck.

Wheeler could not simply take Bingham's word, but had to see the situation for herself. To provide her with a pretext for observing the child, she sought the help of one of the Connolly's neighbors—a woman named Mary Smitt, who was suffering from tuberculosis. The idea was that Wheeler would arrange for Mary Ellen to be sent over each day to check up on the patient. Smitt was reluctant to get involved; however, she had heard the sounds of the beatings and had sympathy for the child and so agreed. Wheeler could then use the excuse that she was merely inquiring about Smitt's condition to check up on Mary Ellen. Wheeler later testified in court, describing what she saw when she knocked on Mary Connolly's door:

It was December and the weather [was] bitterly cold. She [Mary Ellen] was a tiny mite, the size of five years, though, as afterward appeared she was then nine. From a pan set upon a low stool she stood washing dishes, struggling with a frying pan about as heavy as herself. Across the table lay a brutal whip of twisted leather strands, and the child's meager arms and legs bore many marks of its use. But the saddest part of her story was written on her face in its look of suppression and misery, the face of a child unloved, of a child that had seen only the fearsome side of life. . . . I never saw her again until the day of her rescue, three months later.

Social workers often are presented with scenes of poverty, illness, grief, and even cruelty, so Wheeler was not unfamiliar with bad situations. However, in this case the extent of the abuse and the age of the child distressed her so much that she immediately went to the police for help. The police, however, pointed out that for them to intervene, they would need proof of assault. Moreover, the foster parents had all of the legal control over the child that parents were normally granted over their own offspring, and there was no law that prevented parents (whether natural, adopted or foster) from physically disciplining their children. Even very severe discipline and physical punishment could not be challenged as long as it took place inside the home. All this meant that there was nothing that could be done to take Mary Ellen away from her abusers. Any attempts to do so would be viewed by the law as interfering and violating the relationship between a parent and a child—an action that was virtually unheard of at that time.

When appeals to the police did not work, Wheeler turned to various church and charitable organizations for help. Unfortunately, things went no better there. These organizations were sympathetic, and they did offer to care for the child, but first she had to be brought to them through some legal means. Unfortunately there were simply no legal grounds to intervene.

Wheeler returned home frustrated and depressed about not being able to help this unfortunate child. Finally, her niece asked, "If no one else will help this abused child, why not go to Mr. Bergh? He is the man who has looked after the welfare of dogs and other animals, and I have been taught that we humans are nothing but higher animals."

Desperate for some form of aid for Mary Ellen, Mrs. Wheeler acted at once. Within an hour of this conversation, she arrived at the headquarters of the ASPCA. Once there, her pleading that she needed Bergh's help managed to get her an immediate interview with him. Sitting in his well-appointed office, she once again told the story of Mary Ellen.

"If the police say that there are no legal grounds to intervene, Mrs. Wheeler, what would you have me do?" Bergh asked in a concerned tone of voice.

"Mr. Bergh," she replied, "the grounds on which you protect the dumb animals of creation is based upon their absolute helplessness in the face of human cruelty. Tell me, is there anything more helpless than a defenseless child? If you can't interfere on other grounds, possibly you may find some way of reaching this child on the grounds that it is an unfortunate little animal of the human race."

Once before, Bergh had tried to intervene on behalf of abused children—the case of the black children who had been employed to replace the turnspit dogs. In that instance he had failed, so this time he was more cautious. He said to Wheeler, "Very definite testimony is needed to warrant interference between a child and those claiming guardianship. Will you not send me a written statement that, at my leisure, I may judge the weight of the evidence and may also have time to consider if this society should interfere? I promise to consider the case carefully."

Wheeler went back immediately and prepared a statement, including in it the testimony of several of the neighbors that she had spoken to. Bergh carefully read this document and was convinced. He immediately sent a message to his lawyer Elbridge T. Gerry saying, "No time is to be lost. Instruct me how to proceed." The lawyer recommended that Bergh hire a private detective to confirm the child's situation, which he did immediately. It took only an additional day for Bergh to confirm Wheeler's description of Mary Ellen's plight on the basis of the detective's observations. Bergh then acted at once.

Perhaps the best description of the rest of this story comes from Jacob A. Riis, a newspaper reporter and photographer who later became an influential social reformer. In 1874, Riis had held the job of newspaper police reporter for less than a year. He had been assigned to cover "Hell's Kitchen" and New York City's Lower East Side, which included the area where Etta Wheeler worked and Mary Ellen lived. Someone had alerted him that Henry Bergh was going to appear in court that day, which was always an opportunity for some sort of a report. One of Riis's editors had once criticized Bergh in print, writing, "He wanders the landscape looking for abuses levied against dogs and cats, cows and cab horses. In his zeal he will stop a crowded omnibus if he feels that the horse drawing it is overworked. What ill-advised virtue is this when myriad children are being beaten and starved? The young and weak of our own humanity are forced into heavy labor and suffering. Better that Mr. Bergh should tend to our own first, than waste his efforts on four footed beasts created by God to serve man's needs and pleasures."

Given that viewpoint from his editor and his informant's tip that Bergh would be dealing with a case involving a child rather than a dog, Riis's instincts told him that a good story might be about to unfold. Some years later, he described the scene as follows: "I was in a courtroom full of men with pale, stern looks. I saw a child brought in, carried in a horse blanket, at the sight of which men wept aloud. I saw it laid at the feet of the judge, who turned his face away, and in the stillness of that courtroom I heard the voice of Henry Bergh."

Bergh pointed out that there had been laws passed by the State of New York for the protection of animals. The state had also specified that the abuse of animals—all animals—was to be monitored and reported to the courts by the ASPCA, the society that he presided over. He then pointed directly at the frail child, whose bruises could be seen clearly from across the dingy courtroom, and continued. "The child is an animal. If there is no justice for it as a human being, it shall at least have the rights of the dog in the street. It shall not be abused."

Riis was moved by this plea, but in his mind, the mind of a social reformer, he could also see the greater implications of what was unfolding. He said, "As I looked I knew I was where the first chapter of the children's rights was written, under warrant of that made for the dog."

Mary Connolly was convicted of abuse and sentenced to a year in jail. For Mary Ellen, the story would end well. She would be taken to an upstate New York farm to be raised with other children in a safe and happy home. She would later marry and have two children of her own, as well as adopting a third little girl. Two of her children would become schoolteachers, and Mary Ellen would live to be ninety-two and die contented and fulfilled.

However, there was also another outcome, which would have wider implications and would affect many more people. Bergh had successfully extended the laws that he had used to protect dogs from being overworked to cover the abuse of children. Riis was correct about the historical implications of the events; the formal beginnings of the child welfare movement occurred as people filed somberly from that courtroom after the verdict. As they exited through the door, Mrs. Wheeler stopped to thank Bergh. She looked at him with eyes still red from crying and asked, "Could there not be a society for the prevention of cruelty to children, which would do for abused children what has been so well done for animals?"

Bergh took her hand and said in a calm, firm, voice, "Mrs. Wheeler, you need not ask. When first I saw Mary Ellen, I had already decided that there shall be one."

When the new child welfare society was formed, Bergh had wanted it to be separate from the ASPCA. It was to be called the American Association for the Prevention of Cruelty to Children. However, in more than three hundred of the branches of the society that were initially created in North America, the child welfare and animal welfare movements were linked together under one banner, and many still are to this day.

CHAPTER FOURTEEN

THE EMPEROR AND HIS DOGS OF MISFORTUNE

N APOLEON BONAPARTE'S LIFE has the pawprints of many dogs across it. Dogs were responsible for badly damaging his first marriage, for his losing a major ally in war, and ultimately for saving his life. It is difficult to believe, but the bloody Battle of Waterloo that ended his political career would never have taken place had it not been for a dog. Nearly all of Napoleon's encounters with dogs had unpleasant outcomes, and this left him with an abiding dislike for all canines.

Napoleon was born on the island of Corsica in 1769. His father was a lawyer, Carlo Buonaparte, and his mother was the strong-willed and fiery Letizia Ramolino. His father's family had roots in ancient Tuscan nobility, which gave him political connections, but they did not live as aristocrats. They did not hunt with dogs, and there was no family dog to serve as a companion for the eight Buonaparte children.

These were politically turbulent times. France was occupying Corsica, and Napoleon's father was active in the resistance led by Pasquale Paoli. This meant that Napoleon's earliest experiences involved hearing about his father's local guerrilla war activities and associating with his highly political friends. When Paoli had to flee, Carlo managed to win the protection of the governor of Corsica, who was looking for politically connected people to reestablish an orderly government. After being appointed assessor for his district, Carlo was able to obtain the admission of his two eldest sons, Joseph and Napoleon, to the Collège d'Autun. From there Napoleon would transfer to the Military College of Brienne and later to the Military Academy in Paris.

Although Napoleon had charisma and great passion, it appears that he had little warmth and empathy for people in general. Some of this clearly had to do with his early experiences. He was small for his age, and therefore larger children would often try to bully him. He compensated by becoming quite a fighter, and learning to strike first and furiously to gain an advantage. The result was a personality that people saw as impulsive and aggressive. When he arrived in continental France, his Corsican birth, heredity, and childhood associations caused him to regard himself a foreigner, despite the fact that from the age of nine he had been educated in France as other Frenchmen were. This in turn gave him the habit of a self-imposed social distance from others, and this pattern of behavior continued throughout his life. His career and his position, not friends and family, became Napoleon's major focus.

Early in his career he tried to reestablish ties with Corsica and Paoli's independence movement, but this did not work out, and he returned to France to fight during the revolution against the royalists. During military actions, Napoleon served heroically as a commander at Toulon, and for his decisive role in the capture of the city he was made a brigadier general. From then on he became closely identified with the National Convention, the revolutionary assembly that had abolished the monarchy in the preceding fall.

Napoleon reported back to Paris just before the National Convention was about to dissolve and form a permanent government under the new constitution it had drafted. The remaining royalists thought that this time of transition might also be a time of political weakness for the republicans. Sensing an opportunity to restore the monarchy, they instigated a revolt in Paris designed to prevent the formation of the new government. Paul de Barras, who had been entrusted with broad political power by the National Convention, was unwilling to rely on the loyalty of his other commanders at that moment of crisis. Remembering Napoleon's services at Toulon, he appointed him second in command, and it was under Napoleon's leadership that the advancing columns of rebels were fired upon and dispersed. The dissolution of the royalist attack saved the fledgling government of the republic, and made Napoleon a hero of France. He was awarded command of the Army of the Interior for his service and also became the highly respected adviser on military matters to the new government (now called the Directorate). In these positions he was aware of every political development in France, and he would use this information to further his own ambitions.

It must be understood that Napoleon was quite young when he first became a general and found himself in a position of authority where not only the other generals, but also most of the officers that he commanded were older than he was. This age disparity made him uncomfortable. He had always had some difficulty socializing with people in authority, or even with subordinates if they seemed not to recognize his status. He therefore decided to do something to improve his position. This action would give him a wife and bring him into contact with a series of dogs that would greatly reduce the quality of his life.

Napoleon reasoned that he might improve his stature in the eyes of his colleagues if he made the right marriage. He needed a wife with established political and social connections. Love was not an important criterion, although if passion could be incorporated into the match that would be all for the better. Fate played its role at this point. Fearing another armed revolt, the French revolutionary government scoured Paris and confiscated any arms owned by French citizens. Among the weapons taken was the sword of Vicomte Alexander Beauharnais, who had been guillotined during the Reign of Terror. His fourteen-year-old son, Eugene, was determined to retrieve the sword as a family heirloom, so he went to Napoleon, who was the commanding general of the army in Paris. Bonaparte was impressed by the boy's loyalty to his deceased father and had the sword returned. A few days later, Eugene's mother, Marie-Josephe-Rose de Beauharnais, called upon the general to thank him.

This must have seemed like an opportunity falling out of the sky to the twenty-six-year-old general. Here was a mature woman, with a good deal of wealth, and who was well known in the salon and political social circles in France. She was a widow and seemed available—perhaps even attracted to him, since she was inviting him to visit in her home. It occurred to him that if he married a woman such as this, he might appear to be somewhat more mature by association. This could give him a little more respect from his officers, thus easing his difficult social interactions with them. In addition, she could provide contacts with others in society and government and allow him to associate with them in what would appear to be merely a social context. She was also a handsome woman, and Napoleon liked to consort with good-looking females. Her beauty did raise a bit of passion in him, and he also admired her intelligence and social grace, all of which made things easier as he set out to make her his wife.

Napoleon's ego and dominant personality would mark his relationship with his new wife. First he tried to convince Rose (and maybe even himself) that this was an affair of the greatest passion by writing her florid love notes. One penned at seven o'clock in the morning read, "What strange power do you have over my heart. . . . I drink from your lips and from your heart a flame which burns me. Ah, this night has shown me how far your portrait falls short of your true self! You leave at noon: in three hours I shall see you again. Till then, my sweet love, a thousand kisses; but give me none, for they set my heart on fire!" The one difficulty Napoleon had in effecting this self-deception of true love was the knowledge that other men before him had possessed Rose. For this reason he insisted on calling her by a new name that no other man had ever whispered in her ear. In that way, at least in his own mind, he created a new and untainted woman. From that time on, Rose would be known as Josephine.

Josephine was just as deliberate and manipulative in her courting of Napoleon as he was in courting her. She was seeking security and status for herself and her family, and was using her beauty and grace to acquire a well-placed husband or protector. At one point she had even been the mistress of Paul de Barras, one of the five directors who ruled France. This complicated her relationship with Napoleon, because de Barras was Napoleon's chief supporter in the Directorate. However, Josephine succeeded in convincing Napoleon that she and Barras had never been more than good friends. She was particularly interested in Napoleon because he already was well placed as a general, and he seemed to have great promise for the future. During their courtship Josephine wrote to a friend, "I don't know why, but sometimes this absurd self-confidence of his impresses me to the point of believing that anything is possible for this singular man—anything at all that might come into his mind to undertake! And with his imagination, who can guess what he might undertake?"

Only four months after they first met, Napoleon and Josephine were married in a civil service accompanied only by a few friends. The fact that this was more of a career move than an act of passion was illustrated by the fact that Napoleon was several hours late, having been delayed by professional matters. Nonetheless the general was passionate enough to be chagrined when he learned that Josephine already had a bed companion whom she was unwilling to evict. This was her dog Fortune, who has often been described as a small spaniel, but which documents and paintings clearly show was a fawn-colored pug. She would own a number of dogs of this breed (and a few small spaniels in addition) over her life.

Fortune was a particular favorite of Josephine because he had proven to be so helpful at a time of crisis during the revolution. When the revolutionary council had imprisoned her first husband, Alexander, because he was an aristocrat, Josephine was also imprisoned and under threat of execution. Her children and others were barred from communicating with her; however, no one paid any attention to the little dog that came to visit her each day. By hiding messages under Fortune's broad velvet collar, it was possible for Josephine to maintain communication with those outside the prison. Several of the outgoing messages were for highly placed officials she knew, and they managed to intervene to delay her execution. When Robespierre, the most radical of the revolutionaries, fell from power, these friends obtained her release.

On their wedding night, Josephine insisted that the dog remain in the room and apparently on the bed. One does not know what was running through Fortune's mind that night, but the evidence is that this particular pug was very suspicious of strangers and had a tendency to snap and growl when unfamiliar people approached. Perhaps Fortune's motivations were nobler this time, and he felt that he was protecting his mistress. Whatever the motivation, right in the middle of their lovemaking, Napoleon and Josephine were interrupted by the dog's attack. It was a brief but painful assault, and Fortune sank his teeth into the calf of the naked and otherwise involved general. The wound was sufficiently large and deep that he would bear its scars for the rest of his life. This confirmed Napoleon's low opinion of dogs, especially small companion dogs, and certainly left him with an intense dislike for Fortune.

This incident caused several changes in the couple's domestic protocol. For the rest of their marriage, whenever they shared a room, any dogs that Josephine owned were forced to stay in an adjoining room. This did not moderate Josephine's fondness for Fortune or any of her subsequent dogs, and she insisted on keeping them despite Napoleon's distaste for them. This led to some additional difficulties especially on journeys, since Josephine required that her dogs accompany her. Thus when Napoleon and Josephine traveled together, her favorite pug of the day would be placed in a second carriage with a servant selected from the Office of the Wardrobe and whose job was to serve as the dog's personal maid. We do have records as to the cost of this, at least in 1806, where the care of the pugs amounted to the impressive sum of 207,320 francs for the year, or 568 francs per day—quite an extravagant sum for the time. Some of this cost was due to the fact that Josephine insisted not only that her pugs sleep near her, but also that they be provided with cashmere shawls and valuable carpets to rest upon.

Napoleon's dislike for dogs seemed to fester in his consciousness to such a degree that he often referred to it in passing to various confidants. When he would later become emperor of France, he would even have legislation passed making it illegal to name a dog Napoleon (to minimize any associations that might be made between him and any canine). When the famous portrait artist François Pascal Simon Gérard, who had been appointed court painter by Louis XVIII, came to paint Napoleon's image as emperor, he suggested that one of Bonaparte's dogs might be with him. He explained that the presence of a dog suggested the ability to control others, pride of ownership, warmth, and loyalty; in addition, it would help to balance the portrait's composition. When the painter was told that the only dogs available belonged to Josephine, and if Napoleon were required to sit in the same room with one of her dogs there would be no portrait, the artist quickly withdrew his request. In the end, Napoleon did allow the artist to paint a picture of him with a cat resting on his lap. However, this was done solely for the artistic effect that it created, and Gerard supplied his own cat to serve as the model.

While Napoleon was away on military campaigns, he regularly wrote to Josephine and was annoyed by her failure to respond very frequently. He knew that she was a social butterfly, and was concerned that she might be unfaithful to him in his absence. In some respects he was less concerned about the fact of infidelity than about how it would affect his social standing and reputation if the wife of General Bonaparte were known to be having an affair.

He did have reason to be concerned. The morals of French society at the time accepted the fact that when married couples were separated for any extended period of time, each party was likely to take a lover. In fact, in some of Josephine's social circles it was considered to be improper, almost indecent, to appear to be passionately in love with one's own spouse. Soon after Napoleon's departure to take command of the army of Italy, Josephine had started an affair with an army lieutenant named Hippolyte Charles. Ten years younger than Josephine, Hippolyte was the exact opposite of her husband. While Napoleon was careless in dress, quiet and reserved in social situations, and always serious and focused, the handsome Hippolyte was conscious of fashion, was full of small talk, had a cynically polite sense of humor, and lived for the moment. Josephine and Hippolyte consorted openly. When rumors began circulating Napoleon felt that, at least for appearances, he would have to bring his wife to Milan in order to exert some control on her. He wrote her a letter in which he accused her of loving everyone more than her husband—including the dog Fortune. His assessment may have been correct, but this letter also showed his attitude toward the dog.

Under pressure, Josephine agreed to come to Napoleon. A six-carriage convoy was put together to move her household to Italy. Josephine was sure to take her pug Fortune, and also to include Lieutenant Hippolyte Charles as her escort. They sat together in the first coach, accompanied by Napoleon's brother Joseph. Joseph and others on that trip would later tell Napoleon that Fortune's behavior was most strange during this trip. The dog had a reputation for being nasty and snappish toward almost everybody except Josephine (remember that Napoleon bore scars proving this), but he showed no negative behavior toward Hippolyte. Josephine did not usually take Fortune with her to formal or even casual social functions, but the dog was always on her bed when she slept. This clearly raised the suspicion that Hippolyte might achieve his friendship with the dog while lying in Josephine's bed as well. Because of the behavior of the dog a seed of distrust had now been sown in Napoleon's mind.

Fortune had the run of the estate that Josephine and Napoleon were now living on. One day, a great mastiff owned by Napoleon's chef got loose. Fortune, who was often nasty to dogs as well as people, stupidly tried to assert his dominance over the larger dog, who then killed him for his arrogance. Napoleon did not have long to enjoy the removal of this hated dog, because Hippolyte almost immediately tried to console the grieving Josephine by purchasing another pug for her. This aroused the suspicions of Napoleon to such a degree that he instituted a clandestine investigation of his wife to definitively determine whether she and Hippolyte were having an affair. Meanwhile, the poor cook whose dog had killed Fortune was mortified by what had happened. He confined his pet and would not let him out in the gardens, as he apologetically explained to Napoleon one day when he encountered the general walking across the courtyard. Napoleon responded, "Bring him back. Perhaps he will rid me of the new dog too!"

Josephine's devotion to her new dog was as strong as it had been to Fortune. When the pug fell ill some time afterward, she went to her husband and insisted that he call in the most famous Milanese doctor of the day, Pietro Moscati, to attend to it. Napoleon was annoyed, but contacted the distinguished physician to placate her. Although Moscati's specialty was caring for humans, he did manage to cure the dog. Josephine was so grateful that she became his patron. Largely because of her influence, Moscati was confirmed as a member of the Cisalpine Directory, and, after the creation of the Kingdom of Italy he became a count, senator, and grand officer of the Legion of Honor.

Napoleon clearly had no more love for Fortune's successor than he did for the original. On a campaign in Egypt in 1798, he ordered his troops to round up all the local dogs they could find, and then he had them chained along the walls of Alexandria. He explained that the barking of the dogs would provide an early warning of an attack and, to the extent that the larger and more aggressive breeds were used near the entrances, they could also help to delay the progress of the enemy. He further noted that if a few dogs were sacrificed to slow any invaders, it would be little loss indeed. "In fact," Napoleon noted to one of his officers at the time, "I can think of a dog that is probably resting on Josephine's bed at this very moment that I would be glad to see hanging from the end of an enemy lance."

In Egypt, as in Italy, Napoleon's military might won the day, but his joy of victory would be marred. The investigation of Josephine's affair, which had been triggered by Fortune and his successor, finally produced significant information. Not only had Josephine been sexually involved with Hippolyte (which would have been bearable if they had been discreet) but, using her prestige as Napoleon's wife, she and her lover had been dealing dishonestly in government contracts using the name "Bodin Company" as a cover. If word of this got out, it would badly affect Napoleon's reputation. He raged around the room, shouting at the walls while his secretary watched in shocked silence. "So! I find I cannot depend on you! These women . . . Josephine!" Then he turned his wrath on the two things that most angered him, Josephine's various lovers and her dogs. "That she should have thus deceived me . . . Woe to them! I will exterminate the whole race of fops and puppies! As to her . . . divorce! Yes, divorce!"

Napoleon would later return to Paris and then lock Josephine out of their home. Although they would reconcile again, the marriage would remain on shaky ground. The wedge between them that had been started by the pug Fortune on their wedding night, and driven deeper by the dog's later suspicious behavior, would eventually end their marriage. When Napoleon would eventually remarry, this time to Marie-Louise, the daughter of the Austrian emperor, he would call upon the 1770 marriage protocol that had been drawn up when Marie Antoinette married the future Louis XVI. Because Marie Antoinette's public playfulness with dogs was considered an embarrassment to the court, her own dogs (including yet another favorite pug, this one named Mops), were constrained to remain in Vienna. With this action as the precedent, Marie-Louise was forced to forsake her pet dog when she left Vienna as well. Thus Napoleon was spared from having any further canines in his boudoir.

The close of the Egyptian campaign, however, began an odd series of encounters with a breed of dog that would influence Napoleon's life even more than Josephine's pugs. The breed of dog that would be his savior and the bane of his existence was the Newfoundland, a huge dog standing twenty-six to twenty-eight inches at the shoulder and weighing up to one hundred and fifty pounds. It has long hair and is typically solid black, although at that time a black-and-white variety called the Landseer was also very popular. The Newfoundland has powerful hindquarters, a large lung capacity, big webbed feet, and a heavy, oily coat that enables the dog to swim well and to withstand cold waters. Its broad, heavy, mastiff-like muzzle gives it the strength to drag ropes, fishing nets, or drowning people through the water. During this era, Newfoundlands were extremely popular as ship mascots and sailors' companions. There were so many stories about them carrying ropes out to stranded rowboats or rescuing people who had fallen overboard that nautical names (such as Sailor, Seaman, Boatswain and Admiral) became traditional for the breed.

The first event in Napoleon's life involving a Newfoundland dog took place in Carlton House, the home of the Prince of Wales when he is residing in London. The prince regent had a Newfoundland dog with the typically nautical name Boatswain (which was pronounced "Bosun"). The dog had the run of the house, and the prince often referred to him as his "bodyguard."

That night there was a reception for diplomats accredited to British court. There was some tension that evening because of rumors that England was on the verge of taking action against Napoleon's France due to concern over his territorial ambitions. Nevertheless, the French envoy and ambassador had come from Paris specifically for this occasion. Although they seemed to simply be engaged in harmless conversation with various other diplomats, their real task was to ensure the neutrality and goodwill of the Prussian envoy.

The prime minister of England, William Pitt, viewed Prussia as the final piece that he needed to forge a grand alliance against France, and he and the prince had the task of convincing Prussia to join them. For this reason the prince had taken the Prussian into his study (which was just off the salon where drinks and tidbits were being served) for a private conversation. At that moment Boatswain entered the room, happily wagging his tail. The big dog loved to retrieve things and would pick up virtually anything that was dropped on the floor; this time, he was carrying a letter that had fallen out of the pocket of one of the visitors. Thinking that the note was for him, the prince quickly opened it and read its contents. Then, with a thoughtful look, he checked the other side. It was addressed to the French ambassador. He turned to the Prussian diplomat beside him and, in a matter-of-fact tone of voice, said, "I think that this message may be of interest to you. When you are finished with it, I will have the dog return it to its owner."

The Prussian looked puzzled, but took the letter. It read as follows: "Monsieur, I am writing to my envoy at the same time, the matter is of utmost importance. Any rapprochement between the Court of Saint James and the Prussian envoy must—at all costs—be prevented. The latter is a man of a slow-witted and complacent nature. You will have no difficulty in dealing with him." It was signed "Bonaparte, First Consul."

A flush came across the face of the diplomat as he handed the note back. Without any further comment, the prince placed the note back in Boatswain's mouth, and the two of them walked out of the room to where the French ambassador was standing and searching his pockets with a distressed look on his face. The prince said something, and the ambassador took the letter from the dog's mouth with a look of puzzlement, but apparent relief. Six weeks later a new coalition against the military tyranny of France was signed and sealed, with Prussia standing with England and its other allies against Napoleon.

Another Newfoundland would affect Napoleon's peace of mind about a year later, and again the events would occur many miles away from the French imperial court. In 1805 Napoleon, now the emperor of France, sent orders to Admiral Pierre de Villeneuve, who was in command of a combined French and Spanish fleet of thirty-three ships. The orders instructed him to leave Cadiz and land troops at Naples to support the military action in southern Italy. Not far off Cape Trafalgar, Spain, which is between Cadiz and the Strait of Gibraltar, Villeneuve met a British fleet of twenty-seven ships under Admiral Horatio Nelson. The battle of Trafalgar was a disaster for Napoleon, and would end forever any dreams of storming across the English Channel to invade England. By the time the fight was over, Villeneuve himself was captured, and his fleet lost most of its ships, as well as fourteen thousand men, of whom half were prisoners of war that had been taken by the French. Nelson was fatally wounded during the battle, but the victorious British fleets lost no ships at all.

When all of the details of the battle were recounted to Napoleon he learned that a dog, specifically a Newfoundland, participated, at least symbolically, in the Battle of Trafalgar. It was serving on the English frigate *H.M.S. Nymph* as ship's dog. It appears that when the French battleship *Cleopatra* struck her colors and the ships were drawn together to effect the surrender, the dog was the first member of the boarding party to reach the deck. On hearing this detail of the events, Napoleon angrily spat out, "Dogs! Must I be defeated by them on the battlefield as well as in the bedroom?"

Despite his defeat at Trafalgar, Napoleon would go on to engage in a series of brilliant and dangerous military campaigns over the next decade, expanding French control in Europe while opposition from other countries grew more determined. His ultimate downfall would be caused by his ill-advised invasion of Russia, which greatly weakened his forces and took away his aura of invincibility (at least for engagements on land). In 1814 Austria, Russia, Prussia, and Great Britain signed a pact that bound them for twenty years. They agreed not to negotiate separately, and promised to continue the struggle until Napoleon was overthrown. The president of the French provisional government, Talleyrand, proclaimed that Napoleon's reign was over, and without consulting the French people began to negotiate with Louis XVIII, the brother of the executed Louis XVI. Since further resistance seemed useless, Napoleon abdicated. This was not a full surrender, since in the Treaty of Fontainebleau the allies granted him the island of Elba as a sovereign principality. He would be given an annual income of two million francs by France and a guard of four hundred volunteers. He also was allowed to keep his title of Emperor. Unfortunately, his wife, Marie-Louise, and his son were put in the custody of her father, the emperor of Austria, and Napoleon would never see either of them again.

It was on Elba that Napoleon had, for the only time in his life, a dog that belonged personally to him. It was a midsize yellow dog that looked much like a golden retriever and spaniel cross. This dog was not to be a companion, and for that reason we do not even know its name, but it did have a job. Napoleon knew of several British plots to assassinate him. He therefore kept this dog simply as a food taster, to ascertain if there were any poisons being added to his meals. In this way the dog provided comfort, if not companionship.

Napoleon carefully followed the politics and events in France from his exile, and he saw that the people of France were not happy about the return of the monarchy under Louis XVIII. Thus he began to plan his escape and his return to the mainland. The logistics involved in leaving Elba required a great deal of detailed planning and luck, but in February 1815 he was prepared to leave. It was a Sunday morning, and he came out early to attend church. A number of local notables and common citizens had gathered, since there had been talk of his leaving to retake France. These townspeople crowded the steep narrow streets to shout "*Vive l'Empereur!*" as Napoleon and his small retinue passed by. Out in the harbor was a tiny flotilla of boats, made up mostly of local fishermen who had come away from their fishing areas to see what the commotion was about.

The sky was gray and overcast, and the water was choppy. The crew and Napoleon's attendants climbed into the little boat (named *Caroline*) that would carry him out to the warship *Inconstant,* which would then whisk him away before the British patrols knew what was happening. Napoleon was the last into the boat. The sailors were having a bit of difficulty manning the oars because of the swells and wind that was in their faces. While they concentrated on moving the boat away from the shore, Napoleon stood by the gunwale for a last look at the island and its citizens. The boat was now pitching, and the surfaces were slippery.

A few minutes later, the sailors looked back to see how the emperor was faring—and were shocked to see that he was no longer in the boat. Some moments before, he had lost his balance and toppled into the sea. Unfortunately, Napoleon was a poor swimmer, and some say that he had never learned to swim at all. Even had he been a good swimmer he would have had a difficult time, since he was in his full dress uniform and had strapped on the great sword that he had worn at his victory over the combined Austrian and Russian forces at Austerlitz. However, while his predicament was still unnoticed by the sailors, and he was desperately floundering in the water, a dog came to his rescue. This was yet another Newfoundland dog, just like the others that had plagued him earlier, only this one was black and white, rather than the solid black of Boatswain and the ship's dog of the *Nymph.* This particular dog was a fisherman's work mate, and it was frequently used for tasks like recovering fishing nets, towing lines between boats, and, at least once before, it had saved a man from drowning. The dog immediately swam to Napoleon, and the struggling man managed to grab hold of the dog and to keep his head above water.

By now the sailors on the *Caroline* had noticed the problem and were turning the boat. Two seamen leaped into the water to assist him, but they arrived several minutes after the actual accident, and had it not been for the dog, the emperor of France would have long since sunk to the bottom of the Mediterranean Sea. Cold, wet, and sputtering, Napoleon was pulled back into the boat to proceed on the path to his destiny. He was successfully transferred to a waiting warship, managed to reach France, and then marched on Paris. He won over the troops sent to capture him, and then veterans of his old campaigns as well as the many anti-royalists in the country flocked to his support. When in Paris, he passed a new and more democratic constitution, then asked the allies for peace.

Instead, the European coalition declared Napoleon an outlaw. Rather than let his enemies gather strength, he decided to strike first, instituting the chain of events that would lead to his defeat at Waterloo. However, that glorious and bloody conflict would never have taken place had it not been for a great black-and-white dog, whose name we do not know. This dog returned safely to its owner, and it is easy to imagine him standing on the deck of his owner's boat, with water dripping from him and his tail slowly swinging back and forth. He is looking out to sea and surely does not know, nor does he probably care, that the person that he has just saved was one of the most famous men ever to have held his species in contempt.

Napoleon was to have one last encounter with a Newfoundland dog. When the British decided to banish Bonaparte to the tiny volcanic island of St. Helena, he was sent there in *H.M.S. Northumberland,* under the command of Rear-Admiral Sir George Cockburn. The ship's dog, the personal pet of Cockburn, was another black Newfoundland with another nautical name, Tom Pipes (the traditional sailor's nickname for the person who held the post of boatswain). The dog was always with the admiral, and so was there when he dined with Napoleon or at numerous meetings and social interludes. Cockburn later included some strange comments in his reports to the admiralty:

> He complains about the presence of the officers' dog. He suggests that it is kept in his presence to degrade him. He says that its presence during our conversations is but to remind him of his defeat and to denote that he is no more worthy than a dog. When we dine together he bolts

his food and then discourteously leaves the table. I have asked him about this and he claims that he eats quickly lest the dog steal his food or that it be taken from his plate and given to the dog.

There appears to have been only one time that Napoleon ever commented favorably on a dog. This occurred during his last year of confinement on St. Helena, while he was dictating his memoirs to the French historian Emmanuel, the Comte de Las Cases. Napoleon was describing his recollection of the night after the battle of Bassano, which was part of the Italian campaign. Then a young general, he was walking across the battlefield, which was covered with corpses of those who had fallen just a few hours before. Emmanuel transcribed his recollection this way:

> We were alone, in the deep solitude of a beautiful moonlit night. Suddenly a dog leaped out from under the cloak of a corpse. He came running toward us and then, almost immediately afterward ran back to his dead master, howling piteously. He licked the soldier's unfeeling face, then ran back to us—repeating this several times. He was seeking both help and revenge. I don't know whether it was the mood of the moment, or the place, or the time, or the action in itself, or what—at any rate, it's a fact that nothing I saw on any other battlefield ever produced a like impression on me. I stopped involuntarily to contemplate this spectacle. This man, I said to myself, has friends, perhaps. He may have some at the camp, in his company—and here he lies, abandoned by all except his dog. What a lesson nature was teaching us through an animal.
>
> What a strange thing is man! How mysterious are the workings of his sensibility! I had commanded in battles that were to decide the fate of a whole army, and had felt no emotion. I had watched the execution of maneuvers that were bound to cost the lives of many among us, and my eyes had remained dry. And suddenly I was shaken, turned inside out, by a dog howling in pain!

It is likely that Napoleon's emotional response was due to the great incongruity that he saw in this situation. Here was a dog, an animal that he held in contempt, and it was displaying nobility and loyalty beyond that shown by soldiers that he held in high regard. Or perhaps this recollection came to mind be-

cause of the memory of the dog that had saved his own life less than a year earlier, although there is no record anywhere of Napoleon expressing gratitude for
that dog's help.

There are two odd footnotes to the story of Napoleon Bonaparte's relationship with dogs. The first is that on St. Helena he had no dog—not even one to
serve as a taster of his food, like the yellow dog that he had on his previous exile
on Elba. This appears to have been an unfortunate oversight on his part, since
current forensic methods have now shown that Napoleon probably died of ar-
senic poisoning introduced into his food over a period of several months. Had
he again employed a dog as a food taster, he might have been alerted to this plot
in enough time to forestall his death.

The second footnote has to do with the fact that the "canine curse" on the
Bonaparte family seems to have continued through the generations. In fact it
was being felt as late as 1945 in New York City. It was there that Jerome
Napoleon Bonaparte—the last of the original Bonaparte family in America—
had taken his dog out for a walk in Central Park. Apparently the dog became excited at something, and darted across the path in front of the elderly man. This
latter-day Bonaparte stumbled over the dog's leash and crashed to the ground,
sustaining a set of injuries that would eventually prove to be fatal. The dog was
a pug, just like Fortune, the dog who slept in Josephine's bed and was the first
canine to be associated with bad luck and adversity in Napoleon's life.

CHAPTER FIFTEEN

CONVERSATIONS

WITH DOGS

I T IS JULY 15, 1941, in the Gatineau hills of Quebec, on an estate called Kingsmere. If you could look into the master bedroom of the estate some-time after nine o'clock in the morning, you would see a relatively short, somewhat plump man of about sixty years old, pacing around the large master bedroom. He is wearing a shirt crumpled from staying up all night, and his eyes are moist with tears. In his arms he is carrying a small dog. The man is softly, tunelessly, singing the old hymn "Safe in the Arms of Jesus." He finishes the hymn and gently strokes the dog. Then he looks into the dog's eyes and begins to speak.

"Remember the messages that I have given to you. Don't forget to deliver them as soon as you get there." He lists a string of names and repeats the com-munication that was to be given to each. These are names of loved ones and colleagues—and every one of them is dead.

This strange scene was not a glimpse of a madman in an asylum. This was the prime minister of Canada, William Lyon Mackenzie King, in his home. At the time that this extraordinary spectacle was taking place, his country was one of the allies locked in a desperate struggle for survival against the forces of Nazi Germany. The situation looked grim. Poland and the Baltic states had fallen, the British forces were not faring well, and the United States was being dragged into the European conflict. Canada was raising an army, and the issue of conscription was tearing the country apart. A meeting of the cabinet war committee had been scheduled for the previous afternoon to discuss the pressing issue of mobilizing a sixth division of the army, as had been recommended by the minister of national defense. However, King had instructed the secretary of the cabinet to postpone it, because "my Angel Dog" at Kingsmere needed him.

Although this scenario seems to be somewhat extreme, it is not unusual for people to talk to their dogs. Talking to a pet dog as if it were another person does not indicate that a person is mad, demented, or lacking in a reasonable amount of intelligence. More than eighty percent of all dog owners admit to talking to their dogs in a conversational way, much like they would talk to a friend or family member. Many famous people have not only talked to their dogs, but recorded such conversations for posterity. Take, for example, the Nobel Prize–winning novelist John Steinbeck, who wrote such classics as *The Grapes of Wrath*, *East of Eden* and *Of Mice and Men*. He was neither stupid nor crazy, and yet he talked to his dog. At the age of fifty-eight, with his reputation as a writer already well established, Steinbeck decided that he wanted to "rediscover" America. To do this he set out on a twelve-thousand-mile trip that took him through thirty-seven states and Canada. He traveled in a camper truck, accompanied only by his black standard poodle, Charley. Steinbeck took Charley along to provide companionship but also because he wanted some casual way to meet people:

> A dog, particularly an exotic like Charley, is a bond between strangers. Many conversations en route began with "What degree of a dog is that?". . . In establishing contact with strange people, Charley is my ambassador. I release him, and he drifts toward the objective, or rather to whatever the objective may be preparing for dinner. I retrieve him so that he will not be a nuisance to my neighbors—*et voilà!* A child can do the same thing, but a dog is better.

The result of this trip was the warm and gentle book *Travels with Charley,* which really could have been entitled *Conversations with Charley.* Steinbeck talks to Charley about such day-to-day matters as when to stop and camp, when and what to eat, and when to move on to a new place. He also talks to Charley about his feelings at the moment and his observations on the social scene. Sometimes, however, the conversations become quite deep and philosophical, such as when

Steinbeck has a long conversation with Charley about the nature of prejudice and racial discrimination.

Steinbeck records his conversations, and they follow a pattern that has now become familiar to psychologists. You see, our language structure and pattern changes under different circumstances. In formal situations, such as when we are talking to authorities or to an audience, we use more reserved and ceremonial language than we do when we are talking with family and friends. There is also a special kind of language that we use when we talk to children. It is simplified language, often done in a singsong rhythm, sometimes in higher voice tones, with lots of repetitions. Psychologists have called this special language form "Motherese," since it is heard most commonly when mothers are talking to their infants and young children. It is not confined to mothers, however, since virtually everyone, male or female, parent or not, tends to lapse into it when talking to a very young child. Psychologists have found that the way that we talk to dogs is very similar to Motherese, and they have dubbed this form of language "Doggerel."

Doggerel sounds quite different from the speech that we would use around other adults. Sentences are much shorter, averaging around four words (as opposed to ten or eleven words when we speak to adults). We use many more commands to our dogs, saying things like "Come over here" or "Get off the chair." Strangely enough, we also ask twice as many questions of our dogs than we do of humans, even though we really don't seem to expect any answers. The questions are usually trivial conversational questions, like "How do you feel today, puppy?" In addition we use a lot more tag questions when we speak to dogs. A tag question is where one makes an observation and then turns it into a question at the very end, such as saying, "You're thirsty, aren't you?" Also, when we talk to our dogs we are also twenty times more likely to rephrase and then repeat things than we would with humans; an example of rephrasing and repeating would be "You are a good dog. What a good dog."

Doggerel also sounds different because we tend to use a higher tone in our voice, and we emphasize our intonations and emotional phrasings. We also use a lot of diminutives, referring to a walk as a "walkie" or the dog as "cutie." We also distort words and phrases to make them appear less formal, as when we use terms like "wanna" or "gotcha." This means that if you hear someone ask in a singsong tone of voice, "Do ya wanna go for a walkie?" you can probably safely infer that she is talking to her dog. Of course, there is some slight chance that she is talking to a very young child, but certainly little chance that she is talking to an adult friend or family member.

There are also special patterns of conversation that we use when talking to our dogs. Conversations with dogs usually take one of three different forms. The simplest is just a monologue, where the human being does all of the talking in a continuous stream while the dog provides just a friendly presence. The second form is a sort of dialogue, where there is some give and take but only one speaker. In this kind of conversation we look at the dog now and then, pausing at places where the dog might be expected to make a comment, then continue on as if the animal's silence had conveyed some meaning. This form of conversation sounds very similar to what you would hear if you were monitoring one side of a phone conversation.

The third form of human and dog conversation is familiar to many dog lovers, but may seem quite odd to an outsider. This is when we not only talk to the dog but also provide the answers, essentially saying the words that we think the dog might utter in response to our comments. You may have seen a version of this kind of behavior when parents talk to young babies. They might, for example, give the child a toy, saying something like, "Would you like this dolly?" When the baby smiles or reaches, these parents might add (often in another voice), "Oh yes, Mommy. I like that doll." In its full-blown form, however, this tends to produce a conversation that sounds much like a clichéd Hollywood movie sequence where the schizophrenic carries on an argument among his or her various multiple personalities—each with a distinctive voice and character. Steinbeck records one such "conversation" when he found Charley staring blankly off into space. Of course, it is Steinbeck who is providing both sides of the discussion:

"What's the matter Charley, aren't you well?"
His tail slowly waved his replies. *"Oh, yes. Quite well, I guess."*
"Why didn't you come when I whistled?"
"I didn't hear you whistle."
"What are you staring at?"
"I don't know. Nothing I guess."
"Well, don't you want your dinner?"
"I'm really not hungry. But I'll go through the motions."

Such conversations can get to be quite playful, and they may serve to reduce feelings of stress and loneliness on the part of the human. Steinbeck was feeling a bit lonely and out of sorts the day of that conversation, and he had noticed that Charley seemed a little depressed also. So he decided to cheer him up by baking him a birthday cake, even though it wasn't Charley's birthday (or at least probably not, since Steinbeck really couldn't remember when Charley's exact birthday was). In any event, he thought that a festive cake might brighten both of their moods. As he prepared the ingredients, the dog watched the operation with some interest. In his Charley voice, Steinbeck says, *"Anybody saw you make a birthday cake for a dog that he don't even know when's his birthday would think you were nuts."*

Then, acting like the scholar, teacher, and author that he was, he interjects in his own voice, "If you can't manage any better grammar with your tail, maybe it's a good thing you can't talk." At that moment the absurdity of this discussion catches him and he breaks up in laughter. The depressed mood has been broken because of his conversation with his canine friend.

It is as a social companion that dogs often have their greatest impact on both ordinary and historically important people. Scientists have shown that people who live alone, or in periods of personal crisis, are less likely to become depressed enough to require clinical help if they are living with a dog. The social interaction and the safe conversations seem to keep them from developing psychological symptoms, just as Steinbeck's conversations with Charley kept him from becoming depressed and morose on his long trip. Dogs have served the same purpose for many other people suffering from loneliness, stress, fear, longing, and uncertainty. Consider, for instance, the tragic case of Mary, Queen of Scots.

Born as Mary Stuart in 1542, she was the only child of James V of Scotland and his French wife, Mary of Guise. Tragedy seemed to hover around her from her birth until a series of unwise marital and political actions ended her reign and eventually led to her execution. When she was only six days old, her father died, and she officially became queen of Scotland. Henry VIII was king of England at the time and was also Mary's great-uncle. He made an attempt to gain control of her as a child, in the hopes that this would also give him control of Scotland. As Henry was becoming more militant about taking Mary to England, though, her mother arranged for her to be sent to France. From the age of five years she would be brought up at the court of King Henry IV and his queen,

Catherine de Medici, with the support of her mother's powerful family, the Guises. It was there at the Valois court that she developed her lifelong love of dogs.

One must understand Mary's situation. She was immediately betrothed to the dauphin Francis, who was a year younger than she was. Now she found herself a member of the court in a strange land and unable to speak a word of French. The king and queen looked on the young girl with affection and decided to rear her as they would a daughter. She and Francis were allowed to play together as brother and sister, and as further playmates they were provided with twenty-two lapdogs—toy spaniels, pugs, and Maltese. In her first few months in France, she would only speak with her Scottish governess and with the dogs. She was often found in her room or in the garden, talking to the dogs and pouring out her sorrow and frustration. Soon, however, she and Francis began to bond. He also loved the dogs, and would spend hours with them. As he spoke to the dogs the young dauphin instructed Mary, teaching her the meanings of the French words that he used. After a while, she became confident enough to try some of the new French words that she had learned in this way on some human listeners. As her confidence grew, so did her language skills, and she ultimately became even more fluent in French than in English. For all intents, Mary grew up to be the ideal of a French princess. She had been well educated in language, literature, history, and music and also was quite beautiful, with a tall and slender build crowned by red-gold hair and amber-colored eyes.

The marriage between Mary and Francis was originally arranged as an attempt to strengthen the ties between France and Scotland. Later in her life Mary would become a factor in the political and religious tangles affecting England and Scotland, but as the wife of the crown prince of France these did not concern her at the time. Despite the politics, Mary was fond of her boy husband, a fondness gained from years of playing together with their pack of dogs. When he assumed the throne as Francis II, she was proud to be the new queen by his side. She was also devastated by his death only a year later, when she was only eighteen years of age. Despondent over the situation, she returned to assume her crown as the queen of Scotland.

At that time, Elizabeth I was queen of England. Elizabeth's road to the throne had been rocky, since she was the daughter of Henry VIII and Anne Boleyn, and had been declared illegitimate after her mother's execution. It took an act of Parliament to reestablish her in the succession to the throne. As has been so often the case in British history, the religious strain between Catholics and

Protestants would play a role in the events of state. Elizabeth was Protestant, and many Catholics still considered her to be illegitimate, regardless of the act of Parliament, because they regarded Henry VIII's divorce from Catherine of Aragon to be invalid. This reasoning would make any subsequent marriages by Henry void of legitimacy. If that was the case, then Mary would be the lawful queen of England by virtue of her Tudor blood, and Henry IV of France, her father-in-law, thus claimed the English throne on Mary's behalf.

When Mary returned to Scotland, her entourage included a number of the Maltese dogs that she had grown to love during her stay at the French court. Each dog had a blue velvet collar with its name embroidered on it. Each dog also received a ration of two loaves of bread, and there were special servants whose job was to tend to them. These same servants made periodic trips to France to get new dogs.

Mary's arrival in Scotland was not cause for much celebration. Elizabeth distrusted her because of the efforts to seize the English throne on her behalf, and her years in the French court made her appear to many to be foreign. Furthermore, during her absence Scotland had officially been reformed to Protestantism, and Mary refused to give up her Catholic beliefs. She was thus viewed by many, including the leading Calvinist preacher, John Knox, as a foreign queen with an alien religion. For a while, though, aided by her half-brother James, Earl of Moray, and a policy of religious tolerance, the reign went well.

Then Mary made the first of her disastrous marital decisions when she married her English cousin Lord Darnley. Elizabeth disapproved of Mary marrying another Tudor descendant, while her brother Moray was so upset at the match that he rebelled against her, depriving her of her best administrative adviser. Darnley turned out even worse than expected; he was quite brutal and joined a conspiracy of Protestant nobles. He then murdered Mary's secretary and her last trusted counselor, David Rizzio, right before her eyes. Mary soon became convinced that Darnley was planning to take her life as well. The birth of their son, James, did little to reconcile the couple, but since Mary now had the heir that she wanted, she began to look for a way out of her situation.

Here the historical record gets rather confused and tangled. The story seems to be that Mary started an affair with the Earl of Bothwell, who later would be charged with the murder of Darnley. Although he was never convicted of the crime, many felt that Mary conspired with him and knew of the plot to kill Darnley. With no wise counselors around her, she then foolishly married Bothwell. This enraged the nobility and the Scottish population in general, and they flew to arms. Mary was forced to abdicate the throne in favor of her one-year-old son, James, who would go on to become King James I of England; her brother, the Earl of Moray, was appointed as the regent. Bothwell was exiled, and Mary was imprisoned. Her Catholic supporters managed to rally a large force in an attempt to seize the throne again, but with a lack of adequate leadership, Mary's army was defeated in battle at Langside by Moray. Now Mary had to flee for her life, with charges of treason and sedition hanging over her in Scotland.

Acting on impulse, Mary fled to England and sought refuge with Elizabeth. Queen Elizabeth had all of the political cunning that Mary lacked, and appeared to welcome her. However, Elizabeth manufactured a series of complications having to do with the death of Darnley, and thus managed to keep Mary in prison for the next eighteen years. Furthermore, Elizabeth attempted to deprive her of all contact with friends and relatives. Nonetheless, there were occasional secret visitors, including the Jesuit priest Samérie, and one of these visitors managed to bring her a couple of Maltese dogs and a small spaniel from France, which would serve as her true confidants and soulmates.

As in her early life, the dogs became a source of solace and companionship during Mary's stressful isolation. Her jailer, Bess of Hardwick, later reported that Mary spent long hours talking with her little lapdogs. Apparently they spoke of religion, and about her son, James, whom she had not seen since her abdication. The dogs were so important to her that they were included in a miniature painting commissioned to be sent as a gift to James (although it was intercepted before reaching him).

These dogs also accompanied Mary Stuart to her last prison at Fotheringhay Castle. In 1586 a plot by a coalition of Catholic groups to murder Elizabeth had been discovered, and Mary was charged with being an accomplice. She was brought to trial and although she defended herself with eloquence, there was overwhelming evidence of her complicity. Her execution, by beheading, was therefore ordered, and Mary was sent to Fotheringhay to await her death. Her only consolation was that, after a direct appeal to Elizabeth, she was allowed to have her dogs with her.

One of her dogs would serve as her companion one last time, to give her one last bit of comfort at the moment of her death. When the time came, Mary walked to the scaffold with slow steps. None knew that this was done to keep pace with the small white dog concealed under her long skirts and petticoats.

Even after the axe had fallen, the little dog did not move. Mr. Bull, the executioner, who was working with an assistant, finally discovered it. He had been given orders that everything splashed with Mary's blood was to be washed or burned "for fear someone might dip a piece of linen in it, as several of this country have done, who keep it as a relic of this act, to incite to vengeance those concerned for the death of the dead person." It was while untying Mary's garters, which in those days were tied at the knees, that Bull noticed the dog. It refused to leave the body, and even when dragged out by force it rushed back and lay between the severed head and shoulders. The poor beast now had its white coat covered with Mary's blood. One of the executioners took pity on the dog, which was carried away and washed clean. Instead of being destroyed, the dog was given to a French princess who asked for it as a memorial of her friend (and was granted it, on condition that the dog be taken out of the country).

Perhaps now we can return to the Canadian prime minister who is talking to his dying dog during a long and lonely period of crisis. William Lyon Mackenzie King was born in Berlin (now Kitchener), Ontario. He was named after his grandfather, William Lyon Mackenzie, who was an impassioned politician and a fiery journalist best known for his armed rebellion against Canada, and his attempts to drag support from the United States for a takeover of the country. Perhaps it is quintessentially Canadian that the nation later pardoned him, and upon his return he immediately entered politics again and was successfully elected to office. His daughter, Isabel, acquired his interest in politics through simple exposure to what was going on around her, and also developed a network of political contacts that would serve her son well when he embarked on a political career.

Willie, as he was affectionately known by his family and friends, grew up in a fairly typical upper-middle-class family situation. His father, John King, was a lawyer, and his mother, Isabel, kept her political and social contacts going by serving as a popular hostess in the community. He had two sisters, Bella and Jennie, and a brother, Max. The family also had a dog named Fannie, who mainly belonged to the girls and did not play much of a role in Willie's early life.

When he grew up, Mackenzie King was not overtly very impressive. He was a relatively short man, had a tendency toward being a bit overweight, dressed very conservatively, and was rather introverted. He did have a good mind, however, and managed to obtain five advanced degrees, specializing in matters pertaining to labor, economics, and politics. His ability to write and reason clearly, plus his knowledge about labor matters (and perhaps his mother's political friends), brought him to the attention of Sir Wilfred Laurier, who was then the prime minister of Canada. He made King the very first deputy minister responsible for labor. Later, when King had been elected to parliament, Laurier would increase the importance of King's job by expanding it to a full departmental position. King did take a break from Canadian politics, spending a few years in the United States investigating industrial relations. At the urging of Laurier, King returned to Canada, where he was chosen to be Laurier's successor as the leader of the Liberal Party. Two years later he would become prime minister, a post that he would hold (with only two brief interruptions) for twenty-two years, making him the longest-serving elected leader in British Commonwealth history.

This man, who looked like a modest and mousy bureaucrat, actually had an astonishingly successful career, in which he helped define the nature of Canadian politics and social policy. He introduced government social-support systems that became available to all citizens; the old age pension, unemployment insurance, and family allowances for children are all legacies of Mackenzie King. He could do this, in part, because his economic understanding had resulted in fiscal policies that produced a massive reduction in the national debt.

With the outbreak of World War II, Mackenzie King found himself faced with a series of difficult crises. One was the issue of conscription. Throughout World War I, Canadians had been bitterly arguing over the issue of a national military draft. Now with another war raging in Europe, and Canada committed to standing by Britain, Mackenzie King was faced with the divisive problem of conscription again. The country desperately needed more troops, but Canadians remained divided along regional and cultural lines. Somehow, King managed to reach a compromise that maintained national unity. Part of his strategy involved simply delaying long enough to allow external influences to come to bear. Thus he gave speeches with wonderfully meaningless but pacifying phrases, such as "conscription if necessary, but not necessarily conscription."

Meanwhile, King signed several important pacts with President Franklin Delano Roosevelt of the United States, which created a joint board of defense, guaranteed cooperation in the production of military equipment and materials, and ensured an integrated defense of the North American continent. This last act permitted the final bit of compromise over the issue of conscription, since it then became possible to draft citizens for service inside the country rather than sending them overseas "to fight a foreign war." After the war, he would go on to significantly help secure continued peace by serving as the chairman of the Canadian delegation at the conference in San Francisco that drafted the charter of the United Nations and later helped to establish its permanent home and political structure. In 1945, King also helped to set the basis for the nuclear arms controls that we have today when he signed the Washington declaration on atomic energy with President Harry Truman and Prime Minister Clement Attlee of Great Britain.

From a Canadian standpoint, one of King's great contributions was that he helped to define the nation as a separate and independent country. It may seem strange, but although Canada had operated as a separate nation since before the time of the American Revolution, there was no such thing as Canadian citizenship until the middle of the twentieth century. Instead, Canadians were simply considered to be British subjects residing in Canada. It was King's strong sense of nationalism that caused him to establish separate Canadian citizenship. On January 1, 1947, during his last year as prime minister, Mackenzie King was the first person to be granted the status of Canadian citizen under the Canadian Citizenship Act.

Despite his many successes, King also made some errors during his administration. Most of these seem to have been due to inadequate consideration of the moral implications of a situation, or because he succumbed to manipulative flattery. Normally people in politics have advisers, often in the form of family or friends, who might step forward and give a bit of confidential advice when delicate private or ethical matters arise. Thus errors can be caught early before much damage is done. Unfortunately, King lived a rather solitary personal life, so when he had an early infatuation with the policies of Adolf Hitler and his negative attitudes toward Jews, there was no one to dissuade him by pointing out the political dangers and moral consequences. His beliefs and actions were corrected only when external events intervened, such as the commencement of the events that eventually led to World War II.

During his early career, King's mother was a constant presence in his life, helping to guide his decisions and often intervening in his personal life. When her health began to fail, his brother, Max, stepped in as a good friend and a candid critic of his activities, while his sister Bella provided a flow of emotional support. However, by 1922, before the end of Mackenzie King's first year as prime minister, all three of them would be dead. His close friend and mentor Wilfred Laurier had passed away even before this, as had his soulmate from his college,

Bert Harper, who had provided most of his social contacts outside of politics during the first half of his life. This meant that King was alone, shorn of any close and personal relationships.

Mackenzie King never did marry. He seemed to have great difficulty establishing intimate and warm ties with others. At the professional level he was friendly enough, but was never all that revealing. At one point it seemed that it would be professionally expedient for him to have a wife, but even after several years of active searching, he found that there was no one with whom he could carry on a sustained intimate relationship. When the pressures of sexual needs became great enough, he turned to the services of prostitutes. When he finally concluded that this sort of contact was sinful, he would resort to prayer for solace—and, if that didn't help, to drinking. His secret diaries, which were only revealed after his death, showed that he tried to cling to the few successful bonds that he had developed in his life by means of spiritualism. He would hire mediums to conduct séances where he could consult with his deceased loved ones, including his parents, his brother and sister, and of course Wilfred Laurier.

Perhaps the most meaningful human relationships that King had during the last thirty years of his life were with Joan Patteson and her husband, Godfroy. Godfroy was a bank manager, and Joan came from an artistic and well-educated family. They were neighbors of King in the Roxborough apartments, which made friendship natural and easy. A bit older than King, Joan seemed to take over some of the functions that King's mother had fulfilled, such as hosting some of his social receptions and handling his personal calendar. The relationship had a certain formality to it, however, in that long evenings would be spent reading philosophical and literary works out loud, and singing hymns. Joan Patteson was extremely fond of King in a sisterly way, and she became concerned about his lack of intimate relationships after the loss of his mother and brother. The Pattesons felt that given the professional pressures that he was undergoing, and his lack of success in finding a human partner, their bachelor friend would be much better off if he had a household pet to provide affection and companionship. Not only did the idea succeed, but it eventually went well beyond their dreams. The intimacy of the relationship with his dog and its successors would only become clear after King's death, when his personal diaries were discovered, and through the clarification provided by Joan Patteson in some letters and conversations.

The Pattesons had just bought an Irish terrier named Derry and from the same litter they gave Mackenzie King a dog named Pat. It is likely that the little brown dog served to fill many gaps in King's life. He provided constant companionship and someone that King could talk to. It is likely that he also flattered King's ego by paying attention to him and treating him as if everything that he did was important, in much the same way that King's mother had done. King even came to believe that there was some spiritual link between his dead mother and the little terrier. He wrote in his diary that one day, when he was kneeling in prayer before his mother's portrait, "little Pat came up from the bedroom and licked my feet—dear little soul, he is almost human. I sometimes think he is a comforter dear mother has sent to me, [as] he is filled with her spirit of patience, and tenderness and love."

Whenever King was at the estate, Pat was with him continuously. He would talk with the dog about events of the day as he wandered around the house, or walked through the nearby landscape. When he was away from home on diplomatic business, there would be several phone calls each week to Joan Patteson, who often looked after Pat on such occasions. The real purposes of these calls was to check up on Pat and to send his greetings.

Mackenzie King's diaries make it clear that Pat was providing the emotional support that he needed at times of crisis. On the day in 1939 that Great Britain and France declared war on Germany, King noted that "Little Pat always seems to me a sort of symbol of my mother," then went on to say that through the dog she "was giving me assurance of being at my side at this most critical of all the moments."

Sadly for King, Pat was now fifteen years old, and even though the crisis associated with war was just beginning, it was clear that the dog could not be expected to live much longer. King did recognize this when he wrote, "He is a little 'angel dog' that some day will be a little 'dog angel'." He appears to have taken the term from a poem written by Norah M. Holland in 1918:

High up in the courts of Heaven to-day
A little dog-angel waits,
With the other angels he will not play,
But he sits alone at the gates;
"For I know that my master will come," says he:
"And when he comes he will call for me."

Pat did manage to live another two years. At the age of seventeen, though, the poor dog was sick, deaf, and going blind. There were no close confidants in King's life to tell him that the time had probably come to think about euthanasia. Perhaps the possibility of speeding the dog's death never occurred to him because Pat was so closely linked in his mind with his mother, and he certainly would never have thought about euthanasia for her. That summer day in 1941, Mackenzie King arrived at his estate in Kingsmere to find Pat very ill. The bond that he saw between his dog and his mother became clear when he later wrote of this day, "I cried very hard as I realized it could not be long before his little spirit, his brave, noble spirit, would have taken its flight, but my tears were mostly of gratitude for God's mercy in so guiding my steps as to bring me home in time. I thought of dear Mother, and how I had come too late, had stayed too long in New York."

King was now clearly anticipating his dog's death. He briefly returned to Ottawa to conduct some pressing business, then instructed the secretary of the cabinet to postpone the meeting of the war committee scheduled for that afternoon until the next day. Meanwhile, he rushed back home to be with Pat. He held the dog in his arms and sang hymns to him.

The vigil went on all night. "Morning was just beginning to break—I kissed the little fellow as he lay there, told him of his having been faithful and true, of his having saved my soul, and being—like God—thought of how I felt as I knelt at dear Mother's side in her last illness." As the end drew near, he described the scene.

> I sang more hymns, held him to me, his little body warm, legs got cold, his little heart got very weak, almost imperceptible. When 10 past 5 came I sang again, "God be with you till we meet again . . ." It was at that moment . . . that we crossed the bar. . . . My little friend, the truest friend I have had—or man ever had—had gone to be with Derry [*his littermate*] and the other loved ones. I had given him messages of love to take to father, mother, Bella [*his sister*], Max [*his brother*], Sir Wilfred and Lady Laurier, Mr. and Mrs. Larkin [*early political supporters and friends of his mother*] and the grand-parents . . . I felt a great peace when all was ended.

Somehow, King managed to keep his private grief from interfering with his political duties, and on the afternoon of July 15 he held the delayed war committee meeting. No one present knew that he was suffering, nor did they know the reason that the original meeting had been delayed.

The Pattesons had anticipated Pat's death and had developed a contingency plan to fill the gap that they were sure this would leave in their friend's life. After the death of their own dog, Derry, they found another Irish terrier, conveniently named him Pat, and encouraged their friend to come and visit their new pet. Mackenzie King grew to know and like him, originally referring to him as "the other Pat." The Pattesons waited a couple of months, until the initial grief had subsided a bit, and then arranged for King to adopt the new Pat. Since he already knew the dog, the transition was easy for King.

Pat II probably never fully replaced the first Pat, but a clear affection developed, and King often referred to Pat II as "the Little Saint." As in the case of his first dog, Pat II became his confidant. King could again relieve the pressures of being the prime minister of a country at war by having intimate discussions with someone who would listen attentively and not tell tales or ascribe blame. For example, on Christmas Eve of 1944, King noted, "Before going to bed I had a little talk with Pat, in his basket. [The basket rested beside King's bed.] We spoke together of the Christ-child and the animals in the crib."

Pat II did not live as long as the original Pat, and his last illness was also a major time of trial for King. Pat II had cancer, and King was reluctantly convinced to have him put to sleep to spare him the pain. During the last days, King noted that that Pat II was nobler, stronger, and "truly greater" than he was himself. He humbly wrote in his diary, "God grant I may be worthy of him."

Following the death of Pat II, King remained without a dog for nearly a year. However, he seemed to call upon their spirits in times of crisis. At one point, during some economic difficulties that were putting a strain upon his government, he wrote in his diary, "The little dogs have been very near to me all day. When I went to my room tonight I felt I could talk to them as if they were again jumping over my bed in their joyous ways. They are very near to me in times like these."

The importance that this dog had developed in Mackenzie King's life became clear in 1947, when King George VI offered the prime minister membership in the Order of Merit. This is a very high honor in the British Commonwealth, since the order never has more than twenty-four members. Furthermore, no other Canadian in history had ever been appointed to it. The honor was in recognition of the service that King had given during the war as prime minister, and afterward in the establishment of the United Nations and several other com-missions and treaties that seemed destined to help preserve the peace. This placed King in a great conflict, since he was not in favor of titles and distinctions as a matter of principle. In addition, Pat II had recently died, which meant that he did not have his usual confidant to discuss the matter with. However, as he wrote in his diary, "I can honestly say . . . that my thoughts, singular as it may appear, went later to my little dog Pat II [*more*] than anything else. I felt that that little creature deserved an O.M. a thousand times more than I do myself, and then came the thought of the other little Pat who also merited more than I do, and the loyalty of his nature, fidelity, and all that counts for most." In the end, however, King convinced himself that the honor was being bestowed upon his country through him, rather than upon him personally. He therefore accepted the Order of Merit rather than recommending that it should be posthumously bestowed upon his dog instead.

There would be one more Pat in Mackenzie King's life—again an Irish ter-rier, only this time it was a gift from his confidential secretary. Time was running out for King, so Pat III would not be with him long enough to develop the same degree of intimacy that his predecessors had. King would, however, still talk with him, sometimes merely to comment on his own physical condition as his health was failing.

On July 20, 1950, King awakened. Pat III had made his way onto the bed. The old man shook violently and had a sudden chill. "Call them, Pat," he coughed, and he was still repeating the phrase when the household was aroused by the frantic barking of the dog. Shortly thereafter Mackenzie King was ad-ministered a dose of morphine to relieve the pain, and he never recovered con-sciousness again.

We will never truly know just how important these dogs were in the life of Mackenzie King. However, the idea that a person could have sustained a career for so long, and so full of intense crises, without intimate social support seems unlikely. For this lonely bachelor, the only truly constant support came from a series of dogs. The fact that he and others report his conversations with these dogs seems to confirm that they provide badly needed solace and support, if not advice, in difficult times.

To people who have not lived with dogs, the idea of talking to them about intimate matters as if they were another person, such as a friend or counselor, might appear strange. Yet one of the great benefits of a companion dog is that there is someone to share feelings with and to relieve the stress of a crisis, or simply of loneliness. A dog listens with a calm look that says, "Go on, I want to know how you feel." A dog never says, "That's the most stupid thing that I've ever heard." With a dog nearby, you are never alone. Perhaps that is why so many people talk to their dogs. As conversational partners, dogs have been the comforting confidants of many people, including authors, composers, royalty, political leaders, and just ordinary people—such as me, and maybe even you.

CHAPTER SIXTEEN

THE LION DOGS OF THE FORBIDDEN CITY

I T IS THE MIDDLE of the second century A.D., and we are at the court on the main palace grounds of the emperor of China. The huge room is draped in silk banners, and brightly painted walls with metallic trim that looks like gold can be glimpsed behind them. Emperor Ling Ti of the Han Dynasty, the current Son of Heaven, is entering the great hall. He is accompanied by his diminutive bodyguard of four "Lion Dogs," all of a breed that we will come to know as Pekingese. Two of them march ahead of him, with heads up and tails high; they announce his approach at correct intervals with sharp, piercing barks. The other two trail behind, daintily holding the hem of his royal robe in their mouths. These dogs have been part of the royal court of China for so long that they are simply an accepted part of royal life and protocol. They are coddled and venerated as an essential element in the rule of the emperor. However, some seventeen hundred years later, this same breed of dog will play a role in bringing down the Manchu dynasty and end imperial rule in China forever.

The Lion Dogs are a small but constant thread throughout the complicated history of China over the past two thousand years. Their story begins with Buddha. Buddhism began in India more than five centuries B.C. It is not surprising that much of the symbolism in Buddhism, as an Indian religion, involves concepts and animals that are common in that country. Since the most feared animal on the Indian subcontinent was the lion, it became the symbol of violence, aggression, and terrible passions. The story goes that Buddha tamed the lion and taught it to "follow at his heels like a faithful dog," a parable that has come to symbolize the triumph of piety and wisdom. The lion would ultimately become Buddha's faithful servant and companion. Later it would be sanctified through its association with him and endowed with many of his attributes. Because of this, the lion became a major symbol of Buddhism, and the image of the lion appears in many of the legends surrounding the life of Buddha. One of these describes how Buddha would soar into the sky on the back of a lion, and from his fingers he would produce myriads of tiny lions that could gather together as if they were one great beast to attack his enemies.

Buddhism entered China along trade routes from central Asia over the first four centuries A.D. and was gradually assimilated into Chinese culture. Many of its concepts, though, began to be blended with the local Taoist traditions and other regional ideas and symbols. The Chinese were quite willing to accept the lion as the great emblem of their new religion; however, virtually none of the people of China had ever seen a real lion. They had some familiarity with tigers, but the verbal description of a lion as a large, tigerlike beast "with great side-whiskers that surround its head and neck to a length that falls over its shoulders, and with a bare back and a broom of soft hair at the end of its tail" does not give a clear image of what a lion actually looks like. There were a few stylized stone carvings of lions that had made their way into the country, but these models had only a vague resemblance to the real animal since they usually had greatly flattened faces so that they could comfortably be worn as an amulet or as a decorative ornament. Real lions were very scarce, and those few who made it to the emperor's court usually did not survive the harsh winters.

The establishment of Chinese Buddhism occurred when the Han emperor Ming Ti abandoned the teachings of Confucius and accepted the newly arrived religion. He was not only a spiritual man, but was also quite superstitious. Because of this he desired—and psychologically needed—visible symbols to reinforce his faith. The fact that there was no living representation or emblem of the greatness of Buddha—not even in the temple of his most high priest, the emperor himself, was a disaster. Certainly as the designated Son of Heaven, he, like Buddha, should have a lion as a companion. The situation was saved, however, when someone took a good look at the emperor's own small dog. Whoever this person was, he or she concluded that probably nothing on earth looked as similar to the depictions of the lion that they had come to know as the Pekingese dog. A little trimming of the face and some skillful shaving of its tail, and it was now surely a Lion-Dog! Thus these small dogs became both the symbol of Buddha and the symbol of the emperor himself.

It is important to note that small dogs had been popular among the nobility for hundreds of years before they became identified with the lion of Buddha. Around 500 B.C., Confucius writes about a "short-mouthed dog" with short legs and long ears and tails. They are described as *ha-pa* or "under-the-table" dogs. This would make them quite small, since the tables at that time were only about eight to ten inches off the ground in order to accommodate a person sitting or kneeling on a mat or cushions in front of it. Some of these dogs were bred to be so small that they could be carried in the wide sleeves that the nobles wore, thus providing not only companionship but also additional warmth for the aristocrat on cold winter days. Bronze vessels from the Shang and Chou dynasties show running dogs that look very similar to the Pekingese. However, after Ming Ti associated the little square-mouthed palace dogs with the lion of Buddha, the history of these dogs would change drastically.

Now royalty and aristocrats began to encourage the breeding of dogs that looked more like their somewhat distorted mental image of a lion. It is during this era that we see an increase in the feathering, especially around the head, and a widening of the nose and flattening of the face. The idea that the emperor's dogs were representations of Buddha's lion began to affect the popular image of the lion. People began to believe that Buddha's sacred creature was actually a Lion Dog. Statues of *Fo-dogs* (where *Fo* is the Chinese name for Buddha) became popular; they are often found in pairs at the entrance to Buddhist temples. In truth they look very little like any living creature, whether lion or dog, with their rectangular heads, shaggy manes, fantastic curls, short bodies, massive legs, and bushy tails. These Lion Dogs usually wear leashes consisting of silken cords or ribbons, and are adorned with collars from which hang bells and tassels. They are often seated on low ornamental pedestals, covered with richly embroidered cloths. Traditionally the male has the pad of his right front paw resting on a ball covered with embroidered silk, while the female has the pad of her left front paw on the upturned mouth of her cub. The significance of this odd posture comes from the folk belief that lionesses secrete their milk through the pads of their paws, so the cub is actually supposed to be suckling.

By the end of the sixteenth century, the idea that the symbol of Buddha was a vaguely lion-shaped dog, like the Pekingese, had become ingrained in the culture. In Chinese art, the lion that Buddha rode had come to look more like a dog than a lion, even to the point of wearing a collar with dangling bells and ornaments. Now the faithful lions that walk beside the holy man look much like Pekingese dogs and even strike obviously doglike poses (such as a play bow, where a dog crouches with its front legs extended and nearly flat to the floor, while the rear of its body and its tail remain up). Even the folklore had begun to change to confirm this melding of the lion and the dog. Thus in some tales, Buddha was accompanied by dogs who could transform themselves to lions when he needed a steed or a protector. Later, a tale appeared that explained the emergence of the Lion Dog from the lion. The story goes that one day the celestial lion, the very lion that Buddha first tamed, came to his enlightened master with a problem.

"Oh Son of Heaven," he said, "I have fallen in love with a marmoset monkey. She is beautiful, and she loves me dearly and has great admiration of my courage, but she is afraid of my size and strength. Oh most wise one, what am I to do?"

Buddha smiled and said, "Faithful lion, this I will do for you. When you go to see your lady love, I will make you small in body so that she will no longer have need to fear you. Your body will be small, but your spirit and courage will remain great and strong. But remember that you are my companion and my faithful servant, so that when I call upon you, you must return, and if you are not able to do so then the obligation falls upon your heirs and their families."

The now-small lion ran off to marry his lovely lady marmoset. They lived happily all of their lives, and had many children. These children were the Lion Dogs, and these small dogs bear an obligation to serve and to act as the symbol of Buddha for eternity.

The most common, and some claim the most royal, of the breeds to claim the title of Lion Dogs is the Pekingese; in fact the Mandarin Chinese name for this breed is *Xiao Shi Zi Gou,* which literally means "little Lion Dog." However, it is important to remember that these dogs were being bred for their appearance, and the idea of keeping pure bloodlines or breeding records did not yet exist. Therefore, although the Lion Dog of Buddha is most often identified as the Pekingese from China, the Lhasa Apso and the Tibetan spaniel began as alternative attempts, made by Buddhist lamas in Tibet, to capture the look of the celestial lion. When the Dalai Lama sent Lhasa Apsos to the emperor of China as gifts, these were interbred with the Pekingese as an experiment to try to capture a somewhat different image of the lion, and this resulted in the development of the Shih Tzu. Later on, when Buddhism made its way to Japan, the Japanese Chin (where *Chin* is the Japanese word for Chinese) was created by interbreeding the Pekingese with the Tibetan spaniel. This was all a form of biological sculpture, where breeders were trying to shape the dogs to a particular image of the symbolic lion and also trying to capture a miniaturized sense of the celestial lion's spirit personality in the form of a bright and energetic temperament.

Competitions were held every year or so to determine which of the many dogs reared by the servants of the Imperial Palace or many of the noble houses looked like the best example of the Lion of Buddha. The dog that won had its portrait painted and included in the official records of the emperor's reign. In addition, the person who bred the winning dog was given a rank in the civil service that entitled them to a pension for life. Thus there was a high premium on having the perfect Lion Dog. Obviously, this resulted in a lot of experimental mating in an attempt to produce the most desirable shape, size, and color in a Lion Dog. When breeding failed, however, some ambitious and unscrupulous kennel keepers would often resort to other extreme measures to produce the ideal-looking dog. For example, the tail tips of newborn puppies were often bitten off, because the dense fur does not grow toward the tip. With the tail tip gone, there would now be longer fur near the end of the tail, and this could then be trimmed into a more lionlike tuft.

The most prized feature in these Lion Dogs was a broad and flat face. One trick used to achieve this involved feeding the dogs from the inside of a stretched piece of pigskin. As the dogs tried to eat the tiny bits of meat attached to the skin, their noses would be pressed hard against the hide. Since there was not a lot of fleshy material, the dogs had to work at cleaning the hide for hours at a time, so this continuous frontal pressure had the effect of stunting the growth of the nose and muzzle, thereby flattening the face. There are some reports of even more drastic procedures, such as crushing the tender noses of the puppies by hitting their faces with a stick. This was a dangerous technique for both the dog and the breeder, since if one of the royal puppies was found to have died because of violence from a slave, eunuch, or worker, the penalty was death. An alternative procedure, which had less risk but was more labor intensive, involved the employment of servants to spend hours each day massaging the puppies' muzzles so that they would remain short.

Size was another issue that was addressed both genetically and in other, harsher ways. When the Manchu emperors gained control, they developed a fondness for smaller dogs, and that led to the inbreeding of the smallest offspring from each successive litter. Because small puppies often owe their reduced size to some physical problem, though, the number of inbred maladies began to increase. To counter this effect, dogs from outside the royal lines were often brought in to improve the health of the emperor's dogs. Since the size often increased with the introduction of the new and healthier genetic stock, some bizarre procedures were adopted to keep the puppies small. Obviously restriction of food during the early months of growth was tried, but there was also the practice of rearing the puppies in tiny wire cages to stunt their growth. Another procedure (a variation on what was being done to flatten their faces) involved having the puppies grow up while being continually held in the hands of slaves, who were instructed to gently squeeze and knead their bodies to limit their size. A whole cadre of slaves might be needed to do this, since the dogs would be passed from one slave to another after a period of a few hours. This means that some dogs might almost never be allowed to touch the floor until they reached maturity. These more outlandish procedures were reserved to add perfection to dogs that already had desirable colors or markings.

The breeding of the Pekingese and the other varieties of Lion Dogs had now become a royal privilege, and the place where they were bred became the Forbidden City. Built early in the fifteenth century during the Ming dynasty, the Forbidden City was a huge, fortified enclave, covering 864,000 square yards and containing around eight hundred buildings that provided a total of roughly nine thousand rooms. The Emperor and his court lived inside the city. Once the Forbidden City was built, the Lion Dogs of China began to disappear from sight, since nearly all of them were now confined within its boundaries for their entire lives. There was an imperial kennel, with its own high-walled courtyard, and tiers of bamboo cages to house the dogs. A special staff attended to the dogs, and all events occurring in the kennel were reported to the chief eunuch, who in turn would relay information about new litters to the emperor. The kennel was subject to periodic visits by His Majesty, especially when new puppies had arrived, or around the time that the competition for the year's most perfect dog was approaching.

The breeding and ownership of the royal Lion Dogs was by this time legally an imperial prerogative. It was unlawful for them to be owned by anyone except the nobility or certain high-placed priests. If a commoner encountered one of these dogs when they were crossing the courtyard, they were required to avert their eyes in a respectful manner, much the way that they did when encountering a noble person in the street. This was appropriate, since the dogs were often given titles and honors. For example, the Emperor Ling Ti of the Han Dynasty went so far as to bestow upon his favorite dog the hat and belt of office of the Chin Hsien grade—one of the most distinguished of the literary ranks in China. In imperial times, promotion and advancement in the highest levels of the civil service depended upon literacy plus a thorough mastery of historical writings and the volumes of commentary that had been written on them. Thus this rank indicated not only knowledge, but also knowledge of such a degree as to actually confer nobility.

The conferring of titles upon the emperors' dogs became an accepted practice. Typically the winners of the annual competitions, or simply royal favorites, were given the rank of *K'ai Fu*, which is roughly the equivalent of a viceroy. The females were given the titles of wives of the corresponding officials. These dogs were all treated as aristocrats, with soldiers assigned to guard them and servants to care for them. They received the best rice and meat for food, and their beds were valuable carpets and cushions.

While the emperor might find the conferring of rank upon dogs appropriate or amusing, it did not sit well with others. One chronicler of the time noted that it was very bad practice and an insult to those in the service of the emperor to liken high officials to dogs. Imagine then, the reaction in the household of Emperor Ming of the Tang Dynasty around 715 A.D. when he added a favorite and very beautiful "wife" named Wo to his family, and it turned out that this wife was a tiny white Pekingese dog. The facts seem to show that this dog was probably more responsive to Ming's needs than any other family member. She would study him attentively, and if he began to show any stress or anger, she would leap up onto his lap to comfort him. This would almost always calm him and cause him to smile.

A story is told about an incident in which this little ritual rescued the emperor from some embarrassment. The emperor was playing chess with one of his princes, who had been acting in a rather independent manner and making decisions that should have been referred to the emperor for confirmation. This prince had developed the reputation for being very intelligent and ambitious, and Ming did not like the idea of palace gossip suggesting that the prince appeared to have a better intellect than the emperor.

As was often the case, other members of the court had gathered around to see the game. Unfortunately, the game was going badly for Ming, and he was becoming distressed at the fact that so many members of the court would see him lose to his potential rival. This would clearly be good for the prince's prestige, but would diminish the eminence of the emperor. Little Wo had been watching her imperial master and, in her usual effort to comfort him in times of trouble, tried to jump into his arms. As she bounded upward she landed first on the chessboard, scattering pieces all over the floor and completely ruining the game. Although the emperor apologized to the prince for their inability to finish the game, because of the misbehavior of his little wife Wo, it was noted by many that he wore a broad smile, and only a few days later his favorite pet was wearing a new jewel-studded collar.

Although dogs had a special place in the life of the Chinese imperial court for centuries, perhaps their greatest impact on the history of the nation occurred during the reign of Tzu Hsi (also called Cixi), who is best known in the West as the Dowager Empress of China. When she was born in 1835, she was given the name Yehonala. Her father was a captain in the banner corps that guarded the emperor's home, the Forbidden City, during the Manchu dynasty.

Yehonala's family was Manchu, and as such they tended to interact only with other Manchus and had little contact with Chinese people of different heritage. Yehonala was strikingly beautiful and she was in love. She was living the equivalent of an upper-middle-class life and was planning to marry a Manchu garrison commander named Jung Lu. All of this ended when she came to the attention of the emperor, Hsien Feng, who chose her to be one of his many concubines. This meant, among other things, that her new home would be the Forbidden City.

Being only a concubine of the third rank, Yehonala did not receive much respect or trust. If selected on a given night to serve the emperor, she was brought to his room by eunuchs, then stripped naked (to be sure that she had not smuggled a weapon into his bedroom) and left to wait at the foot of the bed. Her fortunes soon changed, however. Although Hsien Feng had many concubines, Yehonala was the only one who had given birth to a surviving son. After the birth of her son, Tsai Chun, she was promoted to consort, or first-rank concubine. Yet although the emperor recognized her intelligence and she did have the credit of mothering his first son, the woman who would one day be known as Tzu Hsi did not have his affection. (That was reserved for Li Fei, the emperor's favorite concubine.) At least she did have the emperor's respect and he gave her the honors due her rank, which included the first of her name changes. From that time on, she would be called by the honorific title *Kuei Fei*, meaning "Concubine of Feminine Virtue."

From the moment that she achieved her new status, Kuei Fei (the former Yehonala) had access to documents of state. She made it her custom to read the reports from the provinces and offer advice on all important questions. Very soon, consultation with the mother of the heir apparent became a necessary preliminary to all decisions in government matters. She had the perfect bureaucratic mind, with a love for order and system, knowledge of precedent, and an attention to details. She also had a number of political assets that would further her personal ambitions, not the least of which was her connection to the military through her father's friends and her former fiancé, garrison commander Jung Lu, who would remain loyal to her for the rest of his life. At the personal level she was willing to use patronage and bribery and even violence, when needed, to advance her own ambitions. Kuei Fei also had a strong loyalty to allies and an unforgiving attitude toward enemies, while her close association with the emperor gave her the ability to mete out rewards and punishments to these groups as she saw fit. Not surprisingly, she soon was at the center of a powerful political coalition.

When Emperor Hsien Feng died at the age of thirty, several things happened in quick succession. Since his primary wife had not given birth to a son, Kuei Fei's son, Tung Chih (the former Tsai Chun), became the emperor even though he was only five years old. Yehonala again had her name changed, this time from Kuei Fei to *Tzu Hsi*, which means "Blessed or Fortunate Mother." The former emperor's first wife was given the name *Tzu An*, which means "Peaceful Mother." It was the plan of these two "dowager empresses" to rule as regents, but they were opposed by a council of influential nobles. It was now that the many allies that Tzu Hsi had assembled around her came into play.

Hsien Feng's brother, Prince Kung, knew of her connections with the army, particularly with the banner corps, which served as the imperial guard. Kung was formulating some schemes of his own, and these would require at least the political support of the banner corps. For this reason, Kung allied himself with the two empresses, and together they seized control of the government. Their enemies were charged with treason and put to death (except for two who were allowed to commit suicide because they were royal). Next, Tzu Hsi addressed herself to the issue of her principal rival when the emperor was alive. Hsien Feng's favorite concubine, Li Fei, mysteriously disappeared and was never heard from again. It was widely rumored that on Tzu Hsi's orders, she was tossed down a well in the Forbidden City (a common means of eliminating rivals).

Tzu Hsi and Tzu An were now without any real opposition. Since they were only regents, however, they couldn't rule openly but had to exert their influence through the child emperor. To do this, Tzu Hsi had a bamboo screen set up behind the child's throne. When various government officials and delegations delivered their reports or made their requests, Tzu Hsi, who sat behind the screen, heard what was said and then told the child emperor what to say in return. Tung Chih dutifully said what his mother instructed him to, and thus Tzu Hsi's words became imperial law.

With two women both acting as empresses, it was inevitable that a power struggle would occur. The final conflict came over the chief eunuch, Li Lienying, who Tzu An felt was being given too much power and accorded too many honors. This was a clear mistake on Tzu An's part, since Tzu Hsi had made it a priority to cultivate an association with the palace eunuchs from her first arrival at the palace. She had quickly recognized that it was the eunuchs that controlled the day-to-day operation of the palace, and hence much of the government. As she rose in rank and stature, she also concluded that they could be used as a private secret-police force to enforce her will. It was the eunuchs whom Tzu Hsi used to make many of her rivals disappear, and she now used them to administer poison to Tzu An, leaving herself as the sole empress and regent.

Tzu Hsi's son, Emperor Tung Chih, would not live very long. He had developed a dissipated lifestyle, and was drinking heavily and consorting with prostitutes. At the age of sixteen he married Alute, the daughter of a Manchu nobleman. He also began to keep concubines. Tzu Hsi could see that Alute was beginning to undermine her control over the young emperor, and there were rumors that she might be pregnant. In addition, one of his concubines was also now pregnant, which meant that there could soon be an heir to the throne to completely displace the empress. Tung Chih came down with a mild case of smallpox, and seemed to be recovering when he took a turn for the worse and died suddenly. His medications were being prepared by the palace eunuchs under the supervision of Li Lien-ying, which suggests that foul play may have been involved. This seems even more likely given the fact that Alute and the pregnant concubine both immediately committed suicide under suspicious circumstances—one by taking an overdose of opium, and the other by throwing herself down a well.

Given the convenient fact that Tung Chih had died and left no children to ascend to throne, Tzu Hsi chose her own three-year-old nephew, Kuang Hsu, to be the next emperor even though he was not even in the direct line of succession to the throne. It was possible for her to do this because of her strong military and political allies. At the same time, she had herself declared the guardian (and later "mother") of the child, thereby maintaining her regency and her control over the government.

For the next fourteen years Tzu Hsi was the voice of the imperial government. It was also during this period of time that she became most interested in the Lion Dogs that were traditionally kept in the palace. Most were Pekingese, but there were also a few Lhasa Apsos, Shih Tzus, Tibetan spaniels, and pugs. It was the Pekingese, however, that she most prized. It was not unusual for there to be well in excess of a hundred of these little dogs in residence in the kennel in the Forbidden City at any given time, while others were scattered in apartments around the palace. A smaller kennel area was also established at the summer palace.

Given the number of these dogs, one might feel that we are dealing with an individual who had a true love for little canines. While it is true that she developed some affection for a few favorites, her real reason for attending carefully to the breeding of these dogs was because of their symbolism. Remember that these dogs represent the Lion of Buddha. Part of the authority assumed by the emperor came from his association with Buddha and the powers of the celestial lion. It is from this association that one of his titles, Son of Heaven, is derived. Tzu Hsi, however, was not born of royalty and so could not claim any association with the Buddha. She believed in the Buddhist interpretation of events, though, and also believed that signs and portents could guide and predict events. She kept around her a bevy of Buddhist priests, astrologers, spiritualists, and various types of fortune-tellers. Through conversations with these individuals, she had been told that these Lion Dogs were sacred and by keeping them in close association with herself, she would begin to absorb some of the qualities and spiritual powers of the Lion of Buddha.

As a consummate politician, Tzu Hsi undoubtedly recognized that by frequently being seen with these Lion Dogs, she would become associated with the Buddha in the minds of those around her. She would further try to reinforce this connection by allowing herself to be referred to as *Lao-fo,* which means "Old Buddha." Tzu Hsi continued the policies of former imperial courts, which restricted access to these now-sacred dogs. Anyone who attempted to sell or export one of the Lion Dogs, or even took it out of the Forbidden City without royal consent, would be sentenced to death. Thus these dogs remained one of the best-kept secrets in the world until the 1860 invasion of international troops during the Boxer Rebellion.

The empress would personally inspect the dogs in the kennels at various intervals. If she ever made the slightest negative comment about any dog (such as "Its back is too long," or "Its hind legs are not the right length"), this was effectively a decree of exile for the animal. Most usually it simply disappeared, perhaps dispatched by a blow on the head or tossed into one of the Forbidden City's wells to rest beside the Empress's enemies.

Tzu Hsi's principal concerns were not only with the general lionlike appearance of the dogs, but also with their color and markings. The white spot on the top of the head was highly desired, since it was associated with spiritual factors and was sometimes called the "Eye of Buddha." It was thought to have the same properties as the "third eye" that priests and lamas often spoke of and permitted the dog to sense gods and spirits and know the future. The color of the dogs was also important, since each color had symbolic and prophetic significance. For example, a red dog was associated with joy and happiness, as well as fire and the direction south. Yellow was the color of the earth, and could therefore represent the country of China. It was also considered to be an imperial color and thus represented the emperor's dynasty; in fact, the Chinese often referred to themselves as *yan-huang-zi-sun,* or descendants of the Yellow Emperor. White was a complex color in China. As the universal funeral color, it could represent death, but just as in the West it could also stand for purity and innocence. In addition, it symbolized the direction west. Black was often associated with guilt, evil, death, mourning, water, cold, and the direction north. Special meanings were also given to dogs marked with more than one color, who were called "flowered" dogs. Thus a dog might have a "three-flowered face" with markings of yellow, black, and white, and the pattern of markings could be interpreted. The color and edging of the eyes could also have significance, and each combination had a name (such as "water-chestnut eyes," "leopard-eyes," or "dragon-eyes").

The birth of each litter of dogs was taken to have special significance that might reflect upon current or future events. The colors and markings of the litter were noted, as well as the number of puppies born, the order in which each puppy appeared, and the sex of each. This information was taken by the imperial kennel keeper and given to the chief eunuch, Li Lien-ying. He would pass this information on to whichever priest or spiritualist was currently in the highest favor of the empress at this time. The priest's job was to quickly interpret the significance of these signs, whether favorable or not, and also to suggest what subtle meanings these might have for matters currently under consideration or the future of the realm. Li Lien-ying would then take the priest's interpretations to the empress, and she would often use these to determine her decisions in matters of state. The actual translation of signs associated with the birth of a litter of Pekingese and their influence on decisions made that day by Tzu Hsi were not recorded as matters of state, but sometimes the empress's confidants, such as the princess Der Ling, would make a note of them. At least two of these dog-influenced decisions would have great significance for the nation.

The new emperor, Kuang Hsu, was not a very impressive individual. He was skinny, sickly, and not very socially adept. He was also a poor politician and could not read people very well. Nonetheless, when he reached the age of seventeen Tzu Hsi theoretically gave up her power and ceased to be regent. She then officially retired and moved to her summer palace, which was only six miles away from the Forbidden City and still allowed her to monitor political events. She moved her cadre of eunuchs and her personal military guard as well. She also stocked her kennel there with her favorite dogs from the palace.

One positive aspect of Kuang Hsu's personality was that he had sought to learn as much about the contemporary world outside of China as he possibly could. Several of his teachers had very modern ideas, and Kuang Hsu began to institute a series of reforms that were designed to modernize and westernize China. He began issuing a rapid-fire series of decrees, which have come to be known as the "Hundred Days of Reform." He ordered the construction of railroads, a modernization of the military (including the removal of hereditary rights to officer's privileges), changes in the public education system (including the conversion of some temples to schools), and reforms of the power of the nobles. Unfortunately, this resulted in his alienation of the army, the priesthood, and the aristocratic Manchus, since he began to dismiss hundreds of officials who opposed his reforms.

Dissident forces began to rally around Tzu Hsi, trying to convince her to do something to control the emperor. Although she knew that Kuang Hsu was lacking in the qualities of leadership, had no personal magnetism or charm, and lacked the driving force to attract supporters, she knew some forces might rally to his support simply because he was the emperor. If she moved against him she would have only one chance, and should she fail her life was over. While she pondered over what to do, information came to her that one of her favorite dogs, named Jade Button, had just given birth. Li Lien-ying listed the information about the event. There had been only one puppy, a female that was yellow in color except for a single white spot in the center of its forehead. The interpretation of this event was made clear to her. The significance was that a female would stand alone. The yellow indicated that this female would represent China, presumably as empress. The centered white spot deviated neither to the east or west, suggesting that China should stay on its current course rather than seeking to be more like the Western nations. Furthermore, it was pointed out to her that the number one (as in the litter of only one puppy) had another meaning, that of "guaranteed" or "assured." Taken together, she interpreted these portents from the kennel as prophesying that she would succeed in her coup, would successfully take over the government of China as its sole ruler, and should stop the attempted social and government reforms.

When she learned that Kuang Hsu was going to try to strip her of all of her power, Tzu Hsi moved quickly to set her plans in motion. As it happened, the commander of the garrison was still Jung Lu, the true love of her youth and always her faithful ally. Together they arranged to have the emperor's palace guard replaced by Jung Lu's men. This permitted Tzu Hsi to return to the palace in the Forbidden City without opposition, and it also allowed her and a small contingent of the guard to storm directly into the emperor's private quarters. It is reported that Kuang Hsu was so terrified by the sight of his former regent that he threw himself on the ground and said, in front of all gathered there, "I am unworthy to rule." Tzu Hsi accepted that statement as his voluntary relinquishment of power. She next had him effectively imprisoned in a palace built in the middle of an artificial lake in the Forbidden City. There he was kept totally isolated from the rest of the court. His servants were put to death, and his supporters were either killed or banished. He was allowed to see no one except four guards and his wife (who was Tzu Hsi's spy), and on rare occasions the empress herself. He was only allowed off the island to perform the ceremonies prescribed by the Book of Rites. Thus Tzu Hsi began her third regency, if you can use the word regency for assuming the full rights of government. One of her first acts was to rescind the emperor's modernizing decrees.

Soon after Tzu Hsi's restoration to power, a violent era began in China that involved a secret society called *I Ho Ch'uan,* which means the "Righteous and Harmonious Fists." Its members practiced a form of martial arts that they thought made them immune to wounds, including those from bullets. Because of the nature of their ritual fighting, they came to be known in English as Boxers. Originally they were mostly seen as an association of athletes and acrobats, and later as bandits.

At that point in time, there was a lot of pressure on traditional Chinese culture. Although Kuang Hsu's attempt to westernize the nation had been stopped by the empress, Americans, English, Japanese, Russians, and others were flooding into China in greater numbers than ever before. Many of these were opportunistic businessmen looking for economic gains, or missionaries who had come to convert the Chinese to Christianity. These foreigners were exposing the Chinese population to the same influences and cultural pressures that the imprisoned emperor had tried to introduce. General Tung Fu-hsiang, the leader of the Boxers, saw a political opportunity in this. He took advantage of the fact that so many of the Chinese people saw these foreigners as a threat to their traditional way of life. He began to recruit those members of the population who were most unhappy with Western influences into the Boxer society, where they were taught military tactics and their hatred of foreigners was cultivated. All that he needed next was imperial approval to rid the nation of the "foreign devils."

Within the Forbidden City, Prince Tuan and his brother, the Duke Lan, represented the Boxers. On the day that these two were to have an audience in which they would request support for the Boxer movement from the empress, she was experiencing grave concerns. She did not know the strength of the forces that the foreigners might be able to muster against her nation, and worried about the efficiency of the Boxer army, with its many partially trained and poorly armed peasants.

On the morning of the scheduled audience with Prince Tuan, the chief eunuch Li Lien-ying came to Tzu Hsi to tell her that another one of her favorite dogs, this one named Flowery-Duck, had given birth to a litter of three puppies. The first one born was red, the second yellow, and the third was also red. Each one had a white spot on its forehead. This was a most fortunate omen. Red is the color of joy and success, and yellow is the color for China, so the sign was interpreted as prophesying that the country and her regime would be surrounded by success. Three is the number of life, so the size of the litter suggested that any decisions made this day would cause the Chinese culture to live on for a long time. The fact that each dog had the white "Eye of Buddha" mark on its head indicated that endeavors started that morning would be blessed. Thus when Prince Tuan presented his request for imperial support for the Boxers, he was met with great optimism and acceptance.

The Boxer Rebellion did seem to be successful at first. The Boxers went rampaging through northeast China, killing foreigners and many Chinese who had converted to Christianity, and they gained resources by seizing the property of their victims and destroying anything that might provide aid to their enemies. However, the international powers whose citizens were under attack soon retaliated. A combined force of American, British, French, German, Japanese, and Russian troops marched on Peking to stop the Boxers from burning churches and murdering Christians. When imperial troops were ordered into action by the empress to save the city, the Western coalition seized several Chinese forts along the coast. Tzu Hsi was furious at this and ordered that all of the foreigners in China should be put to death. At the command of the empress a force of around 140,000 Boxers, with weapons and support coming from the imperial court, attacked the main compound in Peking where diplomats and other foreigners lived. The siege lasted for eight weeks, and was broken when a well-armed and highly trained international force of 19,000 troops was sent to reinforce the allied army already in the country. In August 1900 these international forces captured Peking, broke into the Forbidden City, and looted it.

The speed with which the international forces pushed through Peking and burst into the Forbidden City took the imperial court completely by surprise. Tzu Hsi barely escaped with her life, and left disguised in the coarse blue cotton clothes of a peasant woman, with her long curling fingernails cut short to conceal her rank. But even in that moment of desperation, when the most precious treasures of the palace were being abandoned to the invaders, the Lion Dogs, which were the symbol of the greatness of the Manchu dynasty, were not forgotten. Her favorites were carried off in the first few palanquins that left the city.

However there was neither the time nor enough vehicles and personnel to save them all, so rather than having these sacred dogs fall into the hands of the profane foreigners Tzu Hsi ordered that none of the remaining dogs be left alive. Most succumbed to the fate of her enemies and rivals, and were thrown down a well in the palace courtyard, while others were bludgeoned to death wherever they were found.

In an isolated back room, one of Tzu Hsi's aunts was waiting for transportation out of the palace with the last five of the surviving Pekingese dogs. In the chaos of the invasion, it appears that she had been forgotten. Suddenly the French and English troops burst in. Rather than be taken prisoner she committed suicide, and thus the first living specimens of the Lion Dogs fell into Western hands. All of these would end up in the possession of the British aristocrats.

Captain Hart Dunne gave the smallest of the five surviving Pekingese to Queen Victoria. He included a letter with the gift, saying, "It should be treated as a pet, not a curiosity." However, to the Queen it was just another item, along with a vast amount of jewelry, rich textiles, and works of art that had been taken from the imperial palace. In fact, she even named the dog "Lootie," because it was clearly part of the loot that she had been sent from the Orient. Victoria was really not very interested in Lootie, since at the time she was breeding her own line of small companion dogs (Pomeranians) at Windsor Castle, and the remainder of her kennels at Buckingham Palace were full of large hunting dogs. Unfortunately, when Captain Dunne went to check up on Lootie's well-being he found her at Buckingham Palace, barely holding her own against the large hounds and active terriers that filled the compound. The kennel keeper explained to him, "Her Majesty already has a dog which remains in her room." Dunne was distressed and sadly said, "I only hoped that it would be made more or less a pet of the royal family. . . . If it is not made much of, it will die." The kennel keeper could not change the royal family's feelings for the dog, but took compassion upon the small beast. She received some special care from him and ultimately did live for another eleven years.

Of the other four survivors, one was kept by Admiral Lord John Hay; another was given to his sister, the duchess of Wellington; and the last two were given to the duchess of Richmond. A few years later, two more were smuggled out of China concealed in a crate marked "Japanese Deer." These few dogs were to form the basis for the line Pekingese dogs in the West, augmented much later by a few gifts from the palace.

Meanwhile, the empress and her party fled north to the city of Sian. Ultimately she had to sign a humiliating settlement, called the Peace of Peking, that levied heavy fines on China, imposed amended trade treaties that favored foreign interests, and allowed international troops to be stationed in Peking. Tzu Hsi was enraged at the outcome of the Boxer Rebellion and the subsequent treaty. She blamed those around her, and many officials, advisors, and members of the royal court were exiled, decapitated, or "allowed" to commit suicide. One wonders if one of these was the priest or spiritualist who interpreted the significance of Flowery-Duck's litter as an indication that the Boxers would be successful.

Under the terms of the treaty, Tzu Hsi returned to the Forbidden City. Her political policies changed radically, so that she now favored reforms. Railroads would be built, there would be modern schools, the legal system would be changed so that many of the more severe penalties for minor infractions would be eliminated, smoking of opium would be restricted, and many Western cultural and technological innovations would be adopted. She even moderated the rules pertaining to her Lion Dogs. Although still a rarity and not to be owned by commoners, she did allow the export of a few as gifts to highly placed Westerners. From her personal kennel she offered a Pekingese to Alice Roosevelt, the daughter of the American President Theodore Roosevelt, and another to the banker and financier J. P. Morgan. These dogs were admitted into the National Breeders Registry in 1906 and formed the foundation of the American bloodlines for this breed.

Despite the failure of the prophesy based upon her dog's litter, and the decimation of the breeding stock in the imperial kennels in the aftermath of the Boxer Rebellion, Tzu Hsi still maintained a number of Lion Dogs and still gave them sacred status. This reverence would be diminished during the short reign of her designated successor, Pu Yi, and the Lion Dogs would become virtually extinct in China after the Communists took control of the nation. Such dogs were not to be allowed to live, since they were seen as symbols of the decadent and corrupt aristocracy that the Communists had overthrown. Because of this strange twist of fate, this means that the Pekingese breed of dogs actually owes its survival to the raid on the imperial palace and the subsequent dispersal of survivors to the West.

When Tzu Hsi died, her funeral was a rich and colorful spectacle. There were her pallbearers in red robes, the Buddhist priests in yellow robes, and the royal court in white robes trimmed in silver and gold. In front of the imperial bier marched the chief eunuch, Li Lien-ying, now old and weary. In his arms he carried the empress's last favorite dog, Moo-tan (which means Peony), a yellow and white Pekingese with a white spot on its forehead. The priests had assured the aged empress that this color and pattern combination represented the spiritual purity of China.

The fact that Moo-tan was there conformed to a precedent that had been set nine hundred years earlier on the death of the emperor T'ai Tsung of the Sung dynasty, when his little Lion Dog T'ao Hua ("Peach Flower") had followed that Son of Heaven to his last resting place and died of grief at the entrance to the imperial tomb. The next emperor, Chen Tsung, had issued a decree ordering the little dog's body to be wrapped in the cloth of an imperial umbrella and buried alongside its master. Tradition has it that Tzu Hsi's dog was also supposed to have died of grief, but some say that Moo-tan was smuggled away during the interment and sold by one of the eunuchs.

Tzu Hsi, however, with her attention to detail and her sense of organization, order, and symbolism, left a poem that she wrote about the nature and care of the Lion Dog. It appears on a document modestly headed "Pearls Dropped from the Lips of her Imperial Majesty Tzu Hsi":

Let the Lion Dog be small;
Let it wear the swelling cape of dignity around its neck;
Let it display the billowing standard of pomp in a tail held high above its back.

Let its face be black;
Let its forefront be shaggy;
Let its forehead be straight and low, like unto the brow of a Boxer.

Let its eyes be large and luminous;
Let its ears be set like the sails of a war-junk;
Let its nose be like that of the monkey god of the Hindus.

Let its forelegs be bent;
So that it shall not desire to wander far, nor leave its Imperial home.

Let its body be shaped like a hunting lion, that stalks its prey.

Let its feet be tufted with plentiful hair
That its footfall may be soundless,
And for its standard of pomp
Let its tail rival the whisk of the Tibetan Yak,
Which is flourished to protect the imperial litter from flying insects.

For its color,
Let it be that of the lion—a golden sable,
     to be carried in the sleeve of a yellow robe;
Or the color of a red bear,
Or a black and white bear,
Or striped like a dragon,
So that there may be dogs appropriate to every costume in the Imperial wardrobe
And whose fitness to appear at public ceremonies shall be judged by their color
     and their artistic contrast with the Imperial robes.

Let it be lively that it may afford entertainment by its gambols;
Let it be timid that it may not involve itself in danger;
Let it be domestic in its habits that it may live in amity with the other beasts,
     fishes, or birds that find protection in the Imperial Palace.

Let it venerate its ancestors
And deposit offerings in the canine cemetery of the Forbidden City on each new
     moon.

Let it be taught to refrain from gadding about;
Let it come to know how to comport itself with the dignity of a Duchess;
Let it learn to bite the foreign devils instantly.

Let it wash its face like a cat with its paws;
Let it be dainty with its food so that it shall be known as an Imperial dog by its
     fastidiousness.

Sharks' fins and curlews' livers and the breasts of quails,
On these may it be fed;
And for drink give it the tea that is brewed from the spring buds of the shrub
that grows in the province of Hankow,
Or the milk of the antelopes that pasture in the Imperial parks.

Thus shall it preserve its integrity and self-respect;
And for the day of sickness
Let it be anointed with the clarified fat of the leg of a sacred leopard,
And give it to drink an eggshell from a song thrush
Full of the juice of the custard apple in which has been dissolved three pinches of
shredded rhinoceros horn,
And apply to it piebald leeches.

So shall it remain.
But if it dies,
Remember, thou too art mortal.

CHAPTER SEVENTEEN

THE INDIAN
FIGHTER'S DOGS

THROUGHOUT HISTORY, generals and other leaders in times of war have often sought comfort in the companionship of a dog. In World War II alone, we find the great tank commander General George S. Patton seeking companionship from his bull terrier, Willie, while on the German side armored division commander Erwin Rommel was finding solace in the company of his bevy of dachshunds. Another American, General Omar Bradley, was accompanied through his military activities by his poodle, Beau, and the allied commander in chief, General Dwight D. Eisenhower, found social support provided by two Scottish terriers. The companionship of dogs is not just sought by those who fight on the ground, since in that same war General Claire Chennault of the U.S. Air Force eased his mind with the company of his dachshund, Joe, while on the sea Admiral Frederick Sherman fought the battle of the Coral Sea on the aircraft carrier Lexington with his cocker spaniel, Admiral Wags, beside him. The comfort that men engaged in war derive from dogs is so well recognized that it has become part of our mythology. Thus tradition has it that before his last great battle, King Arthur sat quietly stroking his great hound, Cavall, while another knight of the round table, Sir Tristram, drew strength and courage from his gallant greyhound, Hodain. Such would also be the case in the true life history of the youngest general in the history of the United States.

There are, perhaps, two images that are most likely to spring to mind if one speaks about America's "wild west" period of history. The first is Hollywood's classic and clichéd showdown scene, with the bad guy (dressed in black, of course) standing in the street facing the heroic marshal moments before their climactic gunfight. The second is a group of blue uniformed cavalry soldiers, standing in a tight group, with pistols blazing at the hoards of whooping Indians that now surround them, and will soon overwhelm their outnumbered forces. This last image comes from one of the most publicized and controversial incidents in American history, which has come to be known as Custer's Last Stand.

Perhaps more has been written about George Armstrong Custer than virtually any other American of that era except Abraham Lincoln. When I scan the catalogs of several libraries, it also appears that there may be more books written about Custer's final battle at the Little Big Horn than about the battle of Gettysburg, which probably determined the final outcome of the U.S. Civil War. Our dramatic image is based upon the fact that on June 25, 1876, a total of 263 men of the U.S. Seventh Cavalry died. They were overpowered by the combined force of several Indian tribes who amassed a force of more than two thousand warriors. Among the casualties were 210 men under the direct command of Custer, plus Custer himself and, according to reliable reports, one tall dog. That a dog should fall beside Custer in his final moments should not be surprising; indeed, perhaps the real surprise is that only one dog was with him at the last.

Although Custer would almost become synonymous with the history of the western United States, he was actually born in New Rumley, Ohio, in 1839. His father, Emanuel, owned a blacksmith shop and also served as the local justice of the peace, while his mother, Maria, was the daughter of the town's tavern keeper. Custer had a happy childhood, and he enjoyed the company of a several dogs that were used for hunting or simply companionship. As a young boy, he already showed a fondness for dogs and an ability to select and train good working hounds.

The one unhappy aspect of Custer's early life was his schooling. He was a poor student and hated doing his homework. He bored easily, and therefore he filled his time with practical jokes and pranks that often got him in trouble. His father responded to his poor performance and troublesome antics by taking him out of school and apprenticing him to a furniture maker, an endeavor that was as unsuccessful as his school career. His mother then came up with the idea of sending Custer to Michigan to live with his stepsister, Lydia Ann Reed, who was

Maria's daughter by her first marriage. Lydia was a teacher, and was well organized and gentle. She taught Custer at home and then sent him back to New Rumley three years later with a reformed set of attitudes and priorities. He was now able to continue his education and did well enough to earn a teaching certificate.

Custer's first and only posting as a teacher was at the age of sixteen in Cadiz, a town just a few miles from his family home. This job would only last for a year. During that time he became involved with the school superintendent's teenage daughter. The girl's father, Alexander Holland, was not pleased with this liaison. However, Holland thought that there might be a way to end this relationship without having a heated confrontation with his daughter. He had learned that Custer's real desire was to become an army officer, and that the young man had already applied for an appointment to the U.S. Military Academy at West Point. Unfortunately for Custer, at that time most of these appointments were given as political patronage, and the Custers were Democrats while the current president, Abraham Lincoln, was a Republican. Holland had enough local political influence, however, to persuade a Republican congressman to write to Jefferson Davis, the former Secretary of War, in support of Custer's nomination. Within a few months, Custer received his appointment to the academy and left Ohio (and Holland's daughter) for New York and West Point.

If everything had gone normally, Custer would have graduated from West Point in 1862. Unfortunately, the Civil War broke out in April 1861, and since the government was short of officers, Custer's class was allowed to graduate one year early, just two months after the war started. His class was originally composed of sixty-eight members, but only thirty-four would graduate with their commissions. Of the other thirty-four, more than half resigned prior to commencement to fight for the Confederate States of America. Of the remainder, most had only entered the academy to further their political careers and so opted to return to civilian life rather than risk their lives in actual combat. Custer was a poor student, and graduated with the lowest ranking in his class. (It is interesting to note that his best subject in the academy was artillery tactics, while his worst subject was cavalry tactics!)

Despite his poor showing in the subject, Custer was appointed an officer in the cavalry. During the four years of the Civil War, he would fight in nearly all of the major battles of the conflict. He had only had his commission for two weeks when he was thrown into the battle at Manassas (the first Battle of Bull

Run)—first as a courier, and then with the cavalry standing guard at the Union flank. It was there that the Confederate troops under General Thomas J. Jackson, standing like a "stone wall," managed to stop the Union's push into Virginia. The undisciplined Union volunteers, with their young and untested officers, were forced to flee the field, and only the similar inexperience of the Confederate troops prevented an effective pursuit that might have seen them take the capital, Washington, D.C. A short time later, Custer's expertise at reconnaissance won him the attention of the Union commander General George McClellan, who gave him a position on his staff at the rank of captain. Next, under the command of General Joseph Hooker, Custer served at the second Battle of Bull Run, at Antietam, and also at Gettysburg. During the peninsular campaign, Custer distinguished himself by leading the cavalry in several courageous raids behind enemy lines.

McClellan learned of Custer's exploits and was impressed. He promoted Custer to the temporary rank of brigadier general and assigned him to General Philip Henry Sheridan. At the age of twenty-three years, Custer was the youngest man ever to be promoted to the rank of general in the U.S. Army—a record that remains unbroken to this day. He celebrated his promotion by buying a horse and a dog. This would become a familiar pattern for him; whenever things were going well and the resources were available, he would add another dog to his troop of companions. At the same time Custer also hired a freed slave named Eliza to be his cook, and a young masterless black boy named Johnny Cisco to take care of his personal needs and tend to the dog. Cisco's duties would grow steadily as the size of Custer's dog pack grew larger.

Sheridan found in Custer the bravery and energy of command that he needed. He recognized that Custer was not much of a tactician, but he was the perfect weapon if presented with appropriate opportunities. Although Custer could show sensitivity, warmth and compassion, he could also be cruel and remorseless if his orders, or a specific situation, seemed to require it. The harder side of his nature often showed in the harsh discipline that he demanded of his troops, and the brutal way in which he treated captured Confederate guerrilla raiders. Sheridan knew that this kind of steel will would be needed. He also knew the downside of Custer's personality—namely, that he tended to act impulsively without assessing all of the information available. This characteristic could lead to disasters, but more often it led to quick responses in the chaotic and changing situations associated with combat, allowing brief opportunities to be seized and unexpected victories to be won. Therefore he promoted Custer to the temporary rank of major general and gave him command of the Michigan brigade.

Custer served with Sheridan for the rest of the war, fighting at Chickamauga and Missionary Ridge. His only respite from the war was a short time when he returned to his sister's home in Monroe, Michigan, where he courted and married Elizabeth Bacon. He moved Libbie (as she would come to be known) to Washington to be closer to him while he traveled south with Sheridan's army. His first gift to Libbie after she arrived was a dog to keep her company. It was a large hunting hound, not the small companion dog that a lady of the time might be expected to keep, but Custer did not seem to notice the incongruity, and Libbie didn't seem to mind.

During the wilderness campaign, Custer distinguished himself several times. For example, he led a notable raid that destroyed communications and supplies behind the Confederate lines, greatly weakening the position of General Robert E. Lee's forces. Custer seemed to have incredible luck that often saved him from disastrous consequences of his rash actions. A poorly planned raid at Yellow Tavern cost his brigade many casualties, but it also resulted in the mortal wounding and capture of J.E.B. Stuart, the Confederacy's most brilliant cavalry general.

During the Shenandoah Valley campaign, Sheridan relied heavily upon Custer for help in his scorched-earth tactics, in which he systematically confiscated everything that might be useful as supplies for the South's armies. Anything that could not be immediately used by the Union troops—such as crops, livestock, or entire towns—was burned or otherwise destroyed. It took hardened officers to lay this whole region to waste, since, in addition to denying needed supplies for the Confederate army, it also caused starvation and pain to the civilian population. Custer did his part well and was congratulated by Sheridan, who noted when they were through that "even a crow flying over the Shenandoah will have to take his rations with him."

Toward the end of the Civil War, General Robert E. Lee and the Army of Virginia were in full flight. Lee knew, however, that if he could escape to the south the war could continue for a while, permitting a negotiated settlement that would be more favorable for the Confederacy. Sheridan was in hot pursuit. He sent Custer forward and in a daring but risky confrontation, the young cavalry officer destroyed the last major body of Confederate resistance by defeating General Jubal A. Early at Waynesboro. Sheridan then sent Custer ahead to destroy Confederate communications. Custer's subsequent raids cut off the ability of the various Confederate forces to exchange information, and that success greatly facilitated the Union victory over the weakened Southern army at Five Forks.

The war would end with another of Custer's impulsive actions. Lee was gathering his troops and equipment in order to effect an orderly retreat to the south. Custer, serving as the vanguard of the Union army, stormed forward, bypassing Lee's position at Appomattox by a mile or so. This allowed him to seize the railroad equipment that Lee needed for his escape. Custer then tore up the tracks and commandeered the supplies and weapons that had already been loaded onto the trains. This effectively blocked Lee's retreat, and he was left with no alternative other than to surrender.

Sheridan was so impressed by Custer's gallantry throughout the war that he purchased the table that Lee used to sign the surrender, then presented it as a gift to Custer and his new wife. Sheridan would remain a staunch supporter of Custer for the rest of his career, and on more than one occasion would get him out of the trouble that the young general's rashness got him into.

At the end of the war, Custer's permanent rank reverted to lieutenant colonel, and he was assigned to duty in Louisiana. However, officials in Washington were concerned about a possible threat to Texas from Maximilian's regime in Mexico. Although open-range cattle ranching had become economically important prior to the Civil War, cotton was still the chief crop in Texas. The cotton plantation owners had strong slaveholding interests and their influence put the state into the Confederacy, despite the opposition of Sam Houston and his followers. During the Civil War, Texas was the only Confederate state that was not overrun by Union troops. Because of this it remained relatively prosperous, and it liberally contributed men and provisions to the Southern cause. At the end of the war, the new state government that had virtually been imposed by the victorious Union was not popular. This seemed like an opportune time for Mexico to try to reassert its sovereignty over the state.

Sheridan gave orders for Custer to move his force of forty-five hundred cavalry troops from Hempstead, Louisiana, to Austin, the capital of Texas. He took his entire family with him, which at that time consisted of Libbie and eight dogs.

Texas would change the intensity of Custer's association with dogs forever. Despite the fact that the former supporters of the Confederacy viewed him as the head of an army of occupation, Custer and Libbie were well liked. Custer's sense of discipline and justice were well known and were needed. Many former slave owners and Southern sympathizers had become violent and vindictive, threatening anyone who seemed to be loyal to the Union or who cooperated with the new state government. The presence of federal troops helped to keep the discord in check and prevented an escalation of the level of force and bloodshed. Many financially secure planters—such as Leonard Groce, who owned the Liendo Plantation near Clear Creek—therefore welcomed the Custers as a stabilizing influence.

It was Groce and his friends who introduced Custer to the pleasures of owning and breeding purebred hunting dogs. Many of the dogs owned by these wealthy families had been imported from Europe. There were a large number of sight-hounds, including greyhounds and Irish wolfhounds, and also a number of scent-hounds, including beagles, harriers, and bloodhounds. However, Custer developed a particular fondness for Scottish deerhounds (which were often referred to locally as staghounds or English greyhounds) and for the traditional foxhounds. He quickly purchased some breeding stock of both of these varieties of hounds.

Custer would not stay long in Texas. The southern Cheyenne Indians had begun to attack white settlers, and Custer was ordered to the Midwest to defend the citizens who were threatened. He brought Libbie and the dogs with him again; she and their canine family would go with Custer on a number of campaign treks. They arrived in Kansas by train, and Libbie described the scene that would be repeated a number of times at different cities and forts.

> The other ladies of the regiment went on to the hotel in the town. The general suggested that I should go with them, but I had been in camp so many summers it was not a formidable matter for me to remain, and fortunately for what followed I did so. The household belongings were gathered together. A family of little new puppies, some half-grown dogs, the cages of mockingbirds and canaries, were all corraled safely in a little stockade made of chests and trunks, and we set ourselves about making a temporary home.

The picture of Elizabeth Custer trying to make a temporary home with the puppies and small dogs, while her husband went off with the adult dogs, would become commonplace during the Indian wars. If the threat of conflict was imminent, Libbie would be asked to set up housekeeping in officers' quarters in a not-too-distant fort, and so she was often in residence at Fort Leavenworth or Fort Riley in Kansas. Custer would see her whenever it was possible, and once he was even suspended from duty for "abandoning his command in Fort Wallace" in order to visit Libbie at Fort Riley. Sheridan, however, felt that the charges were motivated by political considerations and personal dislike of Custer, and so had him reinstated.

Custer's court-martial may suggest one reason why the dogs had become so important in his life—he did not have very many close friends in the Seventh Cavalry. This was mostly because he tended to be such a strict disciplinarian. He frequently punished both enlisted men and officers for minor infractions. Penalties were often quite harsh; Custer had a deserter executed, and a fellow officer convicted of mutiny. Some historians have claimed that during the campaign in which Custer gained his reputation as an Indian fighter, the desertion rate within the Seventh Cavalry was double that of any other unit on the frontier due to his harsh discipline. More charitable historians have pointed out that the nature of enlisted men changed drastically following the Civil War, and that Custer simply failed to differentiate between wartime and peacetime soldiers. They also suggest that about half of all enlisted troops were Irish and German immigrants who joined the military only to get fast and guaranteed citizenship. In any event, his men often grumbled about their commander and ridiculed his behavioral quirks and unique style of dress.

With few close and intimate friends, and his wife often a long distance away, Custer filled his need for companionship and social interactions with his dogs. This must have been a very large need, because he required a very large pack of dogs to meet it. Libbie describes a typical scenario:

> The pack of hounds were an endless source of delight to the general. We had about forty: the stag-hounds that run by sight, and are on the whole the fleetest and most enduring dogs in the world, and the fox-hounds that follow the trail with their noses close to the ground. The first rarely bark, but the latter are very noisy. The general and I used to listen with amusement to their attempts to strike the keynote of the bugler when he sounded the calls summoning the men to guard mount, stables, or retreat. It rather destroyed the military effect to see, beside his soldierly figure, a hound sitting down absorbed in imitation.

Despite Custer's strict requirements for discipline and the maintenance of respect and military decorum, the hound whose head was tilted back while it bayed its version of the bugle call was never corrected or chastised. Instead, the Indian fighter simply laughed heartily and then went about his business.

Although Custer had difficulty relaxing around his troops or with his fellow officers, he felt completely at home with his dogs. He would often be seen walking across the encampment with his dogs swirling around him. One soldier described the situation, saying, "I think that he talked to his dogs all the time. I often saw his lips moving as that herd of dogs ran with him across the campground, but the noise that they made made it impossible for me to hear what he was saying. Sometimes he would stop and just stand there, looking at the dogs and smiling. At those times he looked like a human island in a roiling sea of hounds."

Long hours and the constant pressure of command often fatigued Custer. The time that he had to sleep at night was frequently limited, but even in his slumber he would include the dogs. Libbie described what typically happened if he took a few hours off.

The next thing was to throw himself down on the sod, cover his eyes with his white felt hat, and be sound asleep in no time. No matter if the sun beat down in a perfect blaze, it never disturbed him. The dogs came at once to lie beside him. I have seen them stretched at his back and curled around his head, while the nose and paws of one rested on his breast. And yet he was quite unconscious of their crowding. They growled and scrambled for the best place, but he slept placidly through it all.

Some of the dogs slept in his bedroom each night as well, and from his description of them one is left wondering whether another psychological function of the dogs was to provide an outlet for his otherwise-denied parental impulses. His favorite dog was a sandy-colored staghound named Tuck. He referred to her as resembling "a well-cared for and half-spoiled child, who can never be induced to retire until it has been fondled to sleep in its mother's arms. Tuck will sleep so soundly in my lap that I can transfer her gently to the ground and she will continue her slumber, like a little baby carefully deposited in its crib." Another bit of evidence that these were his "children" comes from Libbie's description of how he reacted when a puppy was sick: "He walked the floor half the night, holding, rubbing, trying to soothe the suffering little beast" and all the while searching his book of dog medicine for a remedy.

The dogs were also a constant source of recreation. Custer had hunted with dogs since he was a schoolboy. For him, the joy of riding a horse at full speed behind some coursing hounds in pursuit of some game was the height of excited happiness. Many of his letters sing the praises of the exploits of his favorite dogs, such as the greyhounds Blucher, Swift, and Byron and the Scottish deerhounds Tuck, Cardigan, and Lady.

Unfortunately, hunting behind these swift dogs was often dangerous for a lone man. For instance, once Custer was hunting buffalo with his dogs. The dogs were doing their job and harrying the animal so that Custer was able to draw quite close. He pulled out his gun, and just then the great beast swerved. The gun went off and he toppled to the ground, having just accidentally shot his own horse. Not only was Custer now on foot, but also he had ridden so far that he was also stranded in hostile territory. Fortunately, spotting some dust being raised in the distance, he guessed that it was most likely a patrol from the Seventh Cavalry. He confidently sent both Blucher and Byron in that direction. The dogs went straight out on command, and were recognized by the soldiers, who followed them back and managed to rescue their commander.

On another hunt, the dogs pursued their quarry quite a distance from the encampment, and suddenly Custer found himself surrounded by Indians. It could have all ended there, except that by some stroke of luck it turned out to be a delegation coming to the camp to negotiate with him. The Indians simply presumed that Custer had come out to meet them, accompanied only by his dogs, in order to impress them with his bravery. They all rode back to the cavalry camp together, impressing Custer's soldiers with their commander's bravery as well. This incident so worried Libbie that she began to insist that he stay close to the camp until hostilities were over.

The hostilities, however, were escalating. In 1874 the U.S. government sent Custer on an expedition to investigate rumors of gold deposits in the Black Hills of South Dakota. The region had been recognized by treaty as the sacred hunting ground of the Indians, primarily the Sioux and Cheyenne, and this was a clear violation of that agreement. However, nothing seemed able to stop the gold rush from starting. The political pressures were on the government to protect U.S. citizens and to allow them to profit from any resources, rather than to honor any treaties with "savages." It is not surprising that the Sioux and

Cheyenne Indians felt betrayed and responded aggressively. There were a number of skirmishes, and the issue was still unresolved when Custer was recalled to join a larger effort. Hoping to remove the Indians from the region or at least isolate them, the government issued a directive that all Indians who had not moved onto reservations by the end of January 1876 would be deemed hostile. This led to a number of minor encounters during the early part of the year, but no major battles were fought, since the usual practice of the tribes when confronted with charging cavalry was simply to outrun them and thus escape with few losses.

A comprehensive campaign against the Sioux was then planned for the spring of 1876. Custer's regiment was assigned to commanding general Alfred H. Terry and marched from Bismarck, South Dakota, to the Yellowstone River. At the mouth of the Rosebud Creek, Terry sent Custer forward to locate the enemy while he marched on to join the column under General John Gibbon. Custer, however, advanced much more quickly than he had been ordered to do, and neared what he thought was a large Indian village.

Historians continue to argue about Custer's motives and tactics. Some maintain that his attack on a huge Indian encampment of between seven to ten thousand people—of which as many as two to three thousand were warriors—was simply an attempt to increase his own fame and glory, perhaps as a way to further his political ambitions. Others say that it was an act of arrogance, since Custer seemed to have little respect for Indian warriors and was often quoted as saying that three Indians to one cavalry trooper still represented very favorable odds. According to them, this defeat was just another example of the reckless actions that had characterized his command during the Civil War.

Still other historians note that it was difficult for Custer to fully appreciate the size of the force that he was confronting, since many of the Indians were concealed in ravines a short distance from the main encampment. These scholars suggest that Custer was afraid that the Indians would flee, as they had done so often before, when faced with a military confrontation. In Custer's mind, the idea that the army had come this far west to round up "renegade" Indians, only to have them escape at the last minute, would mean that he had failed in his mission. Not knowing where the support troops were, and having underestimated the number of Indians that he would have to face, he simply did what he felt was needed to save the expedition. The final evidence that he did not realize the overwhelming numerical superiority of the enemy is that he then divided his regiment into three parts, sending two of them (under Major Marcus A. Reno and

Captain Frederick W. Benteen) to attack farther upstream. He himself kept only 210 men to lead the direct charge that he thought would send the Indians into flight.

It was Custer's custom to have his dogs with him at all times, except when battle was almost certain. At the times when the dogs were not with Custer or Libbie, they were assigned to the care of a soldier named James H. Kelly, whose major duties with the Seventh Cavalry seem to have revolved around the welfare of Custer's dogs. Custer was even more careful about his dogs in 1876, since earlier that year one of his greyhounds, Blucher, had been killed during a hostile encounter with the Sioux Indians. For this reason, the night before the battle at the Little Big Horn, Custer sent Kelly away with his dogs. (Kelly would later become the mayor of Dodge City, Kansas, as well as the owner of a saloon there. It is said that his dogs had a free run of the town, and that his greyhounds and staghounds were frequently underfoot. Kelly would often claim that some of the dogs actually were Custer's, and had been given to him by Libbie since they appeared to be so fond of him.)

For some reason, Custer decided to keep one dog, Tuck, with him on that fateful day. The rest of the story is only known through the often contradictory and personalized reports of the survivors, all of whom were members of the Lakota, Cheyenne, Arapaho, and Sioux tribes who fought on that day. The consensus is that the Indians were relatively unprepared for a midday attack, counting on the cavalry tradition of attacking at dawn. The advance force of the charge was stopped at the river ford, and the survivors retreated to a low hill to hold out until the expected arrival of the forces under Reno and Benteen. Reno was in retreat, however, while Benteen adopted a defensive position and did nothing. Most accounts say that the troops maintained discipline and fought on through the hopeless battle that followed. Some Indians reported that they could see Custer issuing commands and firing at the surrounding mass of warriors. Others claimed that Custer was easy to find among the group of soldiers because of the tall, light-colored dog that stood beside him until a few moments before the end.

The final fight lasted only twenty minutes, and it left the entire company of 210 men (and one dog) dead. None had made it across the river. It was not until the next day, when General Terry's forces arrived, that the extent of the tragedy became known. All of the men were buried on the battlefield except for Custer, whose remains were reinterred at West Point. The national monument in Montana lists the names of everyone who died and tries to mark where each man fell. Turk, the Scottish deerhound, is not listed, nor is her grave marked.

On the day before the battle, George Armstrong Custer wrote a letter to his wife, Libbie. That letter would be sent with a scout who was leaving at the same time that James Kelly left camp to take the dogs to safety. Part of the letter read as follows:"Tuck regularly comes when I am writing, and lays her head on the desk, rooting up my hand with her long nose until I consent to stop and notice her. She and Swift, Lady, and Kaiser still sleep in my tent. You need not be anxious about my leaving the column with small escorts; I scarcely hunt any more."

CHAPTER EIGHTEEN

THE VIRGINIA
FARMER'S FOXHOUNDS

EORGE WASHINGTON, the commanding general of the Continental army and later the first president of the United States, had a lifelong association with dogs. His major concern with them had to do with fox-hunting, which was one of his great delights and passions. During his years in Virginia he would ride out with his dogs to hunt foxes at least once every week, and sometimes two or three times. He would ultimately bring a new breed of dog into the world, and in turn, his dogs would make it easier for him to become the leader of the new nation that emerged from the American Revolution.

Washington had spent his early years on his family's estate at Pope's Creek, Virginia, and then later on the plantation of his half brother at Mount Vernon on the Potomac River. Although his early education included the study of such subjects as mathematics, surveying, and the literary, historical, and political classics, he also was learning the basics of farming and animal husbandry. So it is not surprising to find that he used his knowledge of animal care to create a "perfect pack of hunting hounds." Robert Brooke of Maryland had introduced English foxhounds into America in 1650, and since that time American breeders had been "adjusting" the breed by mixing in various proportions of different Irish, English, and German hounds to improve these hunting dogs. For Washington, the breeding of dogs became both a hobby and a passion, and his diaries are filled with painstakingly detailed accounts of his careful crossing and mating of dogs, with a detailed evaluation of each resulting litter. His first true success involved the development of the black and tan "Virginia hounds" that became the special breed of his Mount Vernon kennels. The Virginia hounds were good general-purpose hunters, but had a special penchant for hunting foxes. This breed has now disappeared from the scene, but it was one the foundation breeds for the black and tan coonhounds of today, which represent the crossing of Virginia hounds with the bloodhound and a dash of Irish kerry beagle. It was also the starting point for Washington's most successful breeding experiments, which would not be completed until after the revolutionary war.

Washington's attitudes toward his hounds went well beyond the feelings that farmers typically had for working animals. This can be detected in the names that he gave them, including Sweet Lips, Venus, Music, Lady, and Truelove. (These shared a kennel with dogs named Taster, Tipsy, Tippler, and Drunkard, but we don't have time for a psychological analysis of another one of Washington's loves that may be indicated by these names.) His passion for foxhunting resulted in the strengthening of his political fortunes, but also in the complication of his personal life.

Washington gained his first notoriety through his service in the French and Indian Wars. The death of Washington's half-brother, Lawrence, left open the latter's post as adjutant in the Virginia militia. This post was a full-time position, and brought with it the rank and salary of a major. In addition to some command responsibility there were extensive administrative and organization tasks, such as the inspection, mustering, and regulation of various militia companies. Even though he had no military experience, Washington was confident that he could be a good adjutant, and so he applied for, and was granted the post.

Ultimately Washington was called to take a field command. He had learned that the French had every intention of taking Ohio and all of western Pennsylvania; to that end, the French had built Fort Duquesne on the site that would someday become Pittsburgh. Washington's first command was an attempt to take the fort, but he only had a small force and the effort was a failure. He got another chance at the French fort when he later returned as second in command under General Edward Braddock. During the march Washington became ill, and because of a fever he ended up riding in a covered wagon along with the advance guard. Suddenly the French and their Indian allies ambushed them near the Monongahela River. Outnumbered and in a poor tactical position, the army was facing a massacre even before Braddock was fatally wounded. Despite his illness, Washington coolly took command. Even though he was so weak that he had to use a pillow for a saddle, he seemed to be everywhere directing the action. In the end, he was credited for bringing most of his troops back safely.

At the age of only twenty-three, Washington was promoted to the rank of colonel and made the commander in chief of the Virginia militia. As such, he was responsible for defending the colonial frontier. He gained further experience and a wider reputation in 1758, when he took an active part in General John Forbes's successful campaign that finally toppled Fort Duquesne and replaced it with a new outpost, to be called Fort Pitt.

Washington now felt that he had successfully achieved the strategic objectives that Virginia required for its safety. However, he had become disenchanted with the military because of the poor treatment and lack of respect that colonial officers received from the British regular army command. Thus Colonel Washington resigned his commission and turned his attention to the quieter life of a Virginia planter. He felt little pain in doing so since he liked farming, and wrote that it is "one of the most delectable of pursuits. It is honorable, it is amusing, and, with superior judgment, it is profitable."

Immediately after he resigned his commission, Washington married Martha Dandridge Custis, a charming and wealthy young widow who was the mother of two children and had a number of political connections through her former husband and her father's family. After his marriage, Washington turned his attention toward improving his Mount Vernon plantation. He refurnished the house, put up new buildings, and experimented with new crops. He also built a rather lavish set of kennels and began breeding his Virginia hounds. Meanwhile, he engaged in foxhunting whenever he could, which was often.

Washington's contented life as a gentleman farmer was interrupted by the rising storm of anger against the oppressive nature of British regulation and taxation of the colonies. He entered politics at the urging of some influential friends and became a member of Virginia's House of Burgesses. Thus he was present in 1765 when Patrick Henry introduced his resolutions against the Stamp Act, which many consider the first official act of rebellion against the edicts of the British Crown. Less than three years later he would announce that he was willing to take his musket on his shoulder whenever his country called him. His call to his country's service would come soon, but it would be as a delegate to the Continental Congress, which was convening to organize a united opposition to Britain's colonial policies.

Congress met in Philadelphia, and Washington found the conditions quite difficult since he obviously could not mount his horse at a whim and assemble his dogs to hunt foxes through the streets of the city. However, Samuel Powel, the wealthy mayor of Philadelphia, and his lovely wife, Elizabeth Willing Powel, rescued him.

Elizabeth Powel had originally taken notice of Washington when she had been struck by his handsome elegance. She described him in flattering terms as "straight as an Indian, measuring six feet two inches in his stockings," with "penetrating eyes of blue and gray." She added, "His movements and gestures are graceful, his walk majestic, and he was walking with a tall, exceedingly graceful dog of the hound type as he strode down Walnut Street." The dog was one of Washington's favorites, Sweet Lips, whom he kept as a companion while he stayed in the city. Elizabeth, from her comments, was obviously attracted to both the look of the man and the look of the dog. However, she stopped the Virginia gentleman to comment specifically on the dog. Washington was seldom modest about his dogs, and he proudly informed her that it was a "perfect foxhound" that he himself had bred. It was Elizabeth who brought Washington to her husband's attention. Samuel recognized that this was a man with political as well as military talents, and that it might be in his own political interests to foster an association with him.

When Elizabeth had met Washington and Sweet Lips, he mentioned his disappointment at not being able to hunt while Congress was in session. Elizabeth suggested that her husband might be able to help solve that problem and invited Washington to join them for dinner at their home. It was through the Powels that Washington was offered a chance to ride to the hounds at the Gloucester Hunting Club, across the river in New Jersey. It is usually claimed that the Gloucester club was the first foxhunting club in the New World. Washington impressed everyone in the club as being a "splendid horseman," and his dogs were also deemed as being impressive because of their "stamina and sagacity."

Mayor Powel was very well connected in both the political and financial worlds, and many of his powerful friends were also members of the club. It was there that Washington met Jacob Hiltzenheimer and his associates. Hiltzenheimer would eventually become a principal military supply agent, selling wagons to the army (much the equivalent of today's tanks, trucks and transport). The men that Washington met through his visits to hunt with the club were the men who had the ability to sway the current government, and they liked this man from Virginia. He was intelligent, organized, and had a commanding presence. It also appeared that he was honest and moral, and—not to be ignored— he had a love of dogs and hunting. When Washington made a gift of some of his Virginia hounds to these men, they were pleased and appreciative. Their appreciation would turn itself into a lobbying effort that would help to win Washington the command of the Continental army and later would buy him support from members of the Electoral College, which had been established to elect the President of the United States of America.

Elizabeth, however, seemed to have some additional interests aroused by Washington. It has been suggested by some that she was somewhat of a "political groupie" who had intimate liaisons with a number of prominent politicians and military men. Consistent with this is the fact that for much of the time that he was in Philadelphia, Washington stayed in the Powels' home, even though Samuel was often away for days at a time attending to his real estate interests in New Jersey, Delaware, and central Pennsylvania. Most of the correspondence that was sent by Elizabeth to Washington was destroyed by his wife, Martha, shortly after his death. However, there is suggestive evidence that although Elizabeth had been attracted by the Virginia hound that she saw walking beside Washington on the sidewalk, she was also probably attracted to the idea of petting the Virginia delegate as well. This relationship apparently continued through the time that Washington was President. In the few surviving bits of correspondence between them there are cryptic phrases (such as "considering all that passed between us yesterday" and "in conformity with your passionate judgment") that have aroused the suspicions of some historians. They also cite the fact that at the time of this writing Martha Washington was in Virginia overseeing the plantation, while Elizabeth Powel was known to have had several overnight visits at the presidential residence. It is, of course, possible, that Elizabeth and George spent those long nights discussing foxhunting and hounds.

Through the early months of 1775, Mayor Powel and his foxhunting friends spoke to delegates and the press suggesting that, should the Continental Congress decide to raise an army, the obvious choice for commander was Washington. In June of that year, George Washington was Congress's unanimous choice as commander in chief of the Continental forces.

One of Washington's first acts was to take command of the troops surrounding Boston, where there was a British force of occupation. After he forced the British troops to retreat, he then moved to defend New York. It was here that he would encounter General William Howe, a man who would be his principal opponent during most of the American Revolutionary War.

Like Washington, Howe had earned a reputation as one of the army's most brilliant young generals during the French and Indian War. He had been sent to reinforce General Thomas Gage and fought a costly, but ultimately successful set of battles at Bunker Hill. Shortly after that, Howe replaced Gage as commander of all British troops in America.

As Washington moved into defensive positions in New York, Howe attempted to negotiate a peace—which would have effectively been a colonial surrender with a promise of clemency for the revolutionary forces. When this was rejected, Howe landed on Long Island in August 1776, captured New York City, and defeated Washington's army at White Plains. In 1777, Howe achieved a victory over Washington in the Battle of the Brandywine. After another victory at Germantown in October 1777, he took Philadelphia and established winter quarters there, with Washington's forces huddled and freezing in their winter quarters at Valley Forge, only about a day's travel away.

One of the mysteries of American history is the fact that although Howe had defeated Washington consistently, he never pressed his advantage with the brutal ferocity that the British usually employed to force their opponents to surrender. He always acted as if leniency might encourage the rebels to the peace table and cause them to lay down their arms. This attitude gave rise to rumors that he secretly sympathized with the Americans. It is just possible that this might have been true at some level. It is certainly the case that Howe's apparent softening toward his American opponents became clear shortly after the battle of Germantown, during which there was an incident involving a dog.

At that time the American troops under Washington's command were simply trying to contain Howe's forces and prevent the establishment of new outposts. During the battle of Germantown, which was not going well for the Americans, Washington was encamped at Pennibecker's Mill. On October 6, 1777, a little terrier was seen wandering the area between the American and British lines. It seemed to be foraging for food, or perhaps simply out exploring. One of the colonial soldiers rescued the dog and noticed that a plate on its collar identified its owner as General Howe. An officer then took the small fox terrier to Washington, proposing that perhaps the dog be kept as mascot: "It might raise the men's spirits to learn that we have captured the English general's own dog." This was not acceptable to Washington. He was missing the presence of his beloved Sweet Lips, who had been sent back to Mount Vernon for safety, and he understood how close the bond could be between a man and his dog. In addition, although not a hound, it was a breed of dog that was used in the final phases of foxhunting in Britain (to actually dig the fox out of its burrow), and Washington felt a certain comradeship for both dog and owner on that account.

Washington personally wiped the little dog clean, brushed his fur, and then gave him some food. He ordered a cease-fire, and under a flag of truce an American officer returned the dog to the British side of the battle line. The dog was handed over along with a note that read as follows: "General Washington's compliments to General Howe. General Washington does himself the pleasure to return to him a dog, which accidentally fell into his hands, and, by the inscription on the collar, appears to belong to General Howe."

There may well have been an additional communication of a more personal nature between the opposing leaders, since one of Howe's officers described the dog's return, saying, "The General seemed most pleased at the return of the dog. He took him upon his lap, seemingly uncaring that the mud from the dog's feet soiled his tunic. Whilst he stroked the dog he discovered a tightly folded message that had been secreted under the dog's wide collar. The General read the message, which seemed to have good effect upon him. Although I know not what it read, it is likely to have been penned by the commander of the rebellion."

It is unlikely that we will ever know what that second message may have said, but the dog's return was welcome; Howe would later refer to it as "an honorable act of [a] gentleman."

Howe's later correspondence contained a noticeable change in tone toward his opponent, and henceforth he would refer to Washington with respect. Furthermore, from that date onward, although Howe would still win victories, he never seemed to pursue with the vigor that might have won the war for Britain. Ultimately Howe would resign rather than respond to an order to escalate the brutality of the conflict, and to "show such little compassion to the rebels that they will be afraid to do ought but return to the Crown." His replacement, General Henry Clinton, had poor tactical skills, and Clinton's second in command,

General Charles Cornwallis, was a competent administrator but a poor field commander. Together these two would never have the military success that Howe had, and they would go on to lose the war.

At the close of the war, Washington retired to Mount Vernon to continue his agricultural work, to engage in Virginia politics, and to fulfill his dream of creating "a superior dog, one that had speed, scent, and brains." He had decided that his Virginia hounds were too lightly built and were lacking in the strength needed for a long sustained hunt. In addition, they were too easily distracted from the trail of the fox by other things, and he complained that his dogs were "forever sustaining loss in my stock of sheep." During the war Washington had developed a respect for and a warm personal relationship with the Marquis de Lafayette, the French general and political leader whose assistance was vital to the success of the revolution. In their many private conversations, Lafayette had praised the French staghounds for their stamina and focus when on the trail of a quarry. So Washington began a long correspondence with his old comrade-in-arms to try to obtain a few of these dogs as breeding stock. In 1785 the Marquis wrote, "French hounds are not now very easily got because the King makes use of English dogs as being more swift than those of Normandy." Lafayette continued searching, however, and eventually did manage to find seven large French hounds that he promptly sent off to America. John Quincy Adams, who would go on to become the sixth president of the United States, was given the task of escorting these dogs. Adams, however, had little love or enthusiasm for the dogs, and apparently little sense of duty or responsibility as well. Once reaching New York, he simply abandoned the dogs to the care of the shipping company. Washington, for a while, thought that the dogs were missing, and when he finally located them he did not have pleasant words to say about Adams. "It would have been civil in the young Gentleman to have penned me at least a note respecting the disposal of [the foxhounds]." His concern for the welfare of these dogs is evident when he further notes, "The canine species in New York is friendless." This may have been because New York was then suffering from a rabies scare. There were reports of mad dogs everywhere, and any dog that was unknown or unattended was at risk of being killed on sight.

Washington had mixed feelings about these new French dogs. There were some aspects about them that he truly loved, such as their deep voices on the hunt, which he described as being "like the bells of Moscow." On the other hand, these were very big and strong dogs, with an independent streak that made them much harder to handle than his Virginia hounds.

A story that illustrates how difficult these French hounds could be also shows another side of the man that Americans have come to view as being staid, stodgy, a strict moralist who was also an honest and unflinching patriot, but completely lacking in warmth or humor. However, when it came to his dogs, apparently love, humor and forgiveness were all possible from America's revolutionary hero and revered statesman. This event took place at Mount Vernon, after the war but before Washington's election to the presidency. It is described in a bit of correspondence written by George Washington Park Custis, who was Martha Washington's grandson. Because of the size and strength of the original hounds sent by Lafayette, Washington kept most of these dogs fairly closely confined in the kennel area unless they were out hunting. The one exception was Washington's favorite of the group, a huge dog named Vulcan who had the run of the house. He was so large that Martha's grandchildren and their friends could actually ride him like a small pony. In his own words, Mr. Custis writes as follows:

Of the French hounds, there was one named Vulcan, and we bear him the better in reminiscence, from having often ridden bestride his ample back in the days of our juvenility. It happened that upon a large company sitting down to dinner at Mount Vernon one day, the lady of the mansion (my grandmother) discovered that the ham, the pride of every Virginia housewife's table, was missing from its accustomed post of honor. Upon questioning Frank, the butler, this portly, and at the same time the most polite and accomplished of all butlers, observed that "A ham, yes, a very fine ham, had been prepared, agreeably to the Madam's orders. But lo and behold! Who should come into the kitchen, while the savoury ham was smoking in its dish, but old Vulcan, the hound, and without more ado fastened his fangs into it." Although they of the kitchen had stood to such arms as they could get, and had fought the old spoiler desperately, yet Vulcan had finally triumphed, and bore off the prize, "Aye, cleanly, under the keeper's nose." The lady by no means relished the loss of a dish which formed the pride of her table, and uttered some remarks by no means favorable to old Vulcan, or indeed to dogs in general; while the Chief [Washington] having heard the story, communicated it to his guests, and with them laughed heartily at the exploit of the staghound. The Chief observed, "It appears that Monsieur du La Fayette has sent me neither a staghound nor a foxhound, but rather a French ham-hound!"

Washington quickly set about breeding these large French staghounds to his smaller Virginia hounds. He was very selective in his breeding, carefully mating dogs with desirable attributes to others that had different qualities he also desired. He was looking for a hound whose size was a bit larger than his Virginia hounds but considerably smaller than the French hounds, while still retaining the speed and strength of the French imports. The dog should have better running speed than the English foxhound, since the hunt was generally much swifter in the broader expanses of open ground in the Americas. His experiments were successful, and Washington is credited as being the main developer of the American foxhound. A few additional changes were made to the breed in the early nineteenth century when Washington's friends at the Gloucester Foxhunting Club took his basic foxhounds and crossed them with some English foxhounds to make them look a bit more like the Old World version of the breed. However, Washington had clearly defined the model of what the New World foxhound should be.

Washington's experiments with dog breeding would be cut short by political pressures. In 1787 he headed the Virginia delegation to the Constitutional Convention in Philadelphia and was unanimously elected presiding officer. His presence lent prestige to the proceedings, but he kept himself aloof from the arguments among the other delegates and did not vigorously support any position. During his long stay in Philadelphia, he again spent time with the Powels. He also visited the Gloucester club again to hunt with a few of his newer dogs and to renew acquaintances. As expected, his influential foxhunting friends lobbied very strongly in favor of his election as leader of the country, regardless of what form the government might take. After the new Constitution was ratified and became legally operative, Washington was unanimously elected president. How much of this honor was due to the political support that he gained after the mayor's wife stopped to comment on a handsome dog, we will never know. Washington would never have time to return to continue to shape his "perfect hounds," and the number of dogs in his kennels would shrink until it only contained a few favorites that he used for his early morning hunts.

The breed that Washington created would be known as the American fox-hound. It is faster and lighter than its English counterpart. There is a huge variation in the voices of individual American foxhounds, and owners quickly come to know which dog is baying at the moment. Washington would take great delight in providing a narrative to his hunting companions that might go something like, "That is True Love who has the scent . . . ah, but Heart has now picked it up as well." Washington's foxhound also has a uniquely American personality that contrasts it to its English cousin. The English foxhound thinks only about foxes, and is so pack oriented that it is often difficult to keep as a household pet. In contrast, the American foxhound fits the stereotype that many have of the American people: when working this dog tends to act individually, rather than merely part of a group, with each dog willing to take the lead if circumstances demand it. But that was exactly the kind of canine personality that Washington wanted—staunch, tough individualists who would work together when called upon—a perfect match for this Founding Father's view of the citizens of his new nation.

CHAPTER NINETEEN

THE DOGS IN THE

OVAL OFFICE

THERE IS AN ANECDOTE that seems to circulate around Washington, D.C., each and every time the United States is about to inaugurate a new president. In the story, God speaks to the new president and says, "I have some good news for you and some bad news. The good news is that you will be allowed to bring your dog with you when you move into the White House. There are no lease restrictions on pets there."

"Wonderful," says the new president, "but what is the bad news?"

The great voice from the sky answers, "The bad news is that your dog will be happier there than you."

It is hard to confirm the accuracy of this prediction, but it is certainly the case that many dogs have resided in the presidential mansion. Actually more dogs have lived in the White House than presidents, presidential wives, and presidential children combined. One rough count suggests that the total number of dogs who have lived at 1600 Pennsylvania Avenue is around two hundred and thirty. If we consider all of the dogs that have been owned by U.S. presidents over their lifetimes, we find that the number reaches an astonishing value of close to a thousand. In general, the function of presidential dogs has been to serve as companions for the country's leader, and perhaps as playmates for the president's children. However, the White House dogs have often also played an important role in shaping the public's image of the man in the Oval Office, and thus have sometimes had a major impact on his political success.

For some presidents, the companionship of a dog was simply taken for granted. For example, Theodore Roosevelt was an outdoorsman and often hunted with dogs, although many of these hunting dogs were owned by the comrades and guides that he was hunting with. Roosevelt's ability to relate to the dogs that he met on these expeditions was often commented upon by his associates. His own home was filled with dogs, including Sailor Boy, a Chesapeake retriever that often swam behind the boat when Roosevelt took his children out on the river; Pete, a bull terrier who would prove to be a major political embarrassment later; and Jack, a Manchester terrier that was much loved by the children. There was also a Saint Bernard and a variety of mongrels that the president or his children would adopt in their travels, plus a few canines that arrived as gifts from foreign dignitaries.

Probably Roosevelt's favorite dog was a mixed breed named Skip, which he adopted on a hunting trip. Roosevelt claimed that he liked the spirit of the dog, who was willing to stand his ground against a bear with the confidence that the president would be there to back him up with adequate firepower. Skip was described by Roosevelt as a "little dog—by that I mean a little of this, and a little of that." He certainly was by no means physically large, standing about eighteen or nineteen inches at the shoulder. He had a houndlike nose, retrieverlike ears, a wide body, short legs, and a short, hard blond coat. It seemed useless even to speculate on his genetic heritage.

Skip's short legs were sometimes a problem, since it was difficult for him to keep up with men on horseback when Roosevelt was out hunting. The president would not allow him to be left behind, however, and would bend down and scoop the little dog up to ride in front of him on the saddle. After a while, Skip got to be quite good at jumping up to ride horseback with his master; one day a press photographer even managed to snap a very strange photograph of Skip riding alone. It appears that the dog had formed a friendship with the pony named Algonquin that belonged to Roosevelt's seven-year-old son, Archie. They had created a sort of game in which Skip would chase Algonquin, who would dash away but then slow down just enough for Skip to jump onto his back for a ride. If there happened to be a saddle on Algonquin, Skip could hang on for quite a long time. If not, he would cling as long as he could, then jump or slide off, only to start the game again. The sight of a dog riding a small horse across the White

House grounds, with no human to hold him there, caused many visitors to doubt their eyes.

Apparently, in Skip's mind, Roosevelt's invitation to sit in front of him while he rode his horse was interpreted by the dog as the equivalent of being invited to sit on the president's lap whenever Roosevelt was seated. Whenever the dog was not needed as company by the children (whom Roosevelt called "the bunnies"), Skip would seek out his master. If he was indoors and not socializing or doing government business, Roosevelt could usually be found reading; he often read an entire book each day. On these occasions, Skip would make a running leap and land heavily in Roosevelt's lap. The president would laugh and almost invariably say, "If you lie quietly, I won't deny you the opportunity to educate yourself further by reading with me." He would then prop the book up on the back of the dog, who happily sprawled over the man's legs and would soon fall asleep there. The president's hand would absentmindedly stroke the dog between turns of the page.

Skip entertained the family in many ways. Roosevelt's son, Archie, had worked out a contest with Skip using the smooth, polished floor of the main corridor that ran the length of the second floor of the presidential residence. Roosevelt described this game in a letter: "Archie spreads his legs, bends over, and holds Skip between them. Then he says, 'On your mark, Skip, ready! Go!' and shoves Skip back while he runs as hard as he possibly can to the other end of the hall, Skip scrambling wildly with his paws on the smooth floor."

Skip died the year before Roosevelt left office. The president himself laid the dog in his coffin and sorrowfully watched his interment behind the White House. However, Roosevelt's wife, Edith, knew how important Skip was to her husband. At the end of his second term in 1908, she instructed that the dog's casket was to be exhumed and transported to their estate at Sagamore Hill, where Skip was finally laid to rest. Edith explained this action to a puzzled member of the press by noting, "Teddy couldn't bear to leave him there beneath the eyes of presidents who might care nothing for a little mutt dog."

Theodore Roosevelt was only one of several presidents that found comfort in the presence of dogs. In the absence of a wife or children, James Buchanan, the only bachelor to occupy the White House, was accompanied at all times by his huge Newfoundland, Lara. This 170-pound dog was remarkable for three reasons, according to the press of the time: his huge tail, his remarkable attachment to his master, and his strange habit of lying motionless for hours with one eye open and one eye closed. Buchanan's niece, Harriet Lane, fulfilled the social duties of First Lady during his term of office, serving as a gracious host and minding his appointments, while Lara filled the role of presidential companion and confidant.

Dwight David Eisenhower provided another, rather poignant example of the value of a companion dog, although it came a decade before he won his presidential election. The dog involved was a Scottish terrier, a breed that he had a fondness for throughout his life. In 1943, Eisenhower had recently assumed the post of supreme commander of the Allied forces. He was at that time in North Africa, coordinating the operations that would finally push the German army off the African continent and force them back into their European stronghold. He paused in his duties to write to his wife, Mamie, "The friendship of a dog is precious. It becomes even more so when one is so far removed from home as we are in Africa. I have a Scottie. In him I find consolation and diversion . . . he is the 'one person' to whom I can talk without the conversation coming back to the war."

The "Scottie" that Eisenhower mentioned in his letter was named Caacie. The little dog accompanied him back to England and continued providing companionship during his planning for the D-Day invasion. Once he had established his base at the Allied headquarters on British soil, Eisenhower would have other company as well. There has been much speculation about his relationship with Kay Summersby, the British woman who was assigned to him as his personal driver. Whether there was any truth to the gossip about some romantic involvement between them or not, they certainly did have a strong and warm friendship. Summersby came to know Eisenhower quite well, and also came to appreciate his fondness for Scottish terriers. She was so pleased to see the way that he would relax in the presence of his dog that she gave him another Scottie, named Telek, who could be company for both Eisenhower and Caacie through the end of the war and on his return home.

Another president who found solace and comfort from a dog during a time of crisis was John Fitzgerald Kennedy. The public has a general perception that the Kennedy White House was filled with dogs. While it is true that at the time of his assassination there were nine dogs in residence, the only dog that he brought with him when he first arrived in 1961 was a Welsh terrier named Charlie. The dog was supposed to belong to his daughter, Caroline, but was considered by Kennedy as his own special companion.

As in the case of Teddy Roosevelt's family, dogs were often the focus of games played by the Kennedy family. JFK loved to swim and spent a lot of time in the White House pool, and Charlie was often there too. The poolside was usually littered with balls and floating toys for the president to toss into the water for Charlie to fetch. The Kennedy kids, however, were not satisfied with the simple game of fetch and instead played their own game at the pool. The object of their game was to toss a toy into the water and get it close enough to their father so that when Charlie leaped after it in a burst of enthusiasm, he would land on the president. When he did, there were gales of laughter from the kids as the president splashed about in mock distress over being hit by this furry missile. Charlie developed into such a good swimmer that he eventually became a great threat to ducks that would sometimes land in the fountains or pools surrounding the various presidential residences.

The word went out to the White House staff that in the whole Kennedy menagerie, Charlie was the top dog. The terrier's naturally self-assured nature meant that he could get away with bossing around the other dogs in the house most of the time. The staff was informed that if any problems arose, Charlie was to be protected and was assumed to be in the right. After a while, Charlie developed a trick that did not endear him to the gardeners and outside workers around the White House. He would silently come up behind a worker who was digging or working the soil, pick a moment of vulnerability, and then make a quick rush at the man, nipping him in the seat of the pants or grabbing at his leg. This was a guerrilla operation and was over in a second, with Charlie racing across the lawn in great excitement, well out of reach of his victim. One worker complained to his supervisor that Charlie had actually bitten hard enough to draw blood. "Leave it be," he was told. "If it was one of the other dogs we could do something, but when it comes to that one, it's different. If it came to a choice of who would have to go, you would be packing to leave, not Charlie."

Despite his poor reputation with the White House staff, Charlie was a great comfort to his master. Traphes Bryant, the White House kennel keeper, described a striking example of this. One afternoon, Bryant was called to the president's office at the height of the Cuban missile crisis. Bryant recollected that "everything was in an uproar. I was ten feet from Kennedy's desk as Pierre Salinger [the press secretary] ran around the office taking messages and issuing orders, while the President sat looking awfully worried. There was talk about the

Russian fleet coming in and our fleet blocking them off. It looked like war. Out of the blue, Kennedy suddenly called for Charlie to be brought to his office."

Bryant was astonished by the order, but he raced out and was back in a few moments with the active little terrier, who bounded into the room. The president spread his arms wide as a signal and Charlie leaped at his chest, only to be caught in midair and plunked down onto Kennedy's lap. The room was filled with a swirl of vital information, frantic aides, and fearful indecision. The president sat in the center of it all, petting the dog, who watched the proceeding with an alertness that almost suggested that he knew what was going on. As the long minutes passed, Kennedy continued to stroke the dog and seemed gradually to relax. After what seemed like a very long while, the president signaled to Bryant to take Charlie out. Kennedy smiled as the dog was lifted from his hands—and then, with a look of calm control, he leaned on his desk and said, "I suppose that it's time to make some decisions." Obviously the political crisis had to be dealt with by the officials gathered there, but Kennedy's personal emotional crisis seemed to have been dealt with by a little dog who was scampering down the hallway, probably looking for some sort of mischief to get into.

The presidency is a political office, and presidents are political creatures. Therefore it should not be surprising to find that presidents have often used their dogs as a means for trying to manipulate their public image. The first one to do this was Andrew Jackson, who started his life in a small cabin in South Carolina and rose to be an army general before winning the presidency. To remind the public that he was still a man of the people and had not drifted far from his humble background, he filled the White House with an array of hounds and dogs that were clearly not purebred.

William Henry Harrison, who was the hero of the battle of Tippecanoe during the War of 1812, became the first presidential candidate to actually take his dog out with him during his campaign. Again, the idea was to convey a more human side of the candidate, as well as an association with everyday values and concerns. It seemed to work, since political cartoons of the time often depicted Harrison with his dog (and Harrison's associates with the heads or bodies of dogs), and newspaper coverage never failed to mention the animal. For example, one press report of a campaign swing through Virginia noted, "General Harrison greeted the governor with a warm and friendly handshake, while his dog repeated the welcome with a cordial and significant shake of his tail."

Warren Harding had a well-loved Airedale terrier named Laddie Boy who became a public relations asset. The dog was constantly in the public eye and even attended cabinet meetings, where he sat on a specially designed, hand-carved chair. The dog was often with the president when he greeted official delegations. The national press covered Laddie Boy's birthday party, at which the most honored guests were the dogs owned by a number of congressmen and senators. The special treat for the canine partygoers was a tall, multitiered birthday cake made up of layers of dog biscuits. Laddie Boy became such a public figure that reporters even staged mock interviews with the dog, later publishing amusing articles describing "Laddie Boy's views on crucial federal issues."

Unfortunately, Harding's administration was fraught with scandals and mismanagement. In a desperate attempt to recover some public support, the president resorted to a fairly manipulative use of his dog's popularity by concocting a fictitious correspondence between Laddie Boy and a theatrical dog named Tiger. The collection of "letters" exchanged by the dogs was published in a political magazine called *The National.* The contents of this correspondence were designed to explain and defend Harding's loyalty to several presidential appointees (who would later be proven to have defrauded the government). The letter from Tiger complemented Laddie Boy for sticking by his master despite the hard times and accusations. Laddie Boy replied by explaining that both a man and his dog could have their reputations ruined and their integrity challenged because of the actions of people who used friendship for their own personal gain.

We will never know how successful this attempt to manipulate public opinion was. Immediately after the article was published, Harding and his wife took off on a speaking tour. On this trip the president fell ill, and he died before his return home. It was reported that back in the White House, Laddie Boy seemed to sense that something was wrong. In an atypical manner, he had wandered the grounds despondently, setting up prolonged bouts of howling for three days just prior to Harding's death.

Another president who attempted to use his dog to manipulate public opinion was Herbert Hoover, whose image was that of a strong, cold, efficient "social engineer." Even when he was supporting humanitarian causes, Hoover still appeared to be unyielding and austere. When he was running for president, his campaign managers decided that there was a real need to soften his image, so they sent out thousands of autographed copies of a photo that showed a smiling

Hoover holding up the paws of his German shepherd, King Tut. Some reporters claimed that it looked as if both master and dog were happily begging for support from the voters. It must have worked, since he was elected in a landslide.

Hoover had several dogs, but King Tut was his favorite and frequently ran or walked with the president when he went back and forth between the White House and the executive offices. While his master worked, the dog had the freedom to roam the grounds and thus made friends with many of the staff. Hoover's inflexibility and petty temper was demonstrated one time when he was on his way to lunch and noticed that King Tut was playing with one of the White House guards. Hoover whistled for the dog, and although Tut looked up, he didn't come. Hoover whistled again and the dog still remained with the guard, so the president turned abruptly and went on. That very afternoon, an order was issued prohibiting any of the White House staff from playing with the president's pets.

Unfortunately, both Hoover and King Tut showed a lack of adaptability. Hoover could not deal with the economic crisis that had hit the unprepared country, while Tut became overprotective of his master and, for all intents and purposes, suffered a nervous breakdown as a result. Hoover sent him away to recuperate, but the dog became depressed, refused to eat, and died a short time later. Hoover's reelection campaign therefore went on with no canine companion. Having lost both his reputation for effective management and the warm image that he presented to the public when standing with his handsome dog, Hoover suffered a devastating defeat, winning only six states in the election.

Probably the best-known instance where a president used a dog to improve his public image involved Richard M. Nixon. It was in 1952, and only a few days after the Republican Party chose Nixon as the vice-presidential candidate to run with Dwight Eisenhower, when Nixon's political career seemed doomed. The *New York Post* published a story with the headline, "Secret Rich Men's Trust Fund Keeps Nixon in Style Far Beyond His Salary." There was immediate public outrage, and it looked as if Nixon would be dropped from the election ticket. The truth of the matter is that there was really nothing secret or underhanded about the fund. Nixon was from a working-class background and was far from wealthy. When he won his Senate seat, a group of businessmen had publicly solicited a fund of around $18,000 to allow him to keep in touch with the voters in his home state while he was in Washington, D.C.

Faced with a career-threatening public relations disaster, Nixon recognized that he could use the new medium of television to respond to these charges and restore his public support. His explanatory broadcast was a brilliant acting job, filled with pathos and humble family values. He denied that there was anything improper in his use of the money and pointed out, "My wife, Pat, does not have a mink. She wears only a respectable Republican cloth coat." The showstopper came, however, when he used his family dog to appeal to the sentiments of the television audience. In a voice trembling with emotion, he said, "A man down in Texas heard Pat on the radio mention the fact that our two youngsters would like to have a dog. And, believe it or not, the day before we left on this campaign trip we got a message from Union Station in Baltimore saying they had a package for us. We went down to get it. You know what it was? It was a little cocker spaniel dog in a crate that he sent all the way from Texas—black and white, spotted. And our little girl Tricia, the six-year-old, named it Checkers. An' you know, the kids love the dog, and I just want to say this right now, that regardless of what they say about it, we're gonna keep it!"

The effect was incredible. There were reports that many viewers, including Eisenhower's wife, Mamie, wept sentimental tears at this point, and some of Eisenhower's aides wiped their eyes a bit as well—and this was 1952, when men were not supposed to cry in public! It was a political triumph. The movie producer Darryl Zanuck, who was a strong Republican Party supporter, recognized that this was quite a deliberate attempt to sway public opinion. He called to congratulate Nixon on "the most tremendous performance I've ever seen." Shortly thereafter, when Eisenhower met Nixon on his return, he greeted him with the words, "Dick, you're my boy." Nixon's career was saved, and the value of a dog in swaying public relations was now proven beyond a doubt.

When he occupied the White House from 1989 to 1992, President George Bush also had his public image enhanced by his relationship with dogs. Some even suggest that his election to the presidency had a canine connection. Although Bush clearly cherished the company of his dogs, it was his wife, Barbara, who created his image as a devoted and loving dog owner at a time when Bush needed a more human and "common man" image. When he was still the vice president, it was clear that Bush would be a strong contender for the Republican nomination for president after Ronald Reagan retired from office. Unfortunately for him, there was one potential cloud that hung over his career—the period of time that he served as the head of the Central Intelligence Agency. Many Americans have suspicions about this organization, with movies and television pro-

...ms often depicting CIA agents as evil and manipulative, prone to murdering ...olitical dissenters and fomenting revolutions. In Hollywood films, the head of the agency is typically shown as a villainous mastermind who conceals the real truth from the Congress and the president so that he can take over the country or even the world. Bush's political opponents, both in and out of his party, would often invoke this image to turn public opinion against him.

Bush's wife, Barbara, however, always had a strong social commitment, and she was politically astute as well. While her husband was still vice president, she authored a book entitled *C. Fred's Story* that was supposedly written by the Bush family's cocker spaniel. One clear motivation for the book was to raise funds for a campaign for literacy, and all of the proceeds that the book received went to a foundation attempting to improve literacy. However, the content of the book was a dog's-eye view of the life of the vice president, written in the dog's voice with italicized commentaries by Barbara Bush. It was filled with charming anecdotes about George Bush's ambassadorial service in China, his political activities (especially during the election campaign), and his duties as vice president. There were many charming pictures of Fred and the Bush family, with the vice president often playing with the dog and introducing him to dignitaries. Even Bush's politically vulnerable year as head of the CIA was mentioned in a short chapter that dismisses the entire episode with a light touch, with Fred noting, "George told us nothing. He said Bar [Barbara] and I couldn't keep a secret, therefore he didn't tell us any." This book effectively shifted the public's view of Bush toward that of a caring family member with a spunky pet dog that he loved, rather than that of an evil spymaster.

Once Bush was in the White House, Barbara would write another book, this one in the voice of C. Fred's successor, a springer spaniel named Millie. Again, the proceeds would go to the literacy foundation. Like C. Fred's book, *Millie's Book* gave an intimate verbal and photographic picture of Bush's life from a pet's perspective. It became a national bestseller, raising nearly one million dollars for the literacy programs and also producing a lot of favorable publicity for the president. However, any activities using a dog always have the potential for causing embarrassment as well as improving one's image. During a television show on the ABC network, interviewer Sam Donaldson was speaking with Barbara Bush about the new book, with the canine "author" sitting on the sofa beside her in the Yellow Oval Room of the White House. Suddenly Millie jumped off, marched into the middle of the room, and squatted down to relieve herself.

Donaldson unsuccessfully tried to stop her by shouting "Millie, stop that! We on national television . . . Millie!" Perhaps because the cameras quickly swung away from the actual scene, focusing only on the distressed interviewer and embarrassed first lady, the incident simply served as comic relief and no presidential prestige was lost. By the next morning the White House staff had cleaned up the stain on the carpet, and Barbara Bush appeared on yet another national television program. This time Millie acted with great decorum, and the stain on her reputation also disappeared.

Of course, Bush's detractors did not like all of the favorable public attention that Millie had aroused, and political opponents made many negative comments about "the dog that runs the White House." The *Washingtonian* magazine, in an article about the best and worst in America, even went so far as to name Millie "Ugliest Dog." This item was gladly picked up by newspapers and broadcast media. While Bush never directly replied to press criticism of his political policies, when a reporter from another publication asked him about this particular article, he did say that he had spoken to Millie about the matter, and she thought that this awful labeling of her was both unkind and politically motivated. However, he diplomatically added that being a lady and understanding freedom of the press, Millie would not comment further on the subject. The media broadcast this reply widely. In the end, the magazine's editor, Jack Limpert, was so roundly criticized that he felt the need to make a public apology and sent it to Millie, along with a package of dog treats. The President's public approval ratings soared that week when he graciously replied on Millie's behalf as follows:

Dear Jack:

Not to worry! Millie, you see, likes publicity . . . Seriously, no hurt feelings; you are sure nice to write.

P.S. Arf, arf, for the dog biscuits.

It is important to note that although Millie did play a role in shaping Bush's image as a genial and loving family man, his love for the dog was quite genuine. Because the family knew that it made him happy, Millie was always brought along to greet the president when his helicopter arrived, and he responded by always greeting her first. Bush went so far as to have a dog-biscuit dispenser shaped like a gumball machine installed at Camp David, the presidential retreat in Maryland, especially for her. The president even shared his shower stall with Millie each morning. In the end, though, Millie turned out to be more popular than master. She not only had her picture on the cover of *Life* magazine, but her autobiographical account of White House life actually outsold George Bush's own autobiography, written when he left the presidency. In addition, Millie left a living legacy. Her daughter, Fetcher Spot Bush, who was born during George Bush's administration, got to return to the White House as the dog of President George W. Bush, her master's son.

Whether one believes that C. Fred Bush and Millie were deliberately used to shape public opinion or not, there is evidence that his successor, Bill Clinton, and his aides did try to use a dog as a public relations tool. The events began to unfold prior to the breaking of the sex scandal involving Monica Lewinsky. At that time, Clinton still had the image of a devoted father and husband. Clinton's advisers were concerned about the fact that his daughter, Chelsea, was going to leave Washington in order to start school at Stanford University in California. They felt that the president might lose his image as a family man, since there would no longer be photographs of the presidential helicopter being met by both his wife, Hillary, and his daughter. It occurred to them that one way to solve this problem would be to have Hillary meet him in the company of a family dog.

Since Clinton did not have a dog at the time that this decision was made, obviously, one had to be selected. His advisers reasoned that the dog chosen should have the broadest appeal to the greatest number of voters. At that time the most popular dog in America (in fact, in the world) was the Labrador retriever, so obviously the dog would have to be a Lab. However, it could not be a black Labrador, since they don't photograph very well, and it could not be a yellow Lab, since they photograph so well that it might detract from the president. Thus it was decided that the presidential dog had to be a chocolate-colored Labrador retriever. Fortunately for the dog, who would be given the name Buddy, Clinton did appear to eventually form an attachment to his new pet. The dog began to serve as an important source of needed companionship, since his wife Hillary was elected to the Senate and was frequently away from home. When his longtime pet, a cat named Socks, refused to accept the presence of Buddy, Clinton demonstrated his fondness for the dog by giving away the cat. While Buddy's arrival may have been politically motivated, Clinton did appear to be truly upset at his untimely death in a traffic accident.

Sometimes the president's dogs have served to tarnish rather than improve the image of their master. This was often due to the fact that many presidents seemed to spend little time training their dogs, and so their pets would roam around the White House grounds and find their way into trouble. Of the transgressions were minor and did not warrant any mention outside of immediate family, such as when Yuki, Lyndon Johnson's white terrier, soiled the rug in the Oval Office, or Richard Nixon's Irish setter systematically shredded another carpet in that same room. Much earlier, when John Tyler's Italian greyhound puppy was teething, he damaged some of the antique furniture in the presidential mansion. Tyler's wife, Julia, was so embarrassed by this that she had it privately repaired and paid the cost out of personal funds rather than risk embarrassment by asking Congress for the money and thus publicly exposing the President's dog.

Sometimes the misbehavior of the dogs can be mildly embarrassing by causing the kind of negative press notices that Julia Tyler was trying to avoid. One example of this comes from Lucky, a Bouvier de Flandres who was given to Ronald Regan during his first term in the White House. Bouviers are large dogs that have been specialized to herd cattle. Although quite friendly, they can be dominant and demanding unless trained out of it, and there was little time for dog training on the presidential agenda. Left to her own natural tendencies, the rambunctious dog continually attempted to herd Regan across the lawn by snapping at his heels and bumping at his side. On one occasion, Lucky even drew blood with a nip on the presidential hindquarters, a trick Bouviers use to make cattle move along at a swifter pace. The resultant photograph, which was published nationally, seemed to damage the dignity of the president, so Lucky was sent to Reagan's ranch in Santa Barbara, California, where there was livestock for her to herd instead of politicians.

Calvin Coolidge also suffered from embarrassing press reports associated with his dogs. He had a number of them, and they clearly were well loved. Coolidge frequently used his two white collies, Prudence Prim and Rob Roy, in situations where the press coverage would put him in a most favorable light. For instance, on Easter Sunday, a party was held on the White House lawn, and Prudence Prim appeared, ready to pose for the photographers in her new Easter bonnet. Coolidge's wife, Grace, also insisted that her official portrait be painted with her standing next to the elegant-looking collie, Rob Roy.

The Coolidge dogs were treated like family members, which ultimately resulted in some humorous comments about the current occupants of the White House. Once this happened because of the president's habit of feeding the dogs

...m the table in the dining room as the family was seated there to eat sup-
...He and Grace would have an additional plate set near them, which would
...ntain some special bits of meat that they would feed to the dogs, one piece at
.time, over the course of the meal. Once, the humorist Will Rogers was invited
to the White House for dinner with the presidential family, and he later published an account of the evening that caused some giggles around the country.

"Well," Rogers reported in his typical country-style speech, "they was feeding the dogs so much that at one time it looked to me like the dogs was getting
more than I was. The butler was so slow in bringing one course that I come
pretty near to getting down on my all fours and barking to see if business
wouldn't pick up with me."

Coolidge's canine public relations embarrassment, however, would come
about because of an incident involving his wire-haired fox terrier, Peter Pan. The
dog was untrained and often became uncontrollably excited around visitors and
White House staff members. Coolidge thought that this was rather amusing,
and would sometimes warn visitors about his nipping by saying, "Be careful, Peter is one Republican in the White House who bites." One warm summer day
some visitors arrived, including a woman who was wearing a long skirt made out
of some very light material and cinched with a cordlike belt with tassels that
hung down in the back. The president greeted them out on the White House
lawn, and as the woman turned, either the swishing of the skirt or the bouncing
of the tassels caught Peter Pan's attention. He immediately leaped at her skirt,
catching some of the flimsy material in his teeth. There was a tearing sound, and
the skirt seemed to disintegrate, leaving the poor woman exposed and embarrassed. Although an aide resourcefully stepped in and wrapped his suit jacket
around the waist of the flustered visitor, this was all too much for Coolidge's
wife, Grace. She insisted that Peter Pan be banished from the White House and
sent back to the family home in Massachusetts. When Coolidge saw the lurid
press reports of the incident, he reluctantly agreed.

For Gerald Ford, however, it was a simple act of being a responsible dog
master that brought him bad press. His dog was a handsome golden retriever
named Liberty who had been given to him as a gift by the Pulitzer Prize–winning
photographer David Kennerly. Kennerly was working as the White House photographer and wanted to buy a dog as a surprise for his boss. He phoned a couple in Minnesota who were well-respected breeders, and were also noted for
insisting that their dogs go into good homes. Before they would sell him a puppy

they asked Kennerly some questions, such as whether the people who w
own the dog had a fenced yard. The photographer said that they did. The bre
ers next asked if these people leased, rented, or owned their home. "Well," sai
Kennerly, "they actually live in public housing, but the husband has a good job!"
The breeders were not impressed, and Kennerly finally had to reveal that he was
purchasing the dog for the president of the United States.

The idea of living in "public housing" was not the worst part of Gerald
Ford's public image. Because of a couple of unfortunate incidents that were
caught by the TV cameras, such as when he collided with aides when walking
out of an airplane, or tripped on a step while mounting to a podium, Ford was
given the reputation of being clumsy. Soon this idea was picked up by some co-
medians and columnists and escalated into the concept that he was not very
bright, nor very competent. Unfortunately, Liberty would add to that view.

The good-looking, gentle dog did help people empathize with Ford at first,
and the fact that he obviously was fond of the dog helped even more. However,
one night the regular caretaker for Liberty was unable to be at the White House.
This did not particularly bother Ford, since he had owned several dogs during
his life and liked having Liberty around, so he simply volunteered to take care of
the family pet that night. The caretaker noted that Liberty usually was taken out
to make a late-night "business" trip to the White House south lawn, and Ford
agreed to do this as well. Just before he got ready to go to bed, the president
slipped on his robe and took the dog out to relieve herself. Unfortunately he did
this without bothering to tell the Secret Service agents that guard the residence.
While the honey-colored dog and the president strolled around the grounds, the
security team locked down the White House for the night. When Ford returned
to the elevator that he usually used to return to his private quarters, it did not respond. Climbing the stairs to the second-floor entrance, he found the door se-
curely bolted. So Ford began to pound on the door to get the attention of the
guards. Suddenly lights flashed on, and armed men converged on the noise. The
image of the president in his nightclothes, standing next to his dog while a
searchlight is focused on him and armed federal agents point their guns at him
because he was locked out of the White House obviously only added to Ford's
already negative public persona. Ultimately his political opponents capitalized
on that portrait of him, and he narrowly lost his bid to hold the presidency in
the next election.

Perhaps one of the best-known cases of a president damaging his image be-

: of a dog involved Lyndon Baines Johnson, who loved dogs. Johnson's bea-
s, Him and Her, became celebrities by having their picture on the cover of
ife magazine. In addition to the beagles there was a neurotic, but still cherished,
white collie named Blanco, and a terrier named Yuki. Johnson loved the companionship of dogs so much that he had Christmas cards made up with a picture
of Him and Blanco standing next to the president. Each card was signed with
Johnson's signature and the pawprints of the two dogs. In addition, when his
daughter, Luci, was married at the White House, Johnson planned to have the
dogs be part of the ceremony. His wife, Lady Bird, refused to allow this, but the
president still managed to sneak the dogs into the proceedings as the family
posed for the official wedding pictures.

His pleasure at having the dogs around led to Johnson's press difficulties.
One day he was trying to please some photographers by getting the beagles to do
a trick. Johnson was such a tall man that he had to bend way over if he even
wanted to get near a small dog like a beagle. Because of this, as Him danced
around, the president simply reached down and took hold of the dog by the
most convenient handles—namely his large, floppy ears. Johnson apparently
was thinking about a common Texas scene where farmers reach into a litter of
young beagle pups and lift them by their ears. Picking dogs up by the ears can
only be done with young puppies who are still quite light; when a dog grows a
little older, it puts on more weight than the ears can comfortably support. In any
event, LBJ grabbed Him by the ears, and the dog yelped. "Ya see, pulling their
ears is good for a hound," Johnson said in an attempt at nonchalance. "Everybody who knows dogs knows that that little yelp you heard just means the dog
is paying attention."

Before the day was out, pictures of the yelping dog suspended by its ears appeared in virtually every major news publication. The coverage was not favorable. Most of the articles were accompanied by comments of dog experts
criticizing Johnson for hurting his dogs. The American Kennel Club, the National Beagle Club, the American Society for Prevention of Cruelty to Animals,
and several state and national veterinary associations all went on record to condemn this kind of behavior as harmful. That year in the Rose Bowl parade in
California, there was even a float with a giant beagle whose ears would raise up
in the air as a speaker in its mouth howled "Ouch!"

Johnson's reputation was somewhat tarnished by this situation, but he didn't
let it prevent him from allowing television cameras into the Oval Office, where

he sat his terrier, Yuki, on his lap as both of them began to sing—or how
folk song and then an operatic aria. The press outcry was almost as loud f
music critics, who suggested that having the dog howl classical music was equ
alent to having the president make a demeaning comment about classical music.
Others simply wondered about what all of this was doing to the decorum and respect that people were supposed to have for the holder of the job of president.
Johnson, however, was delighted with the furor. He happily waved a copy of one
article about his performance, noting, "Not all the comments are bad. This one
says that I sing almost as good as the dog!"

Most of the incidents that have been described so far were minor in nature,
even if they did affect the president's public image negatively, at least for a while.
On the other hand, there have been situations involving White House dogs that
have had major political impact and have received international attention. For
example, Theodore Roosevelt's bull terrier, Pete, had a dominant personality,
and if people annoyed him he had no hesitation about responding with his
teeth. When he nipped at a naval officer and snapped at some cabinet ministers,
Roosevelt waved the incidents off as "the nature of the breed" or "his attitudes
toward their political stances." Unfortunately Pete's aggression continued to increase, and one day he chased the French ambassador, Jules Jusserand, down a
White House corridor, ultimately catching up with him and then tearing the
bottom out of his pants. The press made a large fuss about this, the French government complained, and rather than jeopardize U.S. relations with France, Pete
was exiled to the Roosevelt mansion at Sagamore Hill.

It is interesting that Theodore Roosevelt's distant cousin, Franklin Delano
Roosevelt, would suffer a similar embarrassment from a dog. This time the dog
was Major, a German shepherd, and the target was British Prime Minister Ram-
say MacDonald. Major's attack on the ministerial trousers was so vigorous that
MacDonald's pants were nearly ripped off, and a replacement pair had to be
found so that he could decently exit the presidential residence. Although no official complaint was lodged, this was extremely embarrassing for Roosevelt. After all, here was a dog whose breed originated in Germany attacking the prime
minister of Great Britain, just at the time when Germany was bracing itself to go
to war with England, and this occurred in the White House. The press did not
miss the symbolic significance of this, and Major was banished to FDR's mansion in Hyde Park.

It seems that Franklin Roosevelt's dogs were always getting into trouble and ıg consternation. For instance, one morning Roosevelt had arranged for a ̣omatic meeting to be held over breakfast at the White House. There was ̣me time pressure on the participants, as wartime events were unfolding and ̣uick decisions had to be made. As the members of the group were gathering to enter the dining room, the White House staff tried to expedite matters by laying out the plates, each containing a serving of bacon, eggs, and fried potatoes. The serving personnel then opened the door to usher the guests into the room—only to find that Winks, the president's Llewellin setter, was standing on the table. By the time they got to him, he had already gobbled up eighteen breakfasts! Winks would be very sick from this rash action later that day, but the president roared with laughter. The table was cleared and a hasty substitution was made of pastries and coffee. As they ate their minimal breakfast, Roosevelt sipped on his coffee. He looked at his cup and then commented on his dog's behavior, noting, "The only reason Winks didn't wash it down with coffee was because it hadn't been poured yet."

There would be yet another incident involving one of Roosevelt's dogs. This was Meggie, the Scottish terrier that he owned before the arrival of his most famous dog, Fala. Meggie had developed into a pushy dog, but Roosevelt's wife, Eleanor, refused to let anyone discipline her. She terrorized the housemaids by chasing them down the halls and biting at their brooms, mops, and dusters. Word about her rowdy behavior had leaked out, and the famous newspaper reporter Bess Furman decided to explore the story a bit further. During an interview with the president on more serious matters, she brought up the issue of Meggie's delinquency. Roosevelt laughed and said, "I am not with her all of the time. Perhaps you had best ask her about these reports."

Furman patted the seat beside her, and Meggie responded to the invitation by jumping up on the sofa. Then Furman looked directly into the terrier's eyes and asked in a serious voice, "Meggie, have you been a naughty dog? Come now and confess to the public what you have really done." The terrier's response was to give the reporter a sharp bite on her nose. So much for canine openness with the press!

On one occasion, certain members of the press and political opponents deliberately tried to embarrass Roosevelt through his dogs. This involved Roosevelt's Scottish terrier, Fala, who became the president's constant companion and would even sleep on the president's bed at night. Fala was continually in the news, and part of this may have had to do with his ability to sense whenever a press conference was about to occur. As soon as the doors opened to admit reporters, Fala would dash in and settle himself at the president's feet, much he often did at cabinet meetings.

In many ways, Fala became a sort of national symbol. Part of this was simply because he was seen so often with the president. Like other presidents, however, Roosevelt often consciously used his dog in public relations efforts. One instance of this was in a White House campaign to rally public sentiment in support of fundraising activities associated with the war effort. For this purpose Fala became an honorary Army private, the rank being awarded to him because of a cash contribution (of one dollar) made on his behalf. The same option was offered to the public, and as a result hundreds of thousands of dogs across the country became Army privates as well, with the funds that were received used to support military activities associated with the war.

Roosevelt liked having Fala with him, and soon the dog came to expect that he would be present on all occasions. For example, when the presidential entourage was preparing to leave for Roosevelt's third inauguration, Fala hopped into the car beside his master. This time, however, the additional seats had been reserved for a senator and the Speaker of the House, so the president attempted to shoo him out of the car. Fala just snuggled closer to him on the seat. Roosevelt laughed and said to Tommy Qualters, who was in charge of the Secret Service contingent assigned to the White House, "Would you kindly check the credentials of this individual? If he does not have an invitation to be on the inaugural platform, please have him removed." Qualters then gently lifted the black dog out of the car and carried him back inside.

At other times Fala was more successful. He was frequently the president's associate and companion when he attended many international meetings. He was with Roosevelt in 1941 aboard the *U.S.S. Augusta* when FDR and Winston Churchill signed the Atlantic Charter. He was even photographed with the two state leaders and of course with Winston Churchill's poodle, Rufus, who was there also.

During the election campaign of 1944, somebody associated with the Republican party decided that the constant fellowship between Roosevelt and Fala provided an opportunity to attack the president's credibility and reputation as a leader. To do this they started a false rumor, charging that Roosevelt had abused his position as commander in chief of the military on Fala's behalf. According to the rumor, Fala supposedly had somehow been left behind on an island off

ollowing a presidential visit. When this was discovered, Roosevelt al-
y squandered public resources by sending a U.S. Navy warship to retrieve
dog. Unfortunately for his opposition, Roosevelt turned this whole incident
ainst his detractors in a national radio broadcast. In it he explained to the nation, "Republican leaders have not been content with attacks on me, or my wife,
or my sons. No, not content with that, they now include my little dog, Fala.
Well, of course, I don't resent attacks and my family doesn't resent attacks, but
Fala does resent them. You know, Fala is Scotch, and being a Scottie, as soon as
he learned that the Republican fiction writers had concocted a story that I had
left him behind on the Aleutian Islands and had sent a destroyer back to find
him—at a cost to the taxpayers of two or three or eight or twenty million dollars—his Scotch soul was furious. He has not been the same dog since." Roosevelt won the election with his reputation still intact.

For Roosevelt however, Fala was always more important as a personal companion than as a political symbol. On April 12, 1945, the dog accompanied the
president to Warm Springs, on Pine Mountain in Georgia. Roosevelt was feeling
poorly that afternoon and was in bed, with Fala lying on the floor across the
room. At 3:35 P.M., Fala suddenly jumped up and stared in the direction of his
master. He gave a yip and a whimper and turned around quickly. He acted as if
he was looking at something—following something—that was not visible to the
human eye. Whimpering plaintively he raced across the floor, his eyes fixed on
something in the air. The little black dog charged out of the room, down the
short passageway and, with his eyes still pointed skyward, he crashed into the
screen door. At that same moment, the doctor pronounced that the president
was dead.

Fala would make one last trip with his master when they traveled from
Warm Springs to the White House, and then to Hyde Park, where the president
would rest in the rose garden on the banks of the Hudson River. A few years
later, as Roosevelt had wished, Fala would be laid there also, to finally sleep again
beside his beloved master as he had done all of his life.

Perhaps the president that has the greatest emotional appeal for Americans
is Abraham Lincoln. He is credited with preserving the Union during the Civil
War and with ending slavery in the country. Part of the charm that clings to his
life story has to do with his rise from a humble beginning, the drama associated
with his violent death at the hand of an assassin, and his distinctive personality,
which demonstrated such humanity and humor. For historians and politicians,

his relevance has to do with his eloquence as a spokesman for democ
which he described how it was important to save the Union not only for .
sake, but also as an embodiment of the ideal of a democratic government t
upon the principles of equal rights and justice. The story of Lincoln's life, he
ever, is not complete without the telling of some events concerning two dogs

Lincoln was born in 1809 in a log cabin near Hodgenville, Kentucky. His father, Thomas Lincoln, is described as a sturdy pioneer, with a serious personality but devoted to his family. His mother, Nancy Hanks, was a frail woman, often subject to depression, whose main passion seems to have been her religion.

When the title to his Kentucky farm was challenged, Thomas Lincoln took his wife and two children (Abraham and his sister, Sarah) to a new homestead in southwestern Indiana. Abraham helped to clear the fields and to take care of the crops, but they had barely enough to survive, and Lincoln would later stoically remember that things were "pretty pinching at times." In the autumn of 1818 Abraham, then only nine years old, stood in his ragged clothes and watched while his father buried his mother in the forest.

Now alone, without the support of a mother's love, the boy began to spend most of his free time exploring the area surrounding the farm. He soon found an interconnecting set of limestone caves that caught his interest, and he would spend hours exploring them. It was on one of these trips that Lincoln found an injured brown and white dog. The dog had no collar, and Lincoln had never seen it before in this neighborhood. His immediate inclination was to take the dog home and attempt to nurse it to health, but there were two problems with this plan. The first was simply mechanical, in that the dog was about the size of a large hound, and he would have had to carry it over a distance of several miles—an act that was clearly beyond the young boy's strength. The second was that he didn't believe his father would allow him to keep a "useless" animal, probably viewing it just as another mouth to feed. Instead, Abraham built a lean-to shelter near the mouth of one of the caves, and each day brought the dog some food and water. He named the dog Honey and lavished her with all the affection that he had been missing since his mother's death.

Events were changing rapidly, however, and while Honey was still convalescing, Thomas Lincoln went back to Kentucky and returned with a woman who would be a new wife for himself and a new mother for his children. Sarah Bush Johnston Lincoln was a widow with two girls and a boy of her own. She was full of energy and had an affectionate nature, treating all of the children as

borne them herself. She rapidly became especially fond of Abraham, would later refer to her as his "angel mother." As Abraham's affection and grew, he decided to risk bringing Honey to the house.

Much to Abraham's relief, Sarah accepted the dog—but with a condition that the boy spend some of the time reading and learning that he had spent each day caring for the dog in its distant cave. Even then, as he would later describe it, he ended up being educated "by littles," meaning a little now and a little then, and his entire formal schooling probably amounted to only a bit more than one year's attendance in a classroom. He did learn to read and write, as well as the basics of arithmetic, and did become an avid reader. He would borrow books and sit and read them by the fire with his head resting on Honey's side, as if she were a pillow.

The eleven-year-old Lincoln still had a child's thirst for exploration, and he would often return to the caves to engage in "adventures and quests." Honey would accompany him on these journeys. One afternoon Lincoln thought that he heard water flowing in one of the caves, and he remembered a story where a great treasure was hidden in a cave on the shore of an underground river. This excited the young boy, and he recklessly began to climb down toward where he thought the water was flowing. Suddenly he lost his footing and slipped on some damp rocks, rolling downward quite a long way. His torch went out, and he was badly bruised and completely disoriented in the total darkness of the cave. Meanwhile, many feet above him, Honey began to bark frantically. Lincoln desperately tried to orient himself toward the noise of the dog, but it was difficult, since sounds tended to bounce around in the cave. In addition, as he groped around in the dark, he could not find any path or obvious handholds that might provide a way up the steep incline.

Above him, Honey was becoming more excited. Her barking was turning into a broken howl, and she was now rushing out of the mouth of the cave and then returning to the edge of the abyss where she had seen her master fall. This cave was well off the beaten track, but a seldom-used wagon trail passed around a hundred yards from the opening. The person who could someday save the United States from dissolution and would free the blacks from their slavery, however, was lying in pain and confusion in a deep hole in the ground, and his only contact was a loving dog who was loudly sounding the alarm. In one of those fortunate chance occurrences, a farmer and his two sons were passing by. They heard the panicky barks of the dog, and the farmer sent both boys with

their rifles to see if perhaps a dog had cornered a bear nearby. When t
the cave, the boys tentatively entered it. One tried to calm the frantic c
ing, "What have you got cornered in there, girl?"

A faint voice came up from the dark hole and said, "I ain't cornered,
stuck!"

It took the better part of an hour, and the assistance of ropes and the
farmer's mule, to pull Abraham Lincoln out of his potentially lethal trap, thus allowing the history of America to proceed as we know it. When Sarah later
learned what had happened to Abraham, she was upset and frightened. She made
him promise not to explore the caves again, and then said, "You owe that dog an
obligation. The Indians say that if someone saves your life you are responsible for
them for the rest of their life. You saved her life once, and she has returned the
favor to you. Now both of you are bound together in a sacred commitment."

Honey remained with Abraham—even sleeping in his bed despite the gruff
but unenforced protests of his father—until a year before the family migrated to
Illinois. He would later say, "I woke up to find that Honey, the second of my
three mothers, had died during the night. It made me remember how much it
had hurt me the first time I lost my mother."

Lincoln was twenty-one years of age when he moved to Illinois. Once there
he had no desire to be a farmer and instead worked his way through a variety of
occupations, from rail splitter (building fences) to storekeeper, postmaster, sur-
veyor, Indian fighter, and eventually a lawyer after he taught himself law and
passed the bar examination. Finally he got himself elected as a legislator in the
Illinois state assembly.

In the same way that he had many careers, Lincoln lived with many dogs.
Most were dogs that he could not personally lay claim of ownership to; they
were often dogs that simply "came to visit the children." According to Lincoln's
Illinois law partner, William Herndon, if the Lincoln children "wanted a dog-
cat . . . it was all right and well treated, housed, petted, fed, fondled, etc., etc."

While Lincoln would sometimes suggest that the animals were just pets for
the children, they were actually a therapeutic force in his own life. Lincoln was
often subject to bouts of depression that would force him to stop work, and his
dogs and the occasional cat were lifelines that would pull him out of his despair.
Herndon described the situation this way: "If exhausted from severe and long-
continued thought, he had to touch the earth again to renew his strength. When
this weariness set in he would stop thought, and get down with a little dog or

ecover; and when the recovery came he would push it aside to play
own tail."

ncoln's devotion to his dogs earned him his wife's displeasure on at least
occasion. Lincoln liked to tell a story about Jip, who was the only purebred
og that he ever owned. Lincoln was working as a lawyer at the time, and it was
a gift from one of his clients. The dog was a straight-legged, medium-sized terrier. Known commonly at the time as a Fell terrier, this breed was renamed
around 1925, and we know it today as the Lakeland terrier. Although his legal
practice was successful, the work was difficult and often kept him away from his
family. To earn a living, he found it necessary not only to practice in Springfield
(the capital of the state of Illinois), but also to follow the court as it made the
rounds of its circuit. In the spring and fall he would set out in a horse-drawn
buggy to travel hundreds of miles over the thinly settled prairie. He would go
from one little county seat to another, seeking out clients and cases. The hours
were long, the pay not very high, and there were many lonely days and nights.
This loneliness was partly alleviated by Jip's company. The dog would ride on the
seat of the horse-drawn surrey next to him, announcing his arrival in town with
a cascade of barking.

According to Lincoln, one winter day he had stopped the carriage to water
the horse, and Jip had jumped out and was playing on the thin ice shelf that had
formed along the banks of the Wabash River. Some of the ice gave way, and the
dog fell in. Lincoln was afraid that the dog might not be able to climb back out
onto the slippery bank, or that the ice-cold water might paralyze him before he
could swim to safety. So, without hesitation, the future president waded into the
freezing river to save his dog. The dropoff was steeper than Lincoln had expected, and he suddenly found himself chest deep in the freezing water. Somehow, despite the numbing cold, he managed to grab the dog and scramble back
to shore. He would end the story with the quip, "When I got him out, he was
near froze solid and shivering. He was shaking so hard that I wasted half a glass
of whisky trying to aim it for his mouth. Must have got enough of it into him,
though, since it did seem to bring him back to life. It took the rest of the bottle
to thaw out that dog's master, though."

Then Lincoln would continue. "When I told my cherished wife, Mary,
about these events, she became most disturbed. 'Mr. Lincoln,' she said, 'you are
just too concerned with the welfare of that dog and too little concerned about
your own. You could well have died in that freezing water or come down with

new mon fever *[pneumonia]* from the chill. You laugh and say that that is a[...]
as you will ever get. Well let me tell you, sir, if ever you do something as st[...]
as that again on behalf of your dog or anything else, you will learn what it is[...]
be truly cold by sleeping by yourself for the rest of the year!'" Lincoln would[...]
then pause, laugh, and then finish by saying, "Now that is a case of frostbite that
I won't risk—so next time poor old Jip may have to fend for himself."

When Jip died about five years before Lincoln was elected president, a
floppy-eared, rough-coated dog of unknown ancestry or breed that he named
Fido replaced him. As in the case of Jip, Fido was almost always with Lincoln.
The people of Springfield would report that it was a common sight to see Lincoln walking down the street with Fido walking behind, carrying a parcel by the
string tied around it. A regular stop for Lincoln was at Billy's Barbershop for a
haircut. Fido would settle down to wait outside patiently, although he could easily be lured into a game involving jumping and twirling when young children
came by and paid any particular attention to him.

When the news came that Lincoln had been elected president, he immediately began to plan the move to Washington, D.C. His wife, Mary Todd, however, used this turn of events as an opportunity to rid herself of the dog for a
while. She felt that Lincoln was too indulgent, letting the dog into the house
even when he had dirty feet, letting him pester people at the dinner table and
even letting him jump up on to the furniture. "The public will not tolerate a dog,
even the president's dog, if that animal soils the White House carpets, or damages the heritage furniture in that mansion. Those items are public property and
are held in trust by the president and should not be despoiled by any animal."

Lincoln did not like to argue with his wife, and so he sadly agreed to leave
Fido behind. Lincoln, however, arranged to have Fido cared for by John Eddy
Roll, a local carpenter, and his family until he returned from his term in the
White House. The fact that Mary Todd Lincoln might have been correct about
her perceptions about the way that her husband treated the dog is shown by the
instructions that Lincoln left with the Roll family. He specified that the family
was never to scold Fido for entering the house with muddy paws. He was not to
be tied up alone in the backyard. Fido was also supposed to be allowed to enter
the house whenever he scratched at the door, or whenever the family sat down
to meals. People were encouraged to feed Fido tidbits while they ate in the dining room, since the new president explained that Fido was used to being given
food by everyone sitting around Lincoln's table. Finally, to make Fido feel fully

ᵣe, Lincoln gave the Roll family his horsehair sofa, which was Fido's fa-
ᵣe piece of furniture.

Two of Lincoln's sons, Tad and Willy, were very upset about leaving Fido
ᵣehind. Still unwilling to fight with Mary over the presence of the dog, however,
Lincoln took the boys and the dog over to F. W. Ingmire's photographic studio.
Mr. Ingmire draped a piece of fancy material over a washstand and placed Fido
on top. He then took photographs of the dog in several different poses, while the
boys watched but did not participate. Photography was in its infancy then, and
photographs were considered virtually miraculous. Each of the boys was then
given a copy of a photo of Fido and told that this was just as good as having the
dog with them in reality. The boys were unconvinced by their father's logic.
Nonetheless, Fido had now become the first presidential dog ever to be photographed.

The boys needed occasional reassurance that Fido was thriving, which came
in the form of letters from Springfield. For instance, William Florville (better
known as the president's barber, Billy), wrote the Lincolns a letter in 1863 saying,
"Tell Taddy that his (and Willy's) dog is alive and kicking—doing well—he stays
mostly at John E. Rolls' with his boys, who are about the size now that Tad &
Willy were when they left for Washington."

Following Lincoln's assassination in 1865, hundreds of heartbroken mourn-
ers from all over the country came to Springfield for the funeral. They gathered
around the Lincoln home to pay their respects. On impulse, John Roll brought
Fido back to his original home to meet with members of the grieving public.
One who met Fido reported that "touching the President's dog gave me the feeling that I had touched the man himself and seen his humanity. It brought me
comfort in this time of grief, as touching this dog must have brought the President comfort during his life."

Unfortunately, Fido, like his master, would die a year later as a victim of an
assassin. All of his life he had been surrounded by love, and hence Fido grew into
a trusting and affectionate dog. Sadly, it was this friendly aspect that led to his
tragic death in 1866. The big yellow rough-coated dog came across a man who
appeared to be sleeping on the sidewalk in front of his home. He playfully approached the stranger and began to lick his face. The man, who was drunk at the
time, awakened, saw the dog's open mouth near his face, and panicked. He drew
a knife and stabbed what he imagined to be an assailant.

There is, however, one other legacy that Fido has left us with, and i. his photograph. In 1862 Lincoln and his cabinet were considering varic islative programs and proclamations that would deal with the slavery prac in the American South. The more radical elements in the cabinet wanted the . nouncement of a total abolition of slavery, while more conservative members such as Secretary of State William Seward and Postmaster General Montgomery Blair, were suggesting a slower course of action. When it became clear that Lincoln was leaning toward some form of a decree ending slavery, which would be a direct exercise of the president's war authority and thus would not require passage through Congress, these more cautious cabinet members then began to suggest various options. Knowing that they could not avoid the actual decree, many of their suggestions involved merely a change in title of the various proclamations, or a softening of wording so that some slaveholders might feel less disenfranchised and it might lessen the blow in the eyes of their supporters. Lincoln listened to the arguments of the cabinet ministers and then, in his typical fashion, began to tell a story.

"You know, gentlemen, I have learned a lot from my dog Fido, and some of the lessons that he has taught me might be of value here." Lincoln picked up the photo of Fido that he kept in his office and pointed at it. "Now consider this here dog of mine. Mr. Blair, as Postmaster General you must be good at mathematics and counting. Let me pose the following problem for you. If you were to call his tail a leg, then how many legs would my dog have?"

Blair looked at him in a puzzled manner and answered, "Five."

"No," replied Lincoln. "Calling a tail a leg doesn't make it a leg. We will learn this lesson from Fido and call this decree the 'Emancipation Proclamation.' Let it stand on as many legs as God will grant it."

CHAPTER TWENTY

THE COUNTER-FACTUAL
HISTORY OF DOGS

I F DOGS HAVE HAD such an influence on human culture and history, it is quite reasonable to ask, why is it the case that we don't see canine contributions cited in standard political, cultural, and social histories? Many of the stories told here have described events that have pivoted around a dog. The dog's behavior, or sometimes simply its presence in these situations has affected the life of a significant person, and this seems to justify the conclusion that the dog has affected history. There are several premises involved with this idea. One is associated with a technique called *counter-factual reasoning*, which is a "what if?" type of speculation that historians engage in when contemplating pivotal events in history. Thus the historian asks, "If this single event had or had not occurred, would the resulting chain of historical events have been different?" To bring dogs into this, we would have to ask, "If this significant individual had not had an encounter or a relationship involving a dog, would historical events have been different?"

The problem is that historians seldom ask that question. They are interested in great political movements, social conflict, and human decisions and attitudes that have shaped the past and the present. Somehow, the idea that such a mundane thing as a dog may have influenced the whole course of history seems frivolous. Perhaps a person of importance may have had a dog, or even felt fondly it, but the possibility that history may have been changed by that dog is ~ven contemplated as a serious enough possibility to ask the counter-factual ~stions to test its significance.

Perhaps the contributions of dogs to history go unnoticed simply because they are too commonplace. Documents of state and religious records in the past, and newspaper and mass media reports in the present, are concerned with matters of great note. When vast sums of money, tracts of land, military actions, the social stature and reputation of leaders, national honor, religion, or liberty are at issue, these are recorded. However, common activities and concerns are simply presumed to be known to everybody and thus do not make it into the public record. As an example, a colleague of mine wanted to do a history of underwear. While in our time, underwear is a fashion item that gets a lot of attention, in former eras it simply was something that everybody had, used, and knew about. By the time that she had pushed her research back to the middle of the nineteenth century, the trail of underwear began to disappear. It is unlikely that we will ever be able to uncover what type of undershorts, if any, George Washington or Julius Caesar wore. In the end, she had to resort to going through massive amounts of personal correspondence and many volumes of diaries—because it is there, in the personal notations and communications among intimates, that one talks about the commonplace and everyday concerns, such as underwear.

The same goes for dogs. People talk about their pets to friends and loved ones, and it is in letters, diaries, casual reports of conversations, or notations on photographs that we find out about dogs that have been important in the personal lives of individuals. If one is not willing to go through a mountain of trivial scrawlings by a historically important individual or his intimate associates, one will often not find the occasional significant event where a dog has changed a life, and through that life has altered history.

For example, it is only through his letters and the correspondence of others, that we learn of Sir Isaac Newton's dog, Diamond. Newton was, without doubt, the single most important figure in the scientific revolution of the seventeenth century. He discovered the law of gravity, and his three laws of motion have often been referred to as the basic principles of modern physics and mechanics. In addition, he made contributions to optics and to our knowledge of the nature of light, and he created the mathematical system that we now call calculus.

Newton's successful and broadly based scientific life stands in stark contrast

to his rather limited social and personal life. He had very few close relat.
outside of the scientific realm. His contacts with women involved only a
fortunate relationship with his mother, who had seemed to abandon him,
somewhat later his guardianship of a niece. There is no evidence of any love i.
terest in his long life. His relationships with men were also not very successful.

Although he assumed the role of a patron for a circle of young scientists, he
did so with a magisterial attitude, treating the group members as if they were dis-
ciples rather than friends. Most of his relationships with other scientists of his
own age and standing were cool and reserved, since Newton tended to view
these men much more as competitors than as colleagues. In fact, the only evidence for any emotions similar to love or caring that continued for any long period of time is found in Newton's relationship with his dog.

Newton's dog was a creamy white Pomeranian named Diamond. Pomeranians during that era were usually larger than today's breed, but their personalities
were quite similar. Casual descriptions of Diamond suggest that she was a
medium-sized dog (about thirty-five pounds), feisty, and quite protective, at
least to the best of her ability. Thus she made a good watch dog. This latter feature of her behavior, however, once caused Newton considerable trouble.

This story was told in a letter that Newton wrote to explain why his publication of the treatise that contained his law of gravity would be delayed. Newton
was working on the final revisions; he was making significant progress and was
feeling quite good about the work. He had worked all day, and when the sun
went down he needed to light some candles to continue with his calculations. As
usual, Diamond was sleeping nearby. A knock on the door called Newton out of
the room, and apparently Diamond awakened to the sound of talking, which included voices that were unfamiliar to her. Her protective instincts were immediately aroused, and she tried to get to her master. Unfortunately, Newton had
closed the door to his study, so she was reduced to running wildly around the
room, barking in excitement. On one circuit of the room Diamond apparently
collided with the leg of Newton's small writing table, and the shock of her colli-
sion caused the burning candle to tip over, directly onto the manuscript. In the
resulting fire there was actually little damage to the room, but the manuscript
that Newton was working on was completely destroyed.

When Newton returned to the room with the visitor, he was shocked at the
scene that greeted him. Although Newton had a violent temper and was noted

vengeful rages, this time he did not show any anger. Instead he merely the dog from the floor and said to her sorrowfully "Oh Diamond, Diamd, thou little knowest what damage thou hast done."

According to his later account, the shock of the events "so numbed my brain that I was forced to my bed for some weeks." Doctors were called to help bring him out of what we would today call a major depression. Through it all, however, Diamond rested on the bed with him. It would be close to a full year before Newton would reconstruct the theory of gravity in full. Thus an entire year of intellectual life and research, by one of the greatest scientific minds of his era, was lost due to the actions of a dog.

While correspondence tells us about the unfortunate incident involving Sir Isaac Newton's dog, diaries tell us about the dog of Captain Meriwether Lewis. In 1803, Lewis was commissioned by President Thomas Jefferson to put together an expedition to travel across the United States on what would prove to be the first overland expedition to the Pacific Coast and back. The idea was to strengthen the U.S. claims to the Oregon Territories, learn more about the natives and the wildlife, and explore some of the regions that had been acquired by the Louisiana Purchase. Lewis selected as his co-commander Lieutenant William Clark. They carefully chose an expeditionary group of about forty members and made sure that they all had had vigorous outdoor training. Individual members were skilled in the sciences of botany, meteorology, and zoology, while others had more practical skills, including celestial navigation, Indian sign language, carpentry, gun repair, and boat handling. In addition to the men, Lewis also took along a large black Newfoundland dog. His name was Seaman, in keeping with the common practice of using nautical names for the breed in that era. Seaman was quite an expensive dog by the standards of that day, costing Lewis twenty dollars.

The expedition left St. Louis in the spring, and by November they had made the difficult passage up the Missouri River to what later became North Dakota. Foraging or otherwise obtaining food for the rapidly moving groups was difficult, but Seaman proved extremely useful in this regard. As Lewis wrote, "Squirrels appear in great abundance on either side of the river. I made my dog take as many each day as I had occasion for, they were fat and I thought them when fried a pleasant food." Seaman could also pull down large game, as when Lewis later wrote, "Drouillard wounded a deer, which ran into the river. My dog pursued, caught it, drowned it and brought it to shore at our camp." Once the

party had reached the Dakotas, they built a small fort and spent a co.
winter among friendly Mandan Sioux Indians.

Just before leaving that next spring, Lewis employed a French-Canadi.
terpreter, Toussaint Charbonneau, who brought along his seventeen-year-
Shoshone Indian wife, Sacajawea, and their infant son. Sacajawea was an invalu.
able aid to the expedition, serving as an interpreter, guide, seamstress, food
scrounger, and, most important, as an extraordinary diplomat when dealing
with unknown Indian tribes. Sacajawea would often ask for Seaman's company
when approaching various Indian bands. A dog of his size and obvious strength
was unknown in that wilderness and was cause for much wonder, and sometimes
fear. His pleasant nature was reassuring, however, and helped convince many natives that this group of explorers was not hostile—for certainly if they were, they
would have trained this mighty dog to be a fearsome weapon.

Seaman continued to assist the band in hunting, and on one instance this
nearly cost him his life. As Lewis wrote, "One of the party wounded a beaver,
and my dog as usual swam in to catch it; the beaver bit him through the hind leg
and cut the artery; it was with great difficulty that I could stop the blood; I fear
it will yet prove fatal to him."

It was fortunate that Seaman recovered, because not too long afterward he
would be called upon to save the lives of the expedition's leaders. One night, the
expedition was camped beside the river that they had been traveling on. Seaman
was the only one awake, making one of his usual patrols of the camp perimeter.
A large buffalo must have slipped into the water on the other side of the river. It
struggled mightily and managed to make its way to the opposite shore, where it
blundered upon the sleeping camp. The campfires and strange smells simply
added to its rising panic, and the buffalo made a mad dash to escape from the
place. Typically, when buffalo are frightened they rush straight ahead, trampling
anything in their way and ignoring all but the largest of obstacles. This is why
some Indian tribes learned that they could kill many animals by simply stam-
peding them in the direction of a cliff and letting them dive over its side in their
headlong flight. So now the panicked animal let out a bleating roar and charged
forward. Lewis was awakened by the sound of the animal and sleepily lifted the
flap of his tepee, only to be greeted by the sight of maddened beast heading directly toward him. It stood nearly five feet at its shoulder, was over nine feet long,
and probably weighed in excess of 2,500 pounds. Had this animal actually continued in its charge and hit the Indian-style tent, it would have had the same ef-

ickup truck driving over it. Since both Lewis and Clark were sleeping
trail shelter, they both could have suffered serious injury or even death,
g the expedition leaderless.

The animal had already crashed its way over a rowboat and was heading directly toward the men, who were still groggy from being awakened. Suddenly, from the darkness on the right side of the tent there was a loud barking, and Seaman flew out in front of the running buffalo. Presented with what it considered to be a new threat, the big animal veered to avoid the black dog. This action deflected his path by only a few yards, but that was enough to cause the panicky animal to charge past the tent where Lewis and Clark lay. Seaman kept harassing the buffalo, which continued on out of the camp with the dog in pursuit. The big dog returned about five minutes later, completely out of breath, then lay down near the door of his master's tent as if nothing had happened.

The boat that the buffalo had run over required several hours to repair, but Lewis and Clark were safe, and the expedition would continue. The psychological importance of the well-planned, well-executed expedition, on which only one man had been lost (by illness), was enormous. Although it was not the first transcontinental crossing in the north (Alexander Mackenzie had preceded them in a remarkable voyage), it served to open vast new territories to the United States. The maps that it provided made travel safer, the initial friendly contacts with the Indians provided for easier movement of settlers, and the information about the flora and fauna of the area was of great scientific value. Many historians say that it was the event that really opened the far West—but had it not been for a dog, it is likely that a leaderless expedition would have returned home with its task unfinished.

An interesting footnote to the Lewis and Clark expedition with Seaman occurred when the party was finally returning after making its way to the Pacific Coast. They were heading east past the Yellowstone River, and Sacajawea had gone out with Seaman, as she often did, to make contact with a tribe of Indians whose village was not far from the explorers' camp. She was, as usual, hoping to purchase supplies. When they entered the village, the big dog caused quite a stir. The residents of the village first offered to purchase him, or to take him in trade for food and other supplies, but when Sacajawea refused the Indians decided to steal him. To keep the travelers from discovering the theft, they decided to also keep Sacajawea. When Lewis learned of this he was enraged. He fully armed his men, ringed the village, and then sent Clark into the camp to make his demands:

"Return my dog, or we will burn your village to the ground." The vil[lage was] small, and this show of force was stunning to the Indians, so they sheepis[hly] turned Seaman. Furthermore, as a show of good faith and contrition, they [also] returned Sacajawea, whom Lewis had somehow forgotten to include in his ul[ti]matum!

Sometimes the information about a historical role played by a dog comes through material written by third parties, rather than anything written by the dog's owner. These are often close associates or sometimes simply witnesses to an event. Consider, for example, the events surrounding King Henry VIII of England in the year 1527. Henry was born as the second son of King Henry VII and it was his older brother, Arthur, who was in line to assume the throne. Arthur died, however, and Henry then became the Prince of Wales and next in line for succession.

Henry was a clever politician, and he set out to marry Catherine of Aragon, who was Arthur's widow. This marriage would be extremely beneficial politically, since Catherine had many contacts and connections to the royal families in Europe, and the Holy Roman Emperor Charles V was her nephew. In addition she was handsome, intelligent, politically wise, and a clever administrator. She proved her competence in 1513 when Henry was on an expedition to the Continent and she was left as governor of the realm; while the king was away, she organized the successful defense against a Scottish invasion that ended in the English victory at Flodden. Catherine's one major failing was that she did not produce the male heir to the throne that Henry really desired. When the English alliance with Charles V wavered and fell, Catherine's political importance declined. In addition, Henry had become infatuated with Anne Boleyn.

Henry's next move, to clear the way for his liaison with Boleyn, was to seek a divorce from Catherine. Since that was technically impossible within the Catholic Church, he sent Cardinal Thomas Wolsey to see Pope Clement VII to convince him to have his marriage to Catherine annulled. Wolsey was not only a cardinal but was also the lord chancellor of England and had virtually controlled English domestic and foreign policies when Henry was young. He was also the official papal envoy from England, and many felt that he was a serious contender to become pope himself. George Cavendish, an English gentleman who was both the cardinal's usher and a confidant, tells the story of Wolsey's visit to Rome on behalf of Henry's divorce.

The early negotiations with Pope Clement were going well, since Henry was

money and political support, both of which were much needed by the ⌐n to fend off the pressures put on it by Charles V. An audience was ¬ged in which the final details of an agreement that would result in annul-⌐nt of Henry's marriage would be worked out, and the papers would be signed. Wolsey entered the great chamber, accompanied as usual by his favorite grey-hound, Urian. Wolsey left the dog a short distance from the door and ap-proached the dais to pay his respects to the Pope, who was seated on his throne. There was a large throng of cardinals in the room, and a great buzz of conversa-tion as the various clergymen discussed the implications of this momentous event. Urian, who was known to be quite protective when it came to his master, became somewhat upset due to the noise and obvious tension in the room. In-stead of settling down and taking a nap, as he normally did at political meetings, he stood tensely watching the scene. Because the occasion was so significant, and because Clement did not want it to appear that he was being either bribed or co-erced into his decision, the Pope determined that the most formal type of obei-sance and homage should be shown to him. This involved the supplicant kneeling down and kissing the Pope's toe. Wolsey complied, but Urian, already disturbed by the activity of the room, now mistook the Pope's foot hurtling toward his master's face as an assault on the cardinal. In his master's defense the dog sprang forward, pushing aside the clergymen who ringed the dais, knocking over the stool that had been placed for Clement's foot to rest on during the cer-emony, and finally sinking his teeth into the pontiff's bare foot. Clement let out a scream of pain as everyone nearby swarmed around him to pull off the dog and prevent any further attack. Clement unsteadily rose, all the while cursing the En-glish king and his envoy. He grabbed the still-unsigned papers that were resting beside him and then, and in a gesture of anger and disgust, threw them aside. Wolsey's audience was declared over, and the Pope refused to discuss the subject of Henry's divorce further.

Wolsey returned to England without papal agreement, and his failure to ob-tain the annulment of Henry's marriage would ultimately cause his own political downfall. Henry, in turn, now began the events that would lead to the English Reformation and his total break with the Catholic Church. He first required that all ecclesiastical legislation must be subject to royal approval, and then stopped the flow of funds going to the Vatican. Next he had his own nominee, Thomas Cranmer, appointed archbishop of Canterbury. Cranmer, not surpris-ingly, immediately declared Henry's marriage to Catherine to be invalid. In re-

sponse, an angry Pope excommunicated Henry, who responded by pa
Act of Supremacy, which created the Church of England with the king
head. Henry confiscated Catholic monasteries and seized church lands, w.
number of prominent churchmen and associates were executed.

A historian using counter-factual reasoning could quite legitimately rais
the question as to whether the rise of Protestantism and its heated conflict with
the Catholic Church might have been avoided, or at least delayed, if a dog
named Urian had not chosen to sink his teeth into the Pope's toe in a misguided
attempt to protect his master.

While documented information about the influence that dogs have had on
history can be found if one is willing to look long enough, there are instances
where only hints can be found about a canine influence on history. In such situations a tale can still be told, but only with a more conservative suggestion in the
form of "it might be the case" that a dog has changed history here. Take, as an
example, the life of Baron Manfred Freiherr von Richthofen, who would be
known to the world as the Red Baron and would go down in history as Germany's greatest World War I fighter pilot. Richthofen was born into a prosperous family with a long military tradition. His father became a career army
officer, and Manfred and his younger brother, Lother, followed suit. Always ad-
venturesome and with an eye for status and appearances, Richthofen chose the
most glamorous form of service at that time, joining the cavalry. He fought gal-
lantly with the 1st Uhlan Cavalry Regiment in Russia, then went on to participate in the invasions of Belgium and France. This western campaign soon
became a static affair involving trench warfare, and the cavalry was sidelined.

Still craving action and a way to distinguish himself, Richthofen joined the
infantry. In 1915, however, he was told about the formation of the Imperial Air
Service. Airplanes had not been proven to be effective military devices yet, and
were considered to be dangerous and unreliable. However, the title of aviator
during that era carried with it the same aura of excitement, danger and daring
that the title of astronaut would bring with it forty years later. It was a chance to
be a hero, and Richthofen leaped at the opportunity.

Richthofen began his service as a fighter pilot in September 1916, and
shortly thereafter he became commander of Fighter Group 1. His flamboyance
carried over to his combat activities. So that there would be no mistaking him in
combat, he painted his Fokker triplane a bright red, thereby earning his famous
nickname of *der rote Freiherr,* or "Red Baron." Following the example set by their

ier, the entire fighter group painted their planes in bright colors, and
ilted in his squadron getting the nickname "Richthofen's Flying Circus."
Richthofen was a deadly fighter, and one of the top flying aces of all time.
was personally credited with shooting down eighty enemy aircraft, and his
erformance earned him the coveted Blue Max medal in 1917. This was a time
when warfare consisted of massed attacks from trenches, fought between name-
less hordes of soldiers. Because of the nature of such battle tactics, there were few
visible heroes. A fighter pilot engaging in single-combat duels with enemy pilots,
however, could be identified. For this reason Richthofen quickly became a symbol of the German war effort. Every time he shot down another plane, it became
front-page news and cause for rejoicing by the beleaguered German public and
their frontline troops, who needed reassurance that they could still win the war.

During his years as a pilot, Richthofen shared his life and his quarters with
a Great Dane named Moritz. At all hours of the day, the tall aviator could be
seen wandering around the airfield in his leather jacket, with his hands in his
pockets and his large dog marching by his side. On several patrol and observation missions, Richthofen actually strapped Moritz into the second seat of his
plane and took him along. Apparently the noise and the air rushing by the open
cockpit made flying a bit uncomfortable for Moritz. After a few such patrols,
when Richthofen would ask him, "Would you like to fly with me today?" Moritz
would bark loudly and then defiantly lie down, as if to say, "If you want me to
get in that plane, you will have to carry me across the field."

Moritz, however, was extremely loyal to Richthofen. He would go out to the
field with him before each mission, then sit and watch him take off for battle.
Once all of the planes in the group were off the ground and out of sight, he
would look for some spot of shade, near one of the buildings. Typically Moritz
simply lay down and dozed, only waking up occasionally to look at the runway.
There was no radar at that time, and the only way to know that the planes were
returning was to see them. However, Moritz's sensitive ears had apparently become attuned to the sound of the fighter planes. Long before they were visible,
he would get up and move toward the runway, barking as he went. Plane spot-
ters would then immediately start scanning the horizon in the direction that the
big dog was looking, and within a few moments they would almost always spot
the distant incoming group. As soon as Richthofen's plane began its landing approach, Moritz would begin to circle around excitedly, often dashing out to greet
the Red Baron before his plane had rolled to a complete stop.

Richthofen often took Moritz with him on social occasions, and it unusual for him to share a beer with the dog at the officer's club. It is eve that on the same shelf where the pilots kept their personal ornate beer m there was a shallow blue bowl with vertical sides and a gold "M" emblazoned c it for Moritz's portion of beer. The big dog resided in Richthofen's quarters with him, and actually slept on his bed. It may well have been this fact that was Richthofen's undoing.

The battle of the Somme was in progress, and on the morning of April 21, 1918, Richthofen went out to the airstrip to board his plane. He was yawning and looked fatigued. One of his squadron commanders, Lieutenant Hans Klein, asked him, "You look tired. Were you out late last night?"

Richthofen gave a small laugh and replied, "Moritz was very restless last night. He kept waking me, and I doubt that I got two hours worth of real sleep. They will have to give me a bigger bed if they expect me to get enough rest to win this war."

Later that day the famous red triplane sustained damage from ground fire. In a now partially crippled plane, Richthofen had the unfortunate luck to encounter a Sopwith Camel flown by one of Canada's top air aces, Captain A. Roy Brown. This would be the one dogfight that the Red Baron would lose. Richthofen's body was recovered from the wreckage of his Fokker, and he was buried with full military honors by the British and Australian troops occupying that part of the front. Richthofen's death was a great blow to the Germans. General Erich Ludendorff, the commander of the German forces in that battle, said, "His death will have a greater effect on our morale than would the loss of thirty infantry divisions."

It is intriguing to speculate about Richthofen's final night with Moritz. Could it be that the dog's restlessness caused the great pilot to lose enough sleep so that on this day the Red Baron's reflexes and judgment were slightly impaired? Perhaps Moritz was so restless because he felt that his master's death was imminent. In either case, the last night that the Red Baron spent with his dog makes an interesting footnote to the story of his death.

However, one does not have to be particularly speculative to recognize that many times the history of much of mankind has depended upon the actions of a dog. Consider the very straightforward example of Alexander the Great, who was born in 356 B.C, and became king of Macedon and the conqueror of much of Asia. He was the son of Philip II of Macedon and his wife, Olympias. He re-

classical education under none other than the great Greek scholar and ~opher Aristotle, then succeeded to the throne in 336 B.C. after his father assassinated.

It was Alexander's mother, Olympias, who is generally given the credit for introducing mastiffs as guards and military fighting dogs in Greece. These dogs had been developed and used for battles and defense in her native Illyria, which was a Molossian territory. In fact, great savage fighting mastiffs came to be called Molossian dogs and were treated as weapons to be used in time of war against lightly armed infantry and unarmed cavalry horses. Ultimately dogs like these would be effectively turned against the armies of Rome by the invading Celts as they swept down from Gaul. Alexander grew up watching the war dogs being trained, and came to appreciate their tactical uses. His army always traveled with a contingent of these dogs, and they were effectively brought to the front of the battle lines when Alexander's opponents lacked heavy armor.

Alexander also learned about hunting dogs from his father. Philip had a great fondness for pointers, and had some of them imported from as far away as Spain. Alexander liked hunting behind pointers, but he was attracted to the more exciting chase that could be had by racing behind greyhounds, and so he had several greyhounds imported from Gaul. There, in a region that was south and west of the Rhine, was a tribe known as the Segusians who were highly respected for their fine breeding of dogs, particularly for their line of greyhounds, which came to be called *vertragi* ("swift runners"). From these imported Segusian dogs was born Alexander's favorite, Peritas. Trained not only as a hunter but also as a bodyguard, Peritas became Alexander's personal companion. Because he would often accompany Alexander up to the battlefront, a special lightweight armor had been created for him. At such times he would also wear a metal collar with razor-sharp spikes protruding from it to prevent anyone from capturing him by grabbing at the collar and also to protect possible attacks by the war dogs of an enemy.

When Alexander assumed the throne, there was civil unrest around him. He quickly secured Greece and the Balkan peninsula and then crossed the Hellespont (which is now the Dardanelles). At the head of an allied Greek army, Alexander began the war on Persia that his father had been planning. He would fight the Persian forces of Darius III several times, always emerging victorious. Soon most of Asia Minor and Syria had fallen to him. When he entered Egypt,

he met no resistance there. He first proceeded to Memphis, made relig.
rifices there, and was crowned with the traditional double crown
Pharaohs. He then founded the city of Alexandria and proceeded to make
difficult journey to the oracle of the god Amon-Ra at Siwah. There he v
greeted as the son of the god Amon-Ra, and afterward he consulted the goc
about the success of his expedition. He told no one what the god's oracle told
him, but many people assumed he was told that he was truly the son of Zeus,
and he himself would one day be a god.

Regardless of what the oracle actually said, it was now with great confidence
that he returned to Syria and then moved directly to Mesopotamia to confront
Darius once more. The decisive battle against the Persians would take place on
the plains of Guagamela, between Nineveh and Arbela.

Alexander was always impulsive and preferred to be at the head of his troops
when they were in battle. At Guagamela, Alexander thought that he saw the
royal flags of Darius and quickly arranged a cavalry charge into the massed forces
to try to engage the enemy leader. This day Peritas was with him, racing beside
him as the riders forged their way deeply into the enemy's ranks. The close fighting soon slowed Alexander's movements, however, and as he turned to try to find
some space to maneuver, he was startled to see a Persian war elephant charging
toward him. The Persian commander had clearly recognized who was leading
this charge and was willing to sacrifice many of his own troops to capture or kill
Alexander. The huge elephant thundered forward, crushing everything in front
of it, while the Macedonian king struggled to find some clear means of moving
out of its path. Suddenly a tawny figure dashed in front of Alexander and leaped
directly at the elephant. Peritas seemed to fly through the air and amazingly
managed to latch on to the elephant's lower lip. The pain must have been excru-
ciating, since the great beast stopped its charge immediately. The massive animal
swung to its side and reared up, tumbling its riders to the ground as it now
roared its distress. The sweeping movement of the wounded beast left a mo-
mentary opening in the lines. Alexander quickly dashed through it, and thus
managed to escape from the thick of the fighting and make it back to his own
lines. Peritas did not survive the encounter, but the brave dog's desperate attack
had saved Alexander's life.

Alexander was uninjured and was able to continue the battle. It was a hard
fight, but in the end his troops would be victorious. As a result, the mighty army

was so weakened that it would no longer be able to effectively resist his
.e. In subsequent days Darius was hunted down, his cities were burned,
ultimately he would die at the hands of an assassin.

Alexander had been strongly moved by the courage and self-sacrifice of his
og. As the evening fell, he ordered that the battlefield be searched for Peritas.
The dog's body was found and brought to the king. He first insisted that the
body be preserved until the military action was over. When the pursuit of Darius had ended, Alexander then ordered a state funeral for Peritas. In gratitude
and respect for his brave dog he named a city in his honor, and had a statue of
him erected in the central square.

Now let us ask the counter-factual question, "What might have happened if
Peritas had not stalled the elephant's charge and if, as a consequence, Alexander
had been killed at Gaugamela?" Alexander is credited with spreading Greek culture and influence eastward. His expedition led to a vast colonizing wave
through the Near East. Although it did not serve to unify this part of the world
politically, it did create a single economic and cultural world that stretched from
Gibraltar to the Punjab. Alexander's Greek language then became the language
of commerce and scholarship, allowing a flow of trade, knowledge, and social in-
tercourse throughout that broad geographical area. One consequence of this was
that a new religion, Christianity, with its New Testament originally written in
that language could now spread its gospel throughout the known world. None
of this might have happened had it not been for the intervention of a dog.

On the whole, the influence of dogs has been helpful, whether by saving
lives or providing psychological comfort and inspiration for their owners. Sometimes, of course, the influence of a dog has been negative, either by placing lives
at risk or causing embarrassment or social complications. There is at least one incident, however, where the actions of a dog had both negative and positive consequences, and the final resolution as to the course that history would take rested
on the last decision that the dog would make in the chain of events. This incident occurred in Scotland but ultimately would have implications for British
history and also, perhaps, the history of the United States. The story itself is
about Robert the Bruce, the king of Scotland who is credited with freeing the
Scottish from English rule.

In the early half of the twelfth century under King David I, many Anglo-
Saxon families, including the Bruces, moved north to Scotland, where they were
given lands and offices. A number of these families eventually developed ties to

the royal family through marriage. In 1290, the Scottish throne was left
a direct heir, and there were many claimants for the crown. Edward I of En
with whom the Scottish royals had previously enjoyed amicable relations, ag
to arbitrate a decision. The two chief claimants were the sixth Robert Bru
(grandfather to Robert the Bruce) and John Balliol, each descendants of a son o
David I. In 1292 Edward declared John Balliol to be the Scottish king. However,
Edward did not view Scotland as an autonomous nation, and his attempts to exert control over its governance aroused the Scots to rebellion. John Balliol was
forced to submit when Edward marched into Scotland, but the rebellion continued behind William Wallace. When Wallace was captured and executed, Robert
the Bruce assumed the leadership of the uprising and began planning to take the
throne that his grandfather had been denied. In 1306 he assassinated his main
competitor, John "the Red" Comyn, who was a nephew of John Balliol. Robert
then went to Scone to declare himself King Robert I. The sacred Stone of Scone,
which signified the legitimacy of the coronation of the Scottish king, had been
removed by Edward and brought to Westminster Abbey in order to prevent any
attempts to name a new king. However, Robert felt that the traditions associated
with the place itself would be sufficient to ensure that his coronation would be
seen as legitimate in the eyes of the Scots.

Edward was enraged at Robert's actions. He immediately declared Robert a
traitor, and his taking of the throne as a rebellion that must be immediately
crushed. Edward had the advantage of holding many of the major castles and
towns in Scotland, but Robert had a number of personal strengths. He excelled
as a statesman and politician, and he knew how to rally men and gather allies. As
a military leader his major skill was in harrying tactics and surprise raids, not the
standard, fixed-formation fighting of the times. This was demonstrated in 1306,
the first year that he assumed the throne. Prior to this Robert had successfully
raided a number of Edward's garrisons. He would have his forces move in under
cover and attack in an ambush, wounding or killing as many English troops as
they could, then stealing away with whatever supplies they could carry. When
King Robert was forced into two traditional battles, however, he was soundly defeated—first at Methven, near Perth, and the next at Dalry, near Tyndrum. By
the time these disastrous battles were over, his wife and many of his supporters
had been captured, along with three of his brothers (who would eventually be
executed). In the end, though, Robert's greatest triumph was the atypical set-
piece battle that he forced and won eight years later at Bannockburn. This vic-

ld eventually lead to the Treaty of Northampton, which confirmed
n independence.

The events that concern us occurred just after Robert's disastrous encounter
Dalry. His forces were in full retreat, and Edward I had given orders that
Robert was to be hunted down and either captured or killed at all costs. Robert
was now forced to use the skills that had kept him alive this long. During his hit-
and-run guerrilla campaigns he had become quite adept at hiding and escaping
pursuit in the wilderness. Now, unfortunately, his situation would become quite
dangerous, and his life would be in jeopardy because of a dog.

Edward had put the canny fighter John of Lorn in charge of the pursuit of
Robert. John had gotten possession of one of Robert's own dogs—a Talbot,
which is an early version of today's bloodhounds. Robert was fond of hunting
dogs and had an interest in developing dogs that could track game through
dense woods and over the rough terrain that characterized the Scottish countryside. He had been carefully breeding the best tracking dogs of each successive litter to each other in the hopes of achieving a dog that could follow a trail even if
it were hours old and degraded by poor weather. Robert had liked this particular dog that John now had. He had raised it himself to be his companion as well
as a hunter, and it had been given the name Donnchadh (pronounced "DON nu
chu"). Donnchadh had been in the company of Robert's wife when she had been
captured by the English, and so the dog had also fallen into their hands.

John had heard tales about the hunting prowess of this dog, and how on at
least one military operation, Robert had used him to track a small group of English soldiers who were carrying important dispatches to one of the garrisons. He
reasoned that since this dog was Robert's favorite and since Robert had usually
fed him with his own hands, no dog could have been better acquainted with his
scent. John felt that he could turn this fact, and the dog's great tracking ability,
against Robert.

John enlisted the help of Sir Aymer de Valence and a company of some eight
hundred men to give chase. With Bruce's own dog in the lead, the hunt began.
The armed force was told to follow Donnchadh. The dog, who only wanted to
be reunited with his missing master, was led to the place where Robert's forces
escaped into the forest. Donnchadh quickly found his master's track, let out a
happy yelp, and proceeded into the woods. Robert was in full flight and he and
his company hurried ever deeper into the forest, but the pursuit continued.
Robert then began to use the evasive tactics that had worked so well in the past.

He divided his party into three groups, telling them to scatter in different directions. He left the largest group on the main trail, sent one of the groups off at a tangent to the right, and took his own group on a sharp turn to the left, trying to put as much distance as possible between himself and the pursuing English force.

This ploy did not work. Donnchadh was following Robert's party and no other. With the English hard on his heels, Robert split his little band once more. Each group again took a different direction in the hopes of evading the pursuit. Robert was left with only his foster brother, Edward, and they both moved rapidly through the woods. Once more, inexorably, the hound chose the right trail, now baying intermittently as the trail grew clearer and Donnchadh knew that he was coming closer to his loved master.

Robert now listened carefully to the sounds that were drawing closer. He turned to his brother in distress and said, "That is my own dog they have set upon us. I thought I could recognize Donnchadh's voice. Our only hope is speed, and perhaps to find a stream of water which we can use to mask our scent from him."

John of Lorn had no doubts either as to whose trail was being followed. He also knew that the outcome of the chase would be a matter of speed, and his large, heavily armed company was simply moving too slowly. What he needed was a contingent that could find Robert and, if not capture or kill him themselves, at least hold him at bay or slow his party down until the main force could arrive. With that in mind, he hastily handed over the dog to five of his best men-at-arms and ordered them to follow swiftly in Robert's footsteps while he and the rest of the company came up as quickly as they could.

Now a vast amount of history hung on the collar of a dog who was tugging at a leash as it bounded forward after the well-loved and well-remembered scent of its master. Counter-factual reasoning suggests that if the dog succeeded and John was successful as well, then events would have been irrevocably changed. Most importantly, the Stuarts would never have come to the English throne. It was Robert's daughter, Marjory, who first married into the Stuart family, and it was her son Robert who, as King Robert II, became the first Stuart king of Scotland; James VI, who would become the first Stuart king of England, was also part of this lineage. The Stuarts brought with them the fatal dynastic curse of the "royal disease," porphyria—the disease that paralyzed the energies of George III during his most formative years, clouding his mind and making him temperamental. These moods and his hazy thinking led to a number of unwise and rash decisions that would ultimately have an adverse effect on the British subjects in the American colonies. Thus had George's inherited disease not caused him to act so irresponsibly, there might not have been an American Revolution. There almost certainly would never have been an English Revolution, and England might have been reabsorbed into the continent of Europe as she had once been by the Romans. The dog, however, was not trying to change history; he was simply seeking the company of the man who reared him.

Tracked by his own dog, Robert felt that his only alternative was to turn and fight the five men-at-arms while he and his brother still had breath enough. The dog rounded the trees, and the pursuers immediately knew which one was Robert, as Donnchadh raced directly to the Scottish king. One soldier turned to face Robert's brother, while the other four raised their weapons against Robert.

Odds of four to one are a little long even for such a hero, but the dog's role was not yet done. Once the men had engaged in combat, Donnchadh recognized that his master was in jeopardy, and he knew where his true loyalty lay. He sprang forward in Robert's defense, splitting the attack and allowing Bruce to fell one of the combatants. The dog was now in a protective fury and slowed the advance of two attackers while Bruce brought down his second assailant. By this time, his brother had succeeded in his own desperate battle and rushed in from behind just as Bruce turned to attack the remaining two soldiers, who were trying to dispatch the now-raging dog. With their attention on Donnchadh they were slow in responding to their human attackers, and the last two of Lorn's men fell.

Both Robert and his brother were bleeding from minor wounds, as was Donnchadh. However, they were only a few yards from the stream that they had been dashing toward. The three companions plunged into the water and waded down it for a quarter of a mile before emerging on the far side, now confident that they had thrown their pursuers off the scent. Bruce would survive as king, history would follow its ordained course, and a hound named Donnchadh would live to see his master enter Edinburgh as the king of Scotland. The first acts of this dog had placed the course of history, as we know it, in peril of being drastically changed, but his later heroic actions had brought matters back to the historical line of events that we actually have experienced. Robert would later say that he had rightly named the dog Donnchadh, which in the Gaelic language means "Brown Warrior."

Those who use counter-factual reasoning to explore possibilities in history say that small events, occurring at key times and places in history, can have enormous effects in the future. If there is anything that one can say about dogs, it is that they cause many events to happen in their masters' lives. Some of the events are inconsequential and only of interest to their immediate family, but some are significant in changing the lives of their owners. If their owners are people whose actions have changed history, then this fact alone would mean that the dogs have had an influence on historical events.

To find the canine influence on our collective lives and histories, we must sometimes look carefully. The pawprints of many dogs are there, but they are faint, and the winds of time erase them if they are not found and preserved. We cannot ask the dogs to recount their communal stories. Dogs do not write, so there are no diaries or letters that personally recount what an individual dog has done. Dogs do not have museums and libraries dedicated to the conservation of their history. Any wisdom that they have can only pass on in their genes, and history is not stored in their DNA. So dogs entrust to us the task of recording their deeds and their history, and, as we have seen, many of their deeds are important parts of our own human history.

ENDNOTES

A number of books and reference sources have been consulted in many of the chapters. Rather than repeat these references over and over, let me simply note them here. There are a number of good general histories of the dog that I found myself frequently paging through. These include F. Mery, *The Life History and Magic of the Dog* (1968); L. M. Wendt, *Dogs: A Historical Journey* (1996); A. Sloan and A. Farquhar, *Dog and Man* (1925); M. Garber, *Dog Love* (1996); M. E. Thurston, *Lost History of the Canine Race* (1996); M. Riddle, *Dogs Through History* (1987); B. Vesy-FitzGerald, *The Domestic Dog* (1957); C. A. Branigan, *The Reign of the Greyhound* (1997); J. E. Baur, *Dogs on the Frontier* (1978); and R. A. Caras, *A Dog Is Listening* (1993). K. MacDonogh has an extensive history of dogs and royalty in *Reigning Cats and Dogs* (1990), and another good source on that same topic is C. I. A. Ritchie, *The British Dog* (1981). M. Leach, *God Had a Dog* (1961) and P. Dale-Green, *Dog* (1966) are good collections of dog lore. P. Jackson's *Faithful Friends* (1997) is a useful collection of original source materials on dogs.

CHAPTER 1: SENTINELS AND SYMBOLS

Much of the material about the relationships between individuals and dogs is extracted from their letters and the personal correspondence of close associates. A full biography on Pope is by M. Mack, *Alexander Pope: A Life* (1985), and his letters were edited by G. Sherburn in five volumes (1956). Biographical material on William of Orange is from C. V. Wedgwood, *William the Silent* (1944), and the extended quotation is from R. Williams, *Actions of the Low Countries* (1618). The material on the Dalai Lama is from an interview with one of the current Lama's priestly attendants and from Han-chang Ya, *The Biographies of the Dalai Lamas* (1991). Some material about Saint Bosco is drawn from B. Clément, *Père des enfants perdus; vie de saint Jean Bosco* (1956) and H. Thurston and D. Attwater, ed., *Butler's Lives of the Saints* (4 vol., 1956). Florence Nightingale's biographical material comes from studies by M. E. Baly (1986) and Sandy Dengler (1988), while information on her dream comes from her diaries, edited by M. D. Calabria (1987).

CHAPTER 2: THE SAINT AND THE IRISH DOG

Material on the life of Saint Patrick can be found in biographies by J. B. Bury (1905) and Paul Gallico (1958), as well as a study by R. P. C. Hanson (1968). The folkloric material on Patrick and the information on Saint Roche and Saint Margaret comes from G. H. Gerould, *Saints' Legends* (1916); H. Thurston and D. Attwater, ed., *Butler's Lives of the Saints* (4 vol., 1956); and P. McGinley, *Saint-Watching* (1969). D. Attwater, *The Penguin Dictionary of Saints* (1970) and D. Farmer, ed., *The Oxford Dictionary of Saints* (2d ed., 1987) were also consulted here and in the previous chapter for Saint Bosco.

HAPTER 3: THE ANGRY PRINCE AND THE WELSH DOG

Information about this period was drawn from W. Davies, *Wales in the Early Middle Ages* (1982); D. Walker, *Medieval Wales* (1990); and A. D. Carr, *Medieval Wales* (1995). In addition, Alan Carr, late of the University of Cardiff, supplied me with translations from the Welsh of two early accounts of Llywelyn and Cylart that were believed to be written in the thirteenth century.

CHAPTER 4: THE DEVIL DOG OF THE ENGLISH CIVIL WAR

The biographies of Prince Rupert that I relied on were by by Eva Scott (1899), Bernard Fergusson (1952), and Frank Knight (1967). For James, the biographical material came from Christopher Hibbert (1968), and for Charles from D. H. Willson (1956) and David Mathew (1967). Additional material was taken from G. Davies, *The Early Stuarts* (1959); J. P. Kenyon, *The Stuarts* (1958); A. H. Burne and P. Young, *The Great Civil War, a Military History* (1959); and C. V. Wedgwood's two books, *The King's Peace, 1637–1641* (1955) and *The King's War, 1641–1647* (1958).

CHAPTER 5: THE COMPANIONS OF THE PRUSSIAN EMPEROR

There are many good biographies of Frederick the Great, and those that I used for personal and historical details of his life included R. B. Asprey, *Frederick the Great: The Magnificent Enigma* (1986); Nancy Mitford, *Frederick the Great* (1970); and Giles MacDonogh, *Frederick the Great: A Life in Deed and Letters* (1999). Much information about his relationship with his dogs was gleaned from his correspondence, which is a massive amount of material and was collected together in forty-seven volumes as *Politische Correspondenz Friedrichs des Grossen*, (1879–1939). Some other observations were drawn from annotations included with his collected works which were edited by J. D. E. Preuss and published in thirty-three volumes as *Oeuvres de Frédéric le Grand* (1846–57).

CHAPTER 6: THE CONQUISTADOR'S DOGS

A lot has been written on Columbus and the conquest of the Americas. Two excellent general biographies include the classic two-volume work by S. E. Morison, *Admiral of the Ocean Sea: A Life of Christopher Columbus*, (1942, reissued 1962) and F. Fernandez-Armesto, *Columbus* (1991), which places him in the context of his time. The classic work on the Spanish conquest is W. H. Prescott's three volume *History of the Conquest of Mexico* (1843). A scholarly but blood-soaked history of the use of dogs during this era is provided by J. G. Varner and J. J. Varner, *Dogs of the Conquest* (1983). Many useful details were provided by F. Provost, *Columbus Dictionary* (1991) and the two volumes of *The Christopher Columbus Encyclopedia*, edited by S. A. Bedini (1992).

CHAPTER 7: THE DOGS OF THE SCOTTISH WRITER

Probably the be best and most intimate biography of Scott is J. G. Lockhart, *Memoirs of the Life of Sir Walter Scott* (7 vol., 1836–38), while other consulted sources included Edgar Johnson, *Sir Walter Scott: The Great Unknown* (2 vol., 1970) and H. J. C. Grierson, *Sir Walter*

Scott (1932). There is also a tiny book by E. Thornton Cook that specifically focuses on Scott and his dogs, *Sir Walter's Dogs* (1931).

CHAPTER 8: DOGS IN THE OPERA HOUSE

The major sources of intimate information on Wagner and his dogs include Joachim Bergfeld, ed., *The Diary of Richard Wagner* (1980); Martin Gregor-Dellin and Dietrich Mack, ed., *Cosima Wagner's Diaries* (1978); and Wagner's own autobiography *Mein Leben* (2 vol., 1870–81; Eng. trans., *My Life,* 1911). An invaluable biographical source is W. A. Ellis, *Life of Richard Wagner* (6 vol., 1900–08). The Marie (Heine) Schmole quote is from *Letters of Richard Wagner: The Burrell Collection,* edited and annotated by John N. Burk (1972).

CHAPTER 9: THE TALKING DOG

Much has been written about Alexander Graham Bell, but most of this has tended to focus on his work designing and implementing the telephone. Two general biographies that were used are R. V. Bruce, *Alexander Graham Bell and the Conquest of Solitude* (1973) and Catherine MacKenzie, *Alexander Graham Bell* (1928). The Bell-Gallaudet controversy is covered in R. Winefield, *Never the Twain Shall Meet: Bell, Gallaudet and the Communications Debate* (1949). Material about Bell and his dogs has been extracted from letters and articles, which are part of the Bell Family Archives maintained by the U.S. Library of Congress.

CHAPTER 10: THE DOG ON THE THERAPIST'S COUCH

The standard biographical work on Freud is Ernest Jones, *The Life and Work of Sigmund Freud* (3 vol., 1953–57). Observations by friends and contemporaries include Fritz Wittels, *Sigmund Freud: His Personality, His Teaching, & His School* (1924); Hanns Sachs, *Freud* (1944); and Max Schur, *Freud* (1972). Of particular value was material from his diaries, which are available through the Freud Museum in London, and an annotated translation by Michael Molnar, *The Diary of Sigmund Freud, 1929–1939: A Record of the Final Decade* (1992) and some of his letters, *Letters of Sigmund Freud, 1873–1939,* edited by Ernst L. Freud (1961). Material on dog-assisted therapy comes from Boris Levinson, *Pet-Oriented Child Psychotherapy* (1997) and Alan Beck and Aaron Katcher, *Between Pets and People* (1996).

CHAPTER 11: FOR THE LOVE OF DOGS AND OTHER BEASTS

Interesting material on the founders of the humane movement and the consequences of early humanitarian attempts can be found in R. C. McCrea, *The Humane Movement* (1910); Harriet Ritvo, *The Animal Estate: The English and Other Creatures in the Victorian Age* (1987); Maureen Duffy, *Men and Beasts: An Animal Rights Handbook* (1984); and R. Strand and P. Strand, *The Hijacking of the Humane Movement* (1992). Also of interest is the *Report of the Society for the Prevention of Cruelty to Animals, established in Liverpool, Sept. 1833,* which is available through Goldsmiths'-Kress microfilm set (1980), and some general material was taken from the *Encyclopedia of Animal Rights and Animal Welfare,* edited by Marc Bekoff and Carron A. Meaney (1998).

CHAPTER 12: THE DOG SHOGUN

Some excellent sources of information on the Tokugawa regimes, including Tsunayoshi, are Masao Maruyama, *Studies in the Intellectual History of Tokugawa Japan* (1974); Herman Ooms, *Tokugawa Ideology: Early Constructs, 1570–1680* (1985); and Conrad Totman, *Politics in the Tokugawa Bakufu, 1600–1843* (1967). Several of the quotes come from Engelbert Kaempfer, *The History of Japan* (1727) and additional material was provided by Harold Fudai's translation of some handwritten text by Sanno Gaiki that is in the collection of the Australian National Library.

CHAPTER 13: THE DOG LAW AND THE MARY ELLEN CASE

The American Society for the Prevention of Cruelty to Animals has published a number of articles about Henry Bergh over the years, but these are relatively difficult to find. There are, however, two books that summarize his life and the Mary Ellen story—namely, Z. Steele, *Angel in a Top Hat* (1942) and E. Shelman and S. Lazoritz, *Out of the Darkness* (1999). General information on the animal welfare movement can be found in Lyle Munro, *Compassionate Beasts: The Quest for Animal Rights* (2001) and the *Encyclopedia of Animal Rights and Animal Welfare,* edited by Marc Bekoff and Carron A. Meaney. A useful article linking animal welfare with the protection of children is P. Stevens and M. Eide, "The first chapter of children's rights," *American Heritage,* July/August 1990, pp. 84–91 and also L. G. Housden, *The Prevention of Cruelty to Children* (1955).

CHAPTER 14: THE EMPEROR AND HIS DOGS OF MISFORTUNE

As always, one must often rely upon the correspondence and personal notes of individuals, rather than upon formal biographies, for information about dog-related incidents. Fortunately, most of Napoleon's materials have been collected in *The Bonaparte Letters and Despatches, Secret, Confidential, and Official,* (2 vol., 1846); *The Confidential Correspondence of Napoleon Bonaparte with His Brother Joseph* (2 vol., 1855); and *Unpublished Correspondence of Napoleon I, Preserved in the War Archives* (3 vol., 1913). The story about the Prussian ambassador and Boatswain comes from K. Broennecke, *Das Neufundlaenderbuch* (1941), and the story about Jerome Napoleon Bonaparte's death comes from *The New York Times on CD* for the year 1945. Additional information was taken from F. Masson, *Napoleon at Home* (2 vol., 1894), T. Aronson, *Napoleon and Josephine* (1990), and F. McLynn, *Napoleon: A Biography* (1997).

CHAPTER 15: CONVERSATIONS WITH DOGS

Portions of Mackenzie King's diaries have been edited and annotated by J. W. Pickersgill and D. F. Forster, *The Mackenzie King Record* (4 vol., 1960–70). Studies of his personality with several interesting references to his relationship with his dogs are J. E. Esberey, *Knight of the Holy Spirit: A Study of William Lyon Mackenzie King* (1980) and C. P. Stacey, *A Very Double Life* (1976). The fragment of poetry comes from N. M. Holland, "The Little Dog-Angel," in *Spun-Yarn and Spindrift,* (1918, p. 7). John Steinbeck's *Travels with Charley in Search of America* appeared in 1962. Biographical material comes from Jackson J. Benson, *The True Adventures of John Steinbeck, Writer* (1984) and Jay Parini, *John Steinbeck* (1994). Material on Mary, Queen of Scots comes from Antonia Fraser, *Mary Queen of Scots* (1969); T. F. Henderson, *Mary Queen of Scots* (2 vol., 1905); and also some of Mary's own recollections that were dictated to her secretary while she was in captivity, which appear in D. Hay Fleming, *Mary Queen of Scots from Her Birth till Her Flight into England* (1898).

CHAPTER 16: THE LION DOGS OF THE FORBIDDEN CITY

Biographies of Tzu Hsi that were used include Charlotte Haldane, *Last Great Empress of China* (1965); Marina Warner, *Dragon Empress: The Life and Times of Tz'u-hsi, Empress Dowager of China: 1835–1908* (1972); and A. W. Hummel, ed., *Eminent Chinese of the Ch'ing Period, 1644–1912* (2 vols., 1943–44). In addition, more personal material appears in biographies by Princess Der Ling, *Old Buddha* (1929) and *Tz`u-hsi yeh shih* (1994), parts of which were graciously translated for me by Steven Wong.

CHAPTER 17: THE INDIAN FIGHTER'S DOGS

Most of the information and quotations about Custer and his dogs comes from letters, books, and journals written by his wife, Elizabeth Bacon Custer, including *Following the Guidon* (1890), *Boots and Saddles or Life in Dakota with General Custer* (1885), and *The Journal of Elizabeth B. Custer* (edited by A. R., 1992). Information on Custer's life comes from L. Barnett, *Touched by Fire* (1996); F. F. Van de Water, *Glory-Hunter: A Life of General Custer* (1934); and *The Custer Myth: A Source Book of Custeriana,* edited by W. A. Graham (1953).

CHAPTER 18: THE VIRGINIA FARMER'S FOXHOUNDS

There have been a great many collections and books of about various phases and incidents of Washington's career, although comments about dogs and foxhunting are usually short and brief. Probably the definitive biography is by D. S. Freeman, *George Washington* (7 vol., 1948–57). The U.S. Library of Congress also has most of Washington's papers in a searchable electronic form. Several of the anecdotes (including that of Vulcan and the ham) are taken from papers collected by the Ladies Mount Vernon Association, from material at Mount Vernon, Washington's home, and Arlington House, the residence of the family of George Washington Parker Custis, his adopted son. Some of the personal material, especially his relationships, including Elizabeth W. Powel, has been drawn from H. Swiggett, *The Forgotten Leaders of the American Revolution* (1955); L. M. Post, *Personal Recollections of the American Revolution, 1774–1776* (1968); and K. A. Marling, *George Washington Slept Here* (1988).

CHAPTER 19: THE DOGS IN THE OVAL OFFICE

Some initial leads as to the significance of dogs to some of the presidents came from Roy Rowan and Brooke Janis, *First Dogs* (1997) and Niall Kelly, *Presidential Pets* (1992). Material on Theodore Roosevelt came from William H. Harbaugh, *The Life and Times of Theodore Roosevelt* (1975); Nathan Miller, *Theodore Roosevelt: A Life* (1992); and Jean Paterson Kerr's annotated collection of Roosevelt's family letters, *A Bully Father* (1995). Material on Eisenhower is from Stephen E. Ambrose, *Eisenhower* (2 vol., 1983–84) and material from his grandson, David Eisenhower, *Eisenhower at War* (1986). A source of information on Kennedy, Nixon, and Johnson and their dogs is the reminiscences of Traphes Bryant (with Spatz Leighton), *Dog Days at the White House* (1975). Additional material on John Kennedy comes from B. C. Bradlee, *Conversations with Kennedy* (1984). Material on Harding is from Andrew Sinclair, *The Available Man* (1965) and Robert K. Murray, *The Harding Era* (1969). Hoover is dealt with in G. H. Nash, *The Life of Herbert Hoover* (2 vols., 1983–88); Wilton Eckley, *Herbert Hoover* (1980); and Eugene Lyons, *Herbert Hoover, a Biography* (1964). Additional material on Nixon is from J. Aitken, *Nixon: A Life* (1994) and S. Ambrose, *Nixon* (3 vols., 1987–90). Most of the material on George Bush is from material written by his wife, Barbara Bush, *A Memoir* (1994), *C. Fred's Story* (1984), and *Millie's Book* (1990). Material on Clinton is from recent press reports and material provided by a former member of the White House staff, Steven Johnson. The Coolidge material comes mostly from his autobiography (1929) and Donald McCoy, *Calvin Coolidge: The Quiet President* (1988). The Gerald Ford material is from John Osborne, *The White House Watch: The Ford Years* (1977) and a biography by Richard Reeves, (1975). Additional material on Johnson is from R. A. Caro, *The Years of Lyndon Johnson* (2 vols., 1982–90); R. A. Divine, *The Johnson Years* (2 vols., 1987); and Merle Miller's fascinating, *Lyndon: An Oral Biography* (1980). Material on Franklin Roosevelt comes from the marvelous work of Arthur M. Schlesinger, Jr., *The Age of Roosevelt* (3 vol., 1957–60), and also James Macgregor Burns, *Roosevelt* (2 vol., 1956–70) and Frank Freidel, *Franklin D. Roosevelt* (1952); and Russell D. Buhite and David W. Levy, eds., *FDR's Fireside Chats* (1992). Material on Lincoln is mostly from the classic biographies by John G. Nicolay and John Hay, *Abraham Lincoln: A History* (10 vol., 1890) and Albert Beveridge, *Abraham Lincoln, 1809–58* (2 vol., 1928), with supplementary material from the beautifully illustrated Philip B. Kunhardt, Jr., Philip B. Kunhardt III, and Peter W. Kunhardt, *Lincoln* (1992). In addition I must acknowledge many bits and pieces throughout this chapter from the archives of *The New York Times on CD*.

CHAPTER 20: THE COUNTER-FACTUAL HISTORY OF DOGS

The material on Newton and Diamond appears in several entries in H. W. Turnbull et al., eds., *Correspondence* (7 vol., 1959–77), with some biographical material drawn from Richard S. Westfall, *Never at Rest: A Biography of Isaac Newton (1980)*. Material on the Lewis and Clark expedition is mostly drawn from their diaries and from Richard H. Dillon's *Meriwether Lewis: A Biography* (1965). The story of Cardinal Wolsey's dog is drawn from George Cavendish, *Life of Cardinal Wolsey* (1557), with biographical material about Henry VIII taken from J. J. Scarisbrick, *Henry VIII* (1968). Biographical material on Richthofen comes from W. Haiber and R. Haiber, *The Red Baron* (1992) and Peter Kilduff, *Richthofen: Beyond the Legacy of the Red Baron* (1994). Material on Alexander the Great is drawn from translations of rather old sources, particularly *Arrian*, trans. and ed. by P. A. Brunt (2 vol., 1976–83) and *The Romance of Alexander the Great*, which has been ascribed to Callisthenes and has been translated by Albert Mugrdich Wolohojian (1969). Treatments of Robert the Bruce that were consulted include G. W. S. Barrow, *Robert Bruce* (1965); A. M. Mackenzie, *Robert Bruce, King of Scots* (1934); and R. M. Scott, *Robert the Bruce* (1989).

INDEX

Index

About the Author

Stanley Coren is a professor of psychology at the University of British Columbia and author of *The Left-Hander Syndrome*, *The Intelligence of Dogs*, *Sleep Thieves*, *What Do Dogs Know?*, *Why We Love the Dogs We Do*, and *How to Speak Dog*. He lives in Vancouver, British Columbia.

The book has been illustrated with lighthearted drawing by the highly talented artist, animator, and animation director Andy Bartlett, who also lives in Vancouver, British Columbia.